The Brazilian Economy in the Eighties

Pergamon Titles of Related Interest

Agarwala THE NEW INTERNATIONAL ECONOMIC ORDER
Jorge/Salazar-Carrillo/Diaz-Pou EXTERNAL DEBT AND
    DEVELOPMENT STRATEGY IN LATIN AMERICA
Jorge/Salazar-Carrillo/Higonnet FOREIGN DEBT AND LATIN
    AMERICAN ECONOMIC DEVELOPMENT
Jorge/Salazar-Carrillo/Sanchez TRADE, DEBT AND GROWTH
    IN LATIN AMERICA
Salas REFLECTIONS ON POPULATION, Second Edition

Related Journals*

BULLETIN OF LATIN AMERICAN RESEARCH
ECONOMIC BULLETIN FOR EUROPE
LONG RANGE PLANNING
WORLD DEVELOPMENT

*Free sample copies available on request

The Brazilian Economy in the Eighties

Edited by

Jorge Salazar-Carillo
Florida International University and The Brookings Institution

Roberto Fendt, Jr.
Fundacao do Comercio Exterior, Rio de Janeiro, Brazil

PERGAMON PRESS
New York Oxford Toronto Sydney Paris Frankfurt

Pergamon Press Offices:

U.S.A.   Pergamon Press Inc., Maxwell House, Fairview Park,
                         Elmsford, New York 10523, U.S.A.

U.K.   Pergamon Press Ltd., Headington Hill Hall,
                         Oxford OX3 0BW, England

CANADA   Pergamon Press Canada Ltd., Suite 104, 150 Consumers Road,
                         Willowdale, Ontario M2J 1P9, Canada

AUSTRALIA   Pergamon Press (Aust.) Pty. Ltd., P.O. Box 544,
                         Potts Point, NSW 2011, Australia

FEDERAL REPUBLIC   Pergamon Press GmbH, Hammerweg 6,
OF GERMANY   D-6242 Kronberg-Taunus, Federal Republic of Germany

Library of Congress Cataloging in Publication Data
Main entry under title:

The Brazilian economy in the eighties.

   1. Brazil--Economic policy--Addresses, essays,
lectures. 2. Brazil--Economic conditions--1964-1985--
Addresses, essays, lectures. I. Salazar-Carrillo,
Jorge. II. Fendt Júnior, Roberto. III. Title:
Brazilian economy in the 80s.
HC187.B8723   1985   330.981'063   85-12337
ISBN 0-08-031953-X

HC
187
BRA

Printed in Great Britain by A. Wheaton & Co. Ltd., Exeter

TABLE OF CONTENTS

CONTRIBUTORS

WERNER BAER
Professor of Economics
University of Illinois

ALBERT FISHLOW
Professor of Economics
University of California,
  Berkeley

JOSE L. CARVALHO
Professor of Economics
Graduate School of Economics
Fundacao Getulio Vargas

ANTONIO CARLOS LEMGRUBER
President
Central Bank, Brazil

DONALD V. COES
Associate Professor of Economics
University of Illinois

FRED LEVY
Senior Economist
World Bank

CLAUDIO CONTADOR
Professor of Economics
Federal University of Rio de Janeiro

ROBERTO MACEDO
Chairman and Professor
Department of Economics
University of Sao Paulo

STAN CZAMANSKI
Professor of Regional Economics
Cornell University

SAMUEL MORLEY
Professor of Economics
Vanderbilt University

CARLOS von DOELLINGER
Senior Economist
Ministry of Planning, Brazil

JORGE SALAZAR-CARRILLO
Chairman and Professor
Department of Economics
Florida International
  University

RUDIGER DORNBUSCH
Professor of Economics
Massachusetts Institute of Technology

LARRY A. SJAASTAD
Professor of Economics
University of Chicago

TULIO DURAN
Senior Researcher
Foreign Trade Foundation

WILLIAM TYLER
Senior Economist
World Bank

ROBERTO FENDT, JR.
Technical Director, Foreign Trade
  Foundation
Professor, Fundacao Getulio Vargas

JOHN WILLIAMSON
Senior Fellow
Institute of International
  Economics

PREFACE

In this volume several views about the current dilemma of the Brazilian economy and its probable future, solutions and outcomes are explored. Brazil is a leading country in the Western world whose importance will certainly augment in the years to come. In terms of demograpahics, resources and economic activity, Brazil presently constitutes one half of South America and one third of Latin America. In about a generation, Brazil will have approximately the same population as the U.S. has today. Thus, much research and thought about Brazil should be undertaken and possibly will soon be forthcoming. This book will hopefully contribute to generate such efforts.

Moreover, Brazil will eventually provide the best measure of comparison with the United States of any country in the world. Early in the next century their populations will be similar. Their political systems, based on Judeo-Christian morality and Western philosophy, are organized around a Federalist framework, and about the goals of democracy and economic freedom. Other key parallelisms can be found in racial compositions, territorial extension, and natural resource mix. Therefore, the U.S. and Brazil will increasingly constitute the best mirrors on which each other can undertake self examination.

This volume basically focuses on the areas of trade and foreign investment, in Brazil, particularly examining the various economic policies impinging upon them. These topics are examined in the context of the nature and characteristics of the Brazilian economy in the early 1980s, and in the light of its expected growth path for the middle years and the latter part of the decade. At the end, interesting conclusions are derived from the overall discussion, while at the beginning the gist of the arguments presented in the various chapters are summarized and the most recent changes in the Brazilian economy are considered.

This book is the outcome of a substantial effort of reworking and updating a set of papers that were originally prepared at a conference at Florida International University in mid 1982. It has been a long and laborious task to which many have contributed. Thus, our debts of gratitude are many. Particularly we must thank the authors for their papers, and most specifically to Robert Schwarzreich for his organizational and editorial contributions. Thanks should also be expressed to Elaine Dillashaw who was in charge of the final magical touches at word processing. These essential contributions, as well as countless others that have to remain anonymous, provided the authors with the basic intellectual wherewithall to complete this volume of which they accept however, total and final responsibility.

Jorge Salazar-Carrillo - Miami, Florida
Roberto Fendt, Jr. - Rio de Janeiro, Brazil

THE BRAZILIAN ECONOMY IN THE EIGHTIES: AN INTRODUCTION

Jorge Salazar-Carrillo and Roberto Fendt, Jr.

This book is a collection of discussions and papers presented at the Conference on the Brazilian Economy in the 1980s, held in Miami, Florida on May 3 and 4, 1982, and sponsored by Florida International University and the Fundacão Centro de Estudos do Comércio Exeterior of Rio de Janeiro.   The decision to jointly organize this conference was based on the intention to investigate the consequences and options of an international scenario which presaged great disturbances.   The War in the South Atlantic was happening while the conference was taking place, dramatizing these changes abroad, and making it evident that the Brazilian economy, just as other Latin American economies, would not be immune to its effects.

The events after the conference evolved rapidly, showing that the concerns were not unfounded.   The breakdown of the Mexican external indebtedness situation in the second half of 1982 created a balance of payments crisis that affected nearly all of the Latin American countries.   By the end of the year, only two of the major countries in the area had not approached the IMF in order to negotiate adjustment programs for their economies.

The first paper, "Brazil and the Future: Some Thoughts on the Eighties," written by Roberto Fendt, Jr. and Jorge Salazar-Carrillo, after giving the history of the impacts that external shocks had on the Brazilian economy, proceeds to show that the stabilization program in Brazil began almost a year before the formal contract had been signed with the IMF for transitional financing.

When the stabilization program was initiated, some of the macroeconomic variables were out of control.   For instance, the inflation rate in March of 1981 reached an annual figure of 121%; the commercial balance of payments had reached, in April, a record accumulated deficit of approximately US$ 1.4 billion; and the current account deficit was around US$ 12.5 billion, by the end of 1980.

The reshaping of the economy took place in 1981.   The principal short term objective of the economic policies consisted of an attempt to alleviate the pressures on the balance of payments, sacrificing temporarily the growth in national product.

Fendt and Salazar-Carrillo call attention to the doubts which were raised in the country regarding the results obtained from the new stabilization program. In the short run, the questions raised were about the efficiency, instrumentalization and implementation of the program, further it was agreed that there may not have been a necessity to provoke such an abrupt decrease in the national product in order to deter the acceleration of the inflationary process. One line of questioning disagrees with the traditional view, according to which inflation in Latin America is, in principle, a fiscal question, since the approach completely ignores the costs of transition to stabilization. Extending this view in the light of the results obtained, the conclusion was that an effective stabilization program, accompanied by fiscal improvement and some contraction in demand, should include wage control and limiting the real interest rates.

How do short term events effect long term perspectives? Clearly, the two major challenges faced by Brazilian society in the 1980s are the creation of social motivation for the saving effort, and a solution to the problem of political institutionalization, owing to the necessary stability for the investment process.

Examining the relationships between the processes of economic development and institutionalization, it becomes clear that the positive performance in terms of economic development was not sufficient to guarantee political stability in Brazil. Political stability was legitimized by the economic success, by the ample reforms, and by development. The legitimization was basically a result of the political opening process; of the reorganization of the political system in the direction of a multiparty system (which is deeply rooted in Brazilian traditions); of the complete removal of censorship of the press; and of the elections held in November of 1982.

The tensions generated by modernization are not new to Brazil. In the Brazilian context, modernization has been equivalent to industrialization, the only mobilizing force towards the development process observed during this century. The Brazilian experience is also unique in the sense that it has generated a pragmatism which is sufficient to avoid tensions created by the rapid industrialization and modernization.

Brazil, in contrast to semi-industrialized nations of Southeastern Asia and the Mediterranean, is the only country, among others in a similar state of development, that has an internal market capable of assuring an efficient scale of production for several industrial sectors. Politically, it is a nation which is near modernity, and as such it is more stable than it was twenty years ago, even though it is still facing modernization and transition pressures.

The second challenge for Brazil in the 1980s is the issue of financing the Brazilian development efforts, for which the importance of the external sector emerges with clarity. The analysis of issues such as accumulation of capital and technology indicate that they cannot be separated from those related to the integration of the Brazilian into the world economy.

The strategy adopted in the late 1960s and early 1970s explicitly emphasized the role of increasing the balance of trade deficits as a means of enlarging the inflow of external savings. On the other hand, direct foreign investments were sought in order to decrease the technological gap. This strategy could not be sustained after the impact of the oil shock in 1979-80, and the increase in international interest rates. Under these circumstances, it was necessary to obtain increasingly larger and growing trade balance surpluses in order to compensate for the balance of services.

Fendt and Salazar-Carrillo show that the major risks in the mechanisms to mitigate the impact of external restrictions during the next few years are to be found in basic changes of the international scenario. After the oil crisis of the 1970s, the international commercial and financial scenarios became progressively hostile towards the basic concepts which led to the expansion of international trade at rates considerably higher than those observed in the national economies. Protectionism assumed new forms in the developed world during the late 1970s and early 1980s. The multilateralization of commercial and financial flows was endangered.

In reference to trade with fully industrialized countries, the recent experiences of Brazil, and of other developing nations, is that their relations with industrialized nations show a dangerous generalization of the bilateral concept surfacing. On the financial side, multilateral credit institutions have been incapable of facing the challenge of financing a transition for the international financial system which turned to "trade financing" versus "balance of payments financing" of the 1970s. Finally, the functioning of the system of flexible foreign exchange rates adopted at the beginning of the 1970s, has been also highly negative for Brazilian foreign trade.

Fendt and Salazar-Carrillo conclude that modernization in Brazil has been a result of a long historical process, in which industrialization represented the major mobilizing force. Recent external crises, despite requiring an increasing stabilization effort in comparison with previous years, did not lead to a reversal of the principal objectives of political institutionalization and economic development.

Albert Fishlow in his comments on the paper by Fendt and Salazar-Carrillo indicates that their interpretation of the Brazilian response to the oil price shock is too exclusively based upon the external environment. Instead, Fishlow focuses an internal responses, as after all Brazil is a rather closed economy with the capacity initially to have responded to the oil price shock. He points to the lack of direction, the confusion and the alternative targets of government policy that were followed after 1974 as indication of the internal dimensions of the problem. In regard to the prospects for Brazil in the 1980s, Fishlow feels that the optimism over the international environment as a vehicle for Brzilian growth is misplaced. Further, Fishlow sees potential difficulties in regard to the extension of the political process proceeding smoothly. However, he does see a ground for optimism in the capacity for continuing emphasis upon import substitution and the ability to restrain imports over the course of the 1980s, as they were restrained over the previous decade.

Donald V. Coes in his paper, "Imperfect Capital Mobility Risk and Brazilian Foreign Borrowing," develops two models focusing on some of the determinants of capital flows in the context of a less developed country like Brazil. This is necessary since many features of capital mobility particular to the Brazilian case are not reflected in most contemporary models of capital mobility. In particular, the Brazilian situation is marked by an imperfect capital mobility. Most importantly, the greater ease with which capital can enter Brazil than with which it can leave leads to an analysis of risk. In the presence of uncertainty, the constraint on reverse capital flows from the borrowing country becomes binding. In addition, the thinness of markets which permit the transfer of different types of risk from one party to another is a feature of the Brazilian case. Finally, during the past ten years, financial capital flows to Brazil have been subject to a variety of restrictions which limit the extent to which capital that has entered Brazil may leave it.

The first model which focuses on the demand risks, since exchange risk is primarily borne by the borrower, highlights the role of exchange rate policy and the interaction with the monetary correction. In this model, Coes' in order to analyze exchange risks, assumes that all other variables relevant to the decision to borrow or lend can be treated as given and non-stochastic, hence given conditions in the international capital market. The second model supply side in nature, focuses on the lending decision, under the assumption that the return is uncertain. A general model is developed involving repayment risk and subsequently the specific case of full repayment versus complete default is examined.

The common element of both models is that borrowing and lending decisions are made in the presence of uncertainty. Although both models are partial equilibrium models, nevertheless some important policy oriented insights do emerge from Coes' approach. On the lending side, the model indicates the importance of the exchange rate regime followed and its link to the domestic price level. At a more general level, the approach suggests that policies which affect the level of relevant variables may have an impact on capital flows, which is independent of any change in the interest rate differential that is so central to deterministic models of capital mobility.

Rudiger Dornbusch in his comments on Coes' paper finds that it offers a valuable analysis of international capital mobility under conditions of capital controls and is in full agreement with Coes in emphasizing the minimum borrowing constraints, an important modification of standard analysis. Dornbusch raises some objections to a couple of the assumptions in the general model. Firstly, by imposing the assumption that the real price is non-stochastic, matters are being oversimplified. He points out that it is entirely plausible that in some industries the real price and the real cost of external finance are highly correlated. Secondly, Coes' formulation of the minimum investment terms leads to the notion that the real exchange rate has a variance that increases with the investment term. Clearly, such a model of the real exchange rate is not really acceptable. Despite these statements, Dornbusch suspects that the basic message of Coes' paper is nonetheless valid.

Carlos Von Doellinger's paper, "Exports and Foreign Debt in Brazil: Forecasting in the Eighties," tries to demonstrate that if Brazilian exports exhibit a performance similar to that observed during the past 15 years, it would be possible to get the current account of the balance of payments to a gradual adjustment, and to reverse the intense foreign debt growth. He also shows that this adjustment could be obtained even with the expectation of the growth of imports due to a recovery in the industrial sector.

The study presents an evaluation of the Brazilian export performance since 1954, when a new foreign trade policy was adopted. This policy, a result of a combination of fiscal, financial, and exchange rate incentives, was instrumental in that Brazilian exports grew at rates above that of world exports.

When comparing Brazilian exports with GDP and world exports, Von Doellinger shows that Brazil has a great export potential. And since growth in exports is a key variable in adjusting the balance of payments, he concludes that an adjustment can be gradually achieved.

In order to demonstrate his proposition, Von Doellinger constructed a model that tries to reproduce the debt process as a result of deficits in the current account of the Brazilian balance of payments. Based on this model he suggests alternatives in the evolution of the foreign debt as a function of performance of exports.

William G. Tyler found Von Doellinger's paper to be a useful and practical paper which focuses attention on the critical importance of export growth for the Brazilian economy, and on the nature and importance of the parameter estimates and assumptions in the projection exercise. However, he thinks it is an error to treat the years from the mid-sixties until the present as one homogenous period with regard to export performance and therefore, projections made on the basis of the export performance for the entire period appear misleading. He goes on to indicate that understanding the reasons for the decline in Brazilian export growth are to be found on the supply side. In order to cope with the terms of trade shock imposed by the increase in oil prices in the mid-1970s, the government imposed import restrictions, expanded external borrowing, and failed to appreciably adjust the exchange rate. This led to an increase in the anti-export biases in Brazilian commercial policies, which in effect discriminated against export activity. The result is that Brazil is now one of the world's most closed economies. Turning to the Von Doellinger projections, Tyler offers three principal suggestions for future work along similar lines. First, to endogenize some of the more interesting elements. Second, the projection exercise should be carried out in the context of as larger macro model framework. Third, one might gain further insight from a disaggregation of exports and imports.

Jose Carvalho in his paper, "Commercial Policy in Brazil: An Overview," focuses on an analysis of the trade policy adopted by Brazil since World War II. The trade policies were evaluated in terms of protection of domestic production and of the costs of domestic resources when foreign exchange is earned.

The first part of the study is a description of trade policies adopted. This description is divided into historical periods according to their most significant characteristics. During the period of 1946 to 1952, the main characteristic noted was a highly overvalued exchange rate. According to Carvalho, in order for Brazil to maintain the parity of 1937-38 in real terms, the cruzeiro should have been devalued by 42% after World War II. During the period 1953 to 1957, a system of multiple exchange rates and of foreign exchange auctions were utilized. From 1957 to 1960, higher ad valorem tariff rates were charged. The period of 1961 to 1964 was characterized by attempts to contain the balance of payments deficits. From 1964 to 1974, trade was promoted. The period between 1974 and 1979 saw a return to the policy of import substitution of capital goods, and a reduction on the impact caused by the oil price shock could be observed in the Brazilian economy. Finally, the main characteristic after 1979 was the control of the balance of payments deficit.

The second part of the study analyzes the use of each of the political instruments employed by Brazilian authorities to implement the policies mentioned. For giving incentives to the substitution of imports, higher tariff rates were adopted and selective imports which penalized consumer goods and favored capital goods and raw materials. The strategy of export promotion was based on measures of trade liberalization, fiscal incentives and mini-devaluations of the exchange rate.

The general conclusion is that the trade policies adopted by Brazil since 1949, have shifted between import substitution for the increase of industrialization and the attempt to control the balance of payments.

Larry Sjaastad in his comments on Carvalho's paper indicated that is was an excellent and useful summary of the development and current state of Brazilian commercial policy. He then offers some brief thoughts on several topics dealt with in the paper. In regard to commercial and exchange rate policy, Sjaastad indicates that exchange rate policy must be consistent with commercial policy, or internal markets will become distorted. He suggests a basket against which to peg the cruziero that reflects Brazilian trade patterns of approximately an equal division between the dollar bloc and Western Europe. Moving to the consistency of commercial policy, he says that the pre-1972 export subsidies were not inconsistent with the import tariffs. However, more recently both policies are being pursued with considerably more vigor and as a result, both must fail. Nonetheless, Sjaastad states that if a key characteristic of Brazilian foreign policy is to provide a high degree of discretionary latitude in decision-making, then commercial policy may be seen as consistent. Finally, Sjaastad indicates tht if one considers the increase in equilibrium wage rate caused by the combined effect of export subsidies and tariffs that the true effective protective arising is considerably less than is usually stated.

Werner Baer, in his paper, "Foreign Investments in Brazil: Their Benefits and Costs," turns to the question of foreign investment in the light of available empirical evidence.

In historical retrospect, he starts with the sectoral domination of foreign capital in Brazil, particularly British capital. According to Baer, the political pressures that England exerted on Brazil, permitted free access of English products and restricted Brazil to the stage of an exporter of raw materials until the 20th century. The British domination was exercised by a flow of capital for financing exports and imports and control over the shipping companies, the railways, the insurance companies, etc. From the beginning of the 1950s onwards, when Brazil adopted an import substitution strategy, foreign investments shifted from infra-structure to the manufacturing sector.

In the second part of his paper, Baer gives some general considerations regarding the benefits and costs of foreign investment for the development of Brazil. His main conclusions are: (a) the entry of foreign capital has a positive effect on the balance of payments, mainly during the initial stages of development of a new sector and when a sector suddenly begins to expand; (b) another benefit is linked to the rapid transfer of advanced technology, since beyond the production "know how," multinationals also transfer new administrative and organizational techniques; (c) the creation of new jobs and training of skilled manpower is another benefit to be considered; (d) finally, the multinationals established in Brazil make an additional contribution, by opening new markets for exports of manufactured products, utilizing their international marketing channels.

On the other hand, costs refer to (a) the impact on the balance of payments, with profit remittances to their country of origin; (b) the transfer of technology which is not appropriate taking into consideration the factors of production which are abundant locally; (c) the possibility of denationalization, due to the difficulty found by local enterprises to compete with multinational corporations; (d) the production and marketing of goods that could cause distortions in consumption patterns; (e) the political influence of the multinationals on governmental decisions on economic policy.

The author then goes on to analyze, using empirical evidence, the effects of foreign investment in Brazil in relation to:

(a) balance of payments;
(b) technology;
(c) income distribution;
(d) denationalization.

Finally, the policies of the Brazilian government are analyzed in relation to multinationals and their behavior in Brazil.

Baer concludes that the presence of multinationals in Brazil brought benefits and costs, but in the light of the evidence available, any conclusion as to the final balance of these costs and benefits would be subjective.

Tulio Duran in his comments of Werner Baer's paper indicates that the main problem for a country like Brazil with significant multinational presence is to correct the regulations that are causing distortions. He goes on to give some illustrative cases. First, in terms of direct investments versus foreign loans, the legislation is more severe at the margin on direct investments than on foreign loans. Therefore, multinationals prefer to make loans abroad, rather than to engage in direct investments. Second, the limitation of profit and royalty remittances resulting from regulation, provides incentive for MNC subsidiaries to overprice inputs imported from the home country in order to conceal the remittance of profits.

The trade-off between inflation and growth was analyzed by Claudio Contador in his paper, "Inflation and Recession: Fate or Political Choice in Brazil Today."

The orthodox viewpoint expressed by the Phillips Curve, indicates that there is a trade-off between inflation and real growth in the short run. But the author suggests real economic growth can remain positive, even though the objective of reducing inflation is usually accompanied by a temporary decline of GDP growth and higher employment.

One of the most important political implications of the Phillips Curve is that if ther exists a stable trade-off between inflation and unemployment, then it would be possible for the populace and political decision makers to choose and obtain a specific point on the curve representing an optimal combination for that particular society. It would also mean that unemployment could be permanently reduced, if the society were to accept higher inflation rates. Or, conversely, if the population did not want inflation, it could opt for a higher unemployment rate. The latter theoretical revisions that resulted from this line of reasoning suggest that a trade-off would exist only, or mainly, in the short run. Research done in Brazil confirmed this conclusion. Internationally, empirical studies showed that in the long run, the impact of expectation of inflation would compensate for the modification of aggregate demand, and the Phillips Curve would become vertical.

As a consequence of the conclusion obained, one could ask: if growth of the GDP cannot be maintained permanently above its historical level, what role remains for demand policies? Some economists argue that it would be a good political project to accelerate growth in the present, and obtain its benefits in the short run, even at the cost of a higher inflation rate later on.

Contador suggests that the model can describe cyclical movements of inflation and real growth when the disturbance comes from the demand side. If these disturbances come from the supply side, this focus fails to explain and predict the general tendencies of inflation and growth. In order to deal with these cases, another model is necessary. The belief in the inverse relationship between inflation and unemployment in the short run does not apply to situations of supply shocks. In situations of deterioration of the terms of trade, the strategies usually recommended by demand policies fail to reduce inflation and, moreover, bring about greater unemployment.

The inflationary outburst of 1980, followed by the 1981 recession, which only saw a small reduction in inflation, has been designated a consequence of incorrect economic policy, beyond the problems caused by supply shocks. However, these problems made the attempts to find a solution more difficult. Contador believes that better methods of evaluation are necessary to develop strategies that would be effective in dealing with supply shocks.

Samuel A. Morley finds himself in agreement with the case Contador has made regarding the explanation of the recent upsurge of inflation in Brazil as being the result of a series of supply shocks. Morley then attempts to extend Contador's analysis by focusing on the policy responses and possible causes for a supply shock inflation. Government, in response to supply shock, can either confine itself to the traditional tools of demand management, or it can choose to intervene in the wage price system in order to directly change relative prices. Demand management policy may be either neutral, contractionary or accomodating. Brazil chose the latter solution in 1979-80, and as a result Brazil is faced with either high inflation or recession or perhaps both. Looking on the other side of the coin, Morley indicates that although recessions allow the country to live within the bottleneck, they are a very inefficient way to bring about a change in relative prices. He points to the relatively successful stabilization of 1964-66 as offering lessons for the present. During that period, an income policy was imposed through an effective system of wage and price controls, and at the same time, contracting demand policies were in effect. Finally, in regard to indexing and productivity, Morley says that if there are to be productivity adjustments in the general wage indexing system, then there must be an agreement that the total of all the particular adjustments add up to no more than the real rate of productivity growth.

Roberto Macedo in his paper "Remarks on Brazilian Inflation and Wage Policy," deals with wage indexation and inflation, focusing on the transitionary period, 1979-80. In 1979, the government introduced six major changes in regard to wage readjustments; a semi-annual collective readjustment; a natural consumer price index to serve as a basis for the new wage policy; the establishment of rates of adjustment differentiated by wage level; an additional rate of readjustment based on the increase of productivity for each industry group; the announcement at least one month before the base date, of the readjustment to which one is entitled; a compensation for those industry groups which had already passed more than six months from the previous readjustment.

He then turns to analyzing the inflationary impact of the new wage policy. Macedo finds that the wage policy, which was introduced late in the fourth quarter, cannot be blamed for the initial outburst in the rate of inflation which began in the third quarter of 1979. In addition, he indicates that the wage policy did contribute to a further increase in the rate of inflation.

Macedo next discusses one of the demand effects of the wage policy. Workers during the latter part of 1979 had the expectation that their real wage would be higher in the future, and were optimistic that it was going to increase substantially. This led to increased spending in the fourth quarter, although by mid-1980 this effect had been exhausted, as workers knew that inflation had outstripped their wage gains.

In conclusion, although Macedo found that the wage policy led to higher rates of inflation, he nonetheless thinks that the issue of wage policy is basically a political one.

Fred Levy in commenting on Macedo's paper raises the important question "Is the policy sustainable beyond the short run?" Since an answer to this is not found in Macedo's work, Levy undertakes to formulate a response. He refers to the mandated ten percent per annum real wage increase for the large number of workers in the lowest pay categories, and states that quite apart from its impact on aggregate demand, such a rate of pay increase, far in excess of likely productivity gains, could only be non-inflationary if offset by a compression of the wage structure, falling profit rates, and/or the substantial disemployment of low wage labor. All three of these conditions occurred to some degree during the 1981 recession. But, as the economy recovers, new inflationary pressures could arise. Hence, while the wage plicy may not have been a significant factor in the inflation of the past year, it clearly does complicate the future trade off between growth, employment, balance-of-payment and price stabilization.

Antonio Carlos Lemgruber in "Brazil's Foreign Indebtedness--Determinants and Limits," discusses the factors that were responsible for the 22 percent annual growth rate of Brazil's foreign debt between 1975 and 1981. He indicates that the foreign debt growth rate relies primarily on five determinants: (i) the growth of international reserves; (ii) the magnitude of trade deficit; (iii) the magnitude of the services deficit; (iv) the international interest rate; and (v) the volume of foreign investments discounting remittance of dividends. In the Brazilian case, Lemgruber thinks that between 1974-1976; and again in the 1979-80 period, the main factor was clearly the trade balance deficit. However, in recent years, in particular 1982, the major component in Brazil's foreign indebtedness became the international interest rate. He further indicates that based on the current Brazilian situation that foreign debt growth is equal to the international interest rate, if the trade and service balance do poorly. Another element which influences the Brazilian gross demand for funds is the amount of amortizations. Brazil also faces a constraint from the supply side as larger banks are no longer willing to let their international assets grow faster than their capital. Finally, in regard to policy making in the external sector, he suggests that the external debt will be required to grow less than the international interest rate and exports will have to grow more than the international interest rate.

John Williamson in his paper, "Short Run Economic Policy in Brazil," offers considerations on the short term economic policy that should have been pursued at that moment (1982), mainly taking into consideration the indications of severe stagflation.

He emphasizes, initially, that stagflation is a phenomenon that is worldwide, therefore not being specific only to Brazil. It is often the case that short term economic policies are not put into a long term framework. According to Williamson, the basic problem of Keynesian demand administration, as it was practiced in the 1950s and 1960s, has been the lack of such an overall framework. For him, although it might not be possible to achieve an absolute economic harmony, some harmony may evidentally be achieved. As a result, it would not be necessary to go through a depression of the proportions of the one currently being experienced in Brazil.

The article mentions two major long run constraints faced by the Brazilian economy. The first one is inflation, analyzed by Claudio Contador in terms of unemployment through use of the Phillips Curve. With the presence of a supply shock, such as the deterioration of trade terms, there would not exist favorable circumstances for a sharp decline in inflation at a relatively low cost. Therefore, the strategy should be to maintain demand at an appropriate level, avoiding inflationary pressures, but without aiming at sharp reductions, until a favorable supply shock came along (such as a drop in oil prices).

Williamson does not take the Phillips Curve as the sole basis for explaining inflation in Brazil, he also uses a two-sector model: one sector with fixed prices, where participants involved are in a position to demand real income gains, which interacts with a sector of flexible prices, which, in Brazil, is clearly represented by the agricultural sector. With a passive monetary policy, whose objective is to reach a specific level of demand, it becomes impossible to avoid an acceleration of inflation. The adoption of a restrictive monetary policy, contracting demand, would affect the real income of the flexible price sector, and the real product of the fixed price sector. For Williamson, this would be a useful model, not only to understand what was happening in Brazil, but also to understand what was occurring in the world at the time.

Stan Czamanski, in "Long Run Perspectives" focuses on discernible trends in the development of the Brazilian economy. The "Brazilian model," which has become a model of development is based on determined policies aimed at industrialization that invariably involve a lowering of the present standards of living for the sake of benefits likely to accrue beyond the time horizon of political decision makers. The industrial growth of Brazil and its impressive human capital are witnesses to the success of this policy. The process of rapid industrialization and the related governmental policies has raised some significant problems. Firstly, the often exagerrated hopes of finding employment in the rapidly growing cities led to massive rural to urban migration. Secondly, the vast agglomeration of populations and of industrial plants, symptomatic of Sao Paolo and Rio de Janeiro, is, however, inadequately endowed with basic urban servies and suffers from excessive densities. Finally, the rapid industrialization conflicts to some degree with the Brazilian policy of frontier development, particularly in the north-western direction.

BRAZIL AND THE FUTURE:
SOME THOUGHTS ON THE EIGHTIES

Roberto Fendt Jr.
Jorge Salazar-Carrillo

INTRODUCTION

These are times in which the international environment is marked by military conflict in the South Atlantic, political and economic difficulties related to the North-South dialogue, and commodity agreements—such as the new multifiber one, which limited the amount of exports from the developing countries gaining entry into the industrial markets. To use David Rockefeller's apt phrasing, we are living through financial times of "treacherous economic seas and gale force financial winds".

Signs of turbulence are also found in some conflicting and diverging trends in economic and political realities. Economically, the world is probably more interdependent today than at any other point in time since the heyday of trade as the "engine of growth" in the nineteenth century. Yet, politically countries are more apart than ever, and the success of OPEC fits into this broader political diffusion. Socially, divergent trends are also observed between the industrial and developing nations. In the former, population is rapidly becoming older and overeducated. This is not the population willing to produce low-skilled, highly labor-intensive goods. In the latter, the best qualified population is ever eager to produce labor intensive goods for the markets in the industrialized countries. Yet pockets of untrained workers, with low spatial and career mobility, make such adjustment to dynamic changes in comparative advantage very difficult. Inability to cope with such adjustment problems is a vivid example of the divergent trends in economic and political realities.

In the South there is an uneasy feeling about the international environment as still being dominated by the same basic forces that prompted the events occurring at the time of the initial oil shocks. Thus, while one out of eight barrels of oil produced still burn on the American highways, prices kept rising from $13 in 1978, to $19 in 1979, to $31 in 1980, and to $35 in 1981. Those who believe that the old oil glut days are back should take note that the decline in prices in 1982 has a lot to do with the recessionary climate in most industrialized countries, where growth declined from 4.6 percent in 1978, to 3.3 percent in 1979, to 0.3 percent in 1980, to a barely positive level in 1981, to a slightly negative figure of -2.2 percent in 1982.

The basic uncertainties related to the huge financial transfers to the OPEC countries have not yet been properly addressed; and the combination of an orthodox monetary policy in the key currency country (the U.S.), coupled with a decidedly expansionary fiscal policy, has raised LIBOR consistently, from an average of 9 percent in 1978, to 12 percent in 1979, to 14 percent in 1980 and to more than 16 percent in 1981. There are hopes that it might remain around the current levels of 14 percent , but one also should not forget that the real rate of interest today is closer than in any intervening year to the real rates prevailing in the 1930-34 period. Consequences for real output growth and employment in the industrial countries are obvious; and so are the consequences for commodity prices and exports from the developing countries to those countries.

Recently economic, political, and social events in Brazil must be considered against this international background. Now, as always, economic development results from a combination of social motivation, political stability and a properly defined savings investment process. Before addressing the issues related to long term development, let us pause to consider the recent events.

SECTION I.

The external shocks in the early and late seventies were quite severe for Brazil. As the largest importer of oil among the developing countries the rise in the prices of this commodity hit Brazil with uncommon intensity. The compound effect of the first oil shock which alone included terms of trade and export volume losses in the industrialized country markets, at the time in recession, amounted to an average of 2.8 percent of Brazilian GNP for each of the years between 1974 and 1977. The new round of oil price hikes in 1979-80 had similar effects.

Reactions to the external shocks in Brazil took essentially three forms. The more important reaction was a new round of import substitution. Export promotion, although vigorous, was not able to offset the negative effects of the shocks on the demand for Brazilian exports, although setting the basis for a large geographical redirectioning of its export markets. Finally, the decision to finance, instead of adjusting promptly the external imbalances, resulted in a large expansion of external indebtedness. It is not lacking in interest, on this account, to note that real rates of interest in the international financial markets – coupled with an eagerness of international bankers to lend to semi-industrialized countries (not observed since the twenties) made the decision to borrow given the available information, the most rational. Milton Friedman, among others, kept saying that cartels do not last long; and few would have believed that the superpowers would yield to OPEC demands.

The new round of price hikes after Khomeini, the events in Teheran, and the dramatic change in monetary policy in the U.S. in the summer of 1980, prompted Brazil to completely change the strategy then pursued. International rates of interest became highly positive, and prospects were that they would remain so for a long time; there would be no foreseeable oil gluts, except during periods of recession in the OECD countires; hopes for a continuing multilateralization of trade (the great aspirations of the GATT after the War) were being progressively eroded, even at the time when the Tokyo Round negotiations were being completed.

When the new stabilization program started, many of the macroeconomic variables were in disarray. Inflation peaked at a yearly rate of 12 percent in March 1981; by April, the balance of trade was still recording a 12 month accumulated deficit of around $1.4 billion; the current account, by the close of 1980, registered a deficit of $12.5 billion. Domestic credit and monetary policies were not alien to the changing international conditions: the domestic money supply was growing at 85 percent in May 1980, and rising expectations of inflation were widening the gap between the growth in the money supply and inflation. As a result of domestic expansionary policies GDP grew at 7.9 percent in 1980.

In 1981, a reordering of the economy took place. The major short term policy objective became the easing of pressures on the balance of payments. Growth was temporarily interrupted. By the end of the year the results were, if not impressive, at least headed in the right direction. Inflation had declined to 95 percent by December; the balance of trade had recovered from deficit to a $1.2 billion surplus, the largest in the history of the country; international reserves grew, after two years of persistent decline. Money supply growth abated to 72 percent.

Much of the improvement in the balance of payments had to do with the behavior of the balance of trade, since the services account was negatively affected by the rising interest costs. Credit allocations to finance exports received the highest priority in this context crawling peg-devaluations followed closely domestic inflation, thus imparting a real devaluation over parity, and neutralizing the appreciation in the real rate observed in 1980. All in all, exports grew almost 16 percent, with non-coffee exports growing more than 32 percent. These figures compare with an expansion of world trade of only 3 percent. Imports declined by more than 4 percent in current dollars, with non-oil imports declining by 16 percent. The volume of oil imports itself declined by 8 percent, which, given rising prices, was not enough to preclude the oil bill from increasing to $10.3 billion.

If the results in the balance of payments were immediate, other areas were also affected by the new set of economic policies. Results, however, were less impressive, and will certainly take more time to show up. Current strategy comtemplates an overall reindustrialization, away from energy and import-intensive industries, towards activities with a higher positive contribution to the trade balance; the progressive reduction in the rate of inflation; and positive action on the distribution of wealth.

Reindustrialization called for increased priority to be given to agroindustries, mining and alternative energy programs, in addition to, the emphasis on export expansion. Instruments include increased credit allocations - as in the case of exports - and other government support programs, such as support prices for agriculture at higher relative levels. In the case of agriculture, the results that were obtained in accordance with priorities were: agricultural output grew more than 7 percent in 1981, after a very good harvest in 1980. Furthermore, agricultural growth was not concentrated in a few products, as has happened so frequently in the past, but growth encompassed both exportables and food staples consumed in the domestic market. Crucial for this increased output was the elimination of uncertainty associated with support prices, which were indexed for the first time to inflation, in addition to ample credit supplies. Subsidies were reduced, though, without any of the noticeable side-effects, which some had expected.

Energy conservation and increased domestic production also revealed positive results in 1981. Thus, overall oil consumption declined 10 percent, to one million barrels a day. Domestic production grew 43 percent, to 260 thousand barrels a day (tbd); additionally domestic reserves also substantially increased over previous figures, reaching almost 2 billion barrels. With a declining domestic consumption and an increased domestic output, imports declined dramatically. Output continued in the first quarter of 1982 to set record levels; by February, production had reached 282 tbd and will certainly reach 300 tbd before the end of the year. Independent estimates now count on 500 tbd by 1985, when domestic supplies will account for half of the national oil consumption. By that time, oil will account for about one fourth of total energy consumption, as opposed to almost 40 percent today; hydro-electric power will increase its share from 30 to 40 percent; and charcoal and alcohol will account for 20 percent, as opposed to 10 percent presently. The beginning of exploitation at the Carajás project sets new heights for mining in Brazil.

Restructuring also meant that some energy intensive industries were severely hit. In particular, the automobile industry was the center of the recession: output declined by more than one-third, from 1.1 million units to slightly more than 780 thousand. The automobile parts industry, together with iron, steel and other industries down the line, were also severely affected. Part of the explanation for the decline may be attributable to government policy, especially because the maximum terms in the length of car loans were reduced compulsorily, and also as a result of the overall measures aimed at monetary control, which produced record real interest rates.

In all, industrial output must have declined by some 10 percent over the 1980 peak. Although it is true that the basis for comparison is somewhat inflated, overall GNP grew 7.9 percent in that year, it is quite clear that results in 1981 were divergent from previous trends.

These results raise several questions. In the short term what is questioned is the efficacy of the stabilization program and its instrumentalization. Was it necessary for output to have declined so much to halt the acceleration of inflation? What was the role of the stringent monetary growth deceleration observed since the middle of 1980, and what were the effects of both record high real interest rates and the acceleration of the crawling peg?

Rudiger Dornbusch, of MIT, has questioned the traditional view that inflation in Latin America is primarily a fiscal issue, because this approach ignores completely the transition costs to stabilization. Efforts in 1981 brought significant results in bringing down the deficit of the Brazilian public sector from 8.7 percent of GNP to about 4 percent. But one should not necessarily expect substantial results, since, "although fiscal policy certainly sets the trend rate of inflation when there is deficit finance, inflation may be quite independent of the

budget in the short run and enjoy a life of its own".[1] Since expectations
of inflation, coupled with the widespread indexation of the economy,
introduce a feedback mechanism of inflation inertia, stabilization will
not produce the same kind of immediate results as observed, for instance,
during the stabilization program of 1965-66, when indexation was non-
existent. In a sense, the difficulty today is the narrow capacity of the
stabilization program to change relative prices and expectations of
changes in these relative prices. On the other hand, experiments in Latin
America with a managed real appreciation of the exchange rate, by ignoring
the long lags in the process, have been producing either frustation or
balance of payments disequilibria. As Dornbusch has concluded, "the chief
concern, of course, remains the proposition that inflation stabilization
involves inevitably a protracted recession. All the evidence suggests
that there is not sufficient inflation flexibility to allow a collapse of
prevailing inflation rates simply because money growth has fallen.
Because the costs of a protracted recession are vast compared to the
allocation costs of policy activism, one cannot but return to the
suggestion that an effective stabilization program, along with fiscal
sanitation and some contraction of demand, should include wage controls
and real interest ceilings".[2]

SECTION II.

How do these short term events affect long term prospects? The two major
challenges for the Brazilian society in the eighties are the creation of a
social motivation for the savings effort and the problem of political
institutionalization, conducive to the stability necessary for the
investment process.

It was argued that just after the first external shocks in the early
seventies, the carefully programmed political decompression might be
endangered by "lack of time". In a sense, the previous rapid economic
growth in the 1967-73 period had purchased time for the
institutionalization process to follow its own dynamics. A relapse into
slower growth might create the kind of dilemma so often found in Brazilian
history along the first half of the century. As Huntington has pointed
out, modernity is conducive to stability, but modernization is inherently
destabilizing.[3] Although this sort of preoccupation might help to explain
why Brazil refused to adjust promptly to the shocks, its contribution was
probably minor for the reasons previously advanced.

Performance over the 1967-73 period was not sufficient to shield the
system from "contestação" (disagreement). Indeed, the period prior to the
first wave of external shocks coincides with the peak in organized illegal

---

[1] Rudiger Dornbusch, "Inflation Stabilization and Capital Mobility,"
Lecture in Memory of Miguel Sidrauski delivered at the meetings of the
Econometric Society, Buenos Aires, July 1980.

[2] Rudiger Dornbusch, "Inflation Stabilization and Capital Mobility,"
Lecture in Memory of Miguel Sidrauski delivered at the meetings of the
Econometric Society, Buenos Aires, July 1980.

[3] Samuel P. Huntington, Political Order in Changing Societies, New
Haven: Yale University Press, 1968.

opposition to the regime, no doubt very much influenced by the events in France. These lessons were certainly not ignored. In fact, the Brazilian experience both before and after the shocks provided ample evidence that, as Roberto Campos cogently pointed out, "performance in terms of economic development does not in itself assure political stability".[4] Quoting Seymour Lipset, he goes on to point out that "although the validation of a system might come from its efficacy in satisfying the demands of the population, its political stability is better assured by legitimacy, or political loyalty, the latter defined as the capacity of the political system to engender and maintain the belief that its political institutions are the most adequate to the society. Efficacy is an instrumental value, while legitimacy is an effective dimension."[5] Over the recent past, political stability was legitimized by economic success, by the ample reforms and by development. Legitimacy is now the fruit of the general amnesty, the reordering of the political system towards one of multiple parties, (so rooted in Brazilian traditions), by the complete removal of press censorship and by the elections in November.

The tensions generated by modernization are not new to Brazil. In the Brazilian context, modernization has been equivalent to industrialization, the only genuine mobilizing force for development observed throughout the century. The Brazilian experience is also particular in the sense that it has generated enough pragmatism to be able to circumvent the tensions generated by rapid industrialization and modernization. It has already been pointed out that the political process in Brazil became "consensual" probably ahead of time. Not always was economic development able to follow social mobilization. Sometimes the level of frustation went down from the elite to the masses, and in those instances the political party system was not able to reduce the level of frustation through political options. Examples are found not only in several instances of external shocks like the Depression and World War II--but also in domestic events quite unrelated to external events, like the Goulart period.

Pragmatism, especially in economic policy, has helped to rescue the system from circumstances in which there was a potential for disruption and political instability, with their economic dual of reduced savings and investment. As Diaz Alejandro has forcibly argued, the experience of the "large" countries in Latin America during the 1930's, a temporary abandonment of the "orthodoxy", reduced substantially the social costs of adjustment and protected the economy from a long period of economic and political relapse.[6]

Therefore, the institutionalization of the political process in Brazil is again a prime example of Brazilian pragmatism. Brazil is closer today to modernity than at any previous period, and more immune from political

---

[4]Roberto de Oliveira Campos, A Nova Economia Brasileira, Rio de Janeiro: Livraria José Olympio, 1975.

[5]Roberto de Oliveira Campos, A Nova Economia Brasileira, Rio de Janeiro: Livraria José Olympio, 1975.

[6]Carlos Diaz Alejandro, "Lessons of the Thirties for the Eighties," Mimeo, Yale University. Growth Center, 1981.

instability. Return to political participation has become the main form of assuring motivation for the development process.

Most observers have not paid enough attention to the fact that the long period of political decompression will force institutionalization to work within a new social environment, quite unrelated to that of the sixties. Population dynamics is creating new forces for change in contemporary Brazil. These changes go much beyond the fact that GNP per capita grew faster in Brazil than almost everywhere else since the middle sixties. It can be observed through examination of indicators of social welfare, such as access to schooling, homes served by running water and electricity, ownership of the major consumer durables, life expectancy and others, that a massive change has taken place.

The labor force has also undergone substantial changes over the past twenty years. By 1960, population growth was at an all time high, due especially to a large reduction in the death rate. The picture during the seventies shows a still declining death rate, accompanied however by a significant decline in the birth rate.

Table 1. Brazil: Household Characteristics, 1970 and 1980

Number of Households	1970	1980	% Annual Average Growth
Total	17,628,699	26,436,516	4.13
Number of Persons per Household	5.28	4.50	-1.58
Urban	10,276,340	18,213,575	5.89
Owner Occupied*	6,157,744	10,930,675	5.91
With Running Water*	5,592,006	13,810,934	9.46
With Sewer*	2,290,513	6,886,695	11.64
With Gas Stove*	7,124,896	15,170,946	7.85
With Electricity*	7,768,721	16,124,904	7.58
With Radio*	7,439,481	14,435,219	6.85
With Refrigerator*	4,362,681	12,054,999	10.70
With Television*	4,134,312	13,311,504	12.40
With Car*	1,407,028	5,155,716	13.87

Source: Brazilian Census, 1970 and 1980

*Urban Households

Table 2. Brazil Population Growth, Birth and Death Rates, 1940-1980

Census Year	Total Resident Population	*Rates of Population Growth (%)	*Birth Rate (%)	*Death Rate (%)
1940	41,165,289	-	-	-
1950	51,941,767	2.35	4.44	2.09
1960	70,070,457	2.90	4.32	1.42
1970	93,139,037	2.89	3.87	0.98
1980	119,070,865	2.49	3.30	0.81

Source: Decennial Censuses

*Annual averages over the previous ten years

These basic changes in population growth were accompanied by other social developments. Female participation in the labor force increased from 29.4 to 33.6 percent between 1970 and 1980. In absolute terms, female employment rose 116 percent during those ten years, compared with an increase of 78 percent for male employment. Both male and female employment grew faster than population.

Urbanization continued at a fast pace, although showing some abatement when compared with previous trends. But despite this deceleration by 1980 more than two thirds of the Brazilians lived in urban areas, as compared with slightly more than 45 percent in 1960. This shift in the ratio of urban to rural population was accompanied by a dramatic change in sectoral employment. Noteworthy is the reduction in the relative importance of agricultural employment, from providing more than one half of total employment in 1960 to providing less than one third in 1980.

Table 3. Brazil: Urban Population Growth, 1940–1980

Census year	Urban Share In Total	Average Annual Rate of Growth in Urban Population (over the previous ten years)
1940	31.23	–
1950	36.15	3.84
1960	45.15	5.47
1970	55.97	5.16
1980	67.69	4.48

Source: Same as previous tables.

Table 4. Brazil: Age Composition, Literacy and Labor Force Participation, 1940–1980

Census year (%)	% of Population Between 0 - 14 years	Literacy Rate (%)	Labor Force Participation
1940	42.57	43.04	36.85
1950	41.73	48.35	32.95
1960	42.60	60.63	32.47
1970	42.01	67.95	31.73
1980	37.36	74.50	36.78

Source: Same as previous tables.

Table 5. Brazil: Percentage of the Labor Force Employed in Each Productive Sector

Census year	Agriculture and Mining	Manufacturing	Construction	Commerce	Communications	Public Administration	Other*
1940	65.88	7.45	1.76	4.67	3.16	2.74	14.32
1950	59.90	9.40	3.42	5.51	3.73	2.99	15.05
1960	53.96	8.59	3.43	6.50	4.30	2.13	20.09
1970	44.28	10.97	5.82	7.60	3.95	3.90	23.48
1980	29.93	15.55	7.19	9.39	4.15	4.14	29.54

Source: Same as previous tables.

*Other Industrial and Service Activities

What do all these developments in demographic dynamics mean for Brazilian political institutionalization and economic development? It is clear that the picture which emerged from the 1980 census, is that of a predominately urban society, with a young labor force; the most qualified labor force in Brazilian history.

Unlike the Southeast Asia and the Mediterranean rim semi-industrialized nations, Brazil is the only one with a domestic market large enough to ensure an efficient production scale for several industrial sectors. Politically it is, a nation closer to "modernity" and, therefore, much more stable than twenty years ago, although still under the pressures of "modernization" and all its inherent problems.

SECTION III.

Having addressed the issue of institutionalization, the major remaining challenge for Brazil in the eighties is the issue of financing the Brazilian development effort. It is in this context that the importance of the external sector appears more clearly.

We will not pursue in detail the issues of foreign debt or commercial policy and foreign investment, since the papers of Fendt-Lemgruber, Carvalho and Baer discuss them extensively. It is sufficient to point out that the issues of long-term capital accumulation and technology cannot be disentangled from the issue of the integration of the Brazilian economy into the world economy.

On the other hand, debt acquired in the past will continue to press the "transfer problem" for Brazil, much in the same way as World War I created a reparations problem for Germany. The strategy pursued in the late sixties and early seventies emphasized explicitly the role of a widening trade gap as a way to enlarge the inflow of foreign savings. To bridge the technological gap, direct foreign investment was also stimulated. The newly acquired political stability and the new instrumentalization of economy policy, such as the monetary correction, brought about the recovery of domestic savings. All these real resources allowed a rate of investment unequaled in the past. This strategy became unattainable after the second oil shocks in 1979-80 and the rise in international interest rates. What is needed now is a progressively larger trade surplus in order to cope with the service account deficit.

The need to produce larger and larger trade surpluses puts in check the very nature of the real resources transfer mechanism and raises questions about the ability to generate domestically, enough additional savings to substitute for the previous inflow of foreign resources. Of course the key variable for policy-making is export growth. On the capital account, enlargement of multilateral sources of credit may help substantially to alleviate the transfer problem, since the key point here is the extension of maturity periods.

Recent experience has shown that Brazilian exports are highly responsive to changes in profitability and have grown above the rates of growth of net external debt. On the other hand, net external debt has decelerated its rate of growth, in spite of the increase in interest rates. It is reasonable to expect that over the coming years, as the von Doellinger simulations show, the Brazilian net external debt will not exceed, on the average, the rate of expansion of international banks capital plus reserves.[7]

What are the possible risks on the way to alleviating the external constraints over the coming years? Probably the main risk resides in the basic changes in the international scenario. After the oil shocks of the seventies, the international trade and financial scenarios have become progressively hostile to the very basic concepts which led to the expansion of international trade at a rate far above that of the expansion of the national economies. Protectionism has taken new forms in the developed world in the late seventies and eighties. One cannot discard the idea that the floating of the major exchange rates might lead to interlocking problems like those observed in the thirties, and which led to Bretton Woods. Multilateralization of trade and financial flows is in jeopardy.

On trade matters, the recent experience of Brazil and other developing nations in their trade relations with the industrial countries has shown that we are flirting dangerously with the idea of bilateralism. Bilateral negotiations are so widespread as to put in check the very concept of the "most favored nation." The Tokyo Round negotiations were unable to provide a solid basis for a code on non-tariff barriers, and these have escalated since. It is incongruous that tariff rates are so low, when they matter so little. Other signs of relapse into bilateralism are the growing importance of the concepts of "conditional reciprocity" and retaliation measures. "Fair trade" is progressively replacing "free trade".

On financial grounds, the multilateral credit institutions have been unable to face the challenge of the lenders in light of the fundamental imbalances raised by the huge financial transfers to OPEC countries. It helps very little to say that the developing countries resist the conditionality of IMF and other multilateral agencies. There simply would not be enough resources had the non-oil developing nations decided to accept those conditionalities.

In the particular case of Brazil and other industrializing developing nations, the issue of "graduation" poses yet another threat to international economic relations. Recently Brazil has faced "graduation" in the application of the Generalized System of Preferences (GSP) and at international lending agencies, like the Inter-American Development Bank (IDB). These procedures run counter to the very purpose of enlarging free trade areas and of serving as supplementary sources of balance of payments adjustment. Frustation over raised expectations becomes inevitable.

Finally, the working of the floating exchange rate system, adopted by the international monetary authorities in the early seventies, has also been highly detrimental for Brazilian foreign trade, as mentioned earlier. Apparent comparative advantages are created and destroyed by appreciations and depreciations, turning profitable investment for export into a new

---

[7]Carlos Von Doellinger, "Exports and Foreign Debt in Brazil: Forecasting the Eighties". Paper for the workshop on the Recent Developments and Future Perspectives of the Brazilian Economy, (included in this volume) Florida International University, 1982.

source of required susidization. Uncertainty precludes a higher level of investment in the tradeables sector, and delays desired adjustments.

Some concluding comments are in order. Modernization in Brazil has been the fruit of a long historical process in which industrialization has been the major mobilizing force. Economic development has proceeded on a relatively smooth path, no doubt due to the pragmatic conduct of economic policy in Brazil.

The recent external shocks, although requiring a new stabilization effort over the past years which remains ongoing, have not induced a relapse from the major objectives of political institutionalization and economic development. Increased political participation is now providing a major motivation for the process and creating the necessary stability for the savings-investment mechanism to continue operating. Brazil has been through times of "treacherous economic seas and gale-force financial winds" before, always, pragmatically transforming challenges into opportunities. These times will be no different.

SOME ADDITIONAL THOUGHTS ON BRAZILIAN TRADE,
PRICES AND EXCHANGE RATES

Jorge Salazar-Carrillo
Roberto Fendt Jr.

In this chapter an attempt is made to consider a couple of important aspects of foreign trade and policy-making in Brazil. The first part addresses the characteristics of Brazilian-American trade during the last decade and a half, bringing to the fore rather lightly used statistical information. Hopefully, this will provide a cue for further pondering with respect to the commercial relations between these two nations.

The second part considers the relationship between price and exchange rates in Brazil in the context of the relevant economic policies, and its competitiveness in the world markets. Again, new data is introduced which throws a different light into well treaded research subjects. This part brings to the forefront the important role that the balance between internal and external prices has for international economic relationships.

RECENT TRENDS IN THE TRADE BETWEEN BRAZIL AND THE U.S.

Traditionally, the U.S. market has been of fundamental importance to Brazil. Although in the late fifties and early sixties a process of erosion of this U.S. preponderance was evident, a recovery took place in the late sixties and early seventies, as is evident in Table 1.

The rate of growth in the volume of exports to the U.S. during the two triennial periods spanning the years 1967 to 1973 were nothing short of spectacular. It should be considered, however, that 1967 signals the recovery of the Brazilian economy from practically half a decade of slow growth.

As shown in the same table, the expansion of the real G.D.P. for Brazil expressed in 1975 U.S. dollars, was very high. This is remarkable given that the figures were submitted to a double deflation process. First, they have been translated into real U.S. dollars through purchasing-power-parity rates. Thus, the increase in gross product has been adjusted to reflect the same purchasing power over total G.D.P. that the U.S. dollar has. Second, the G.D.P. figures have been expressed in constant prices of 1975, by adjusting the real, but current gross products of U.S. and Brazil, to constant values of 1975. Thus, the G.D.P. figures for Brazil appearing in Table 1 are expressed in terms of the purchasing power of the U.S. dollar in 1975.

Contrasting the expansion in the quantity of exports from Brazil to the U.S. with that of Brazilian overall product, it is apparent that they have been quite similar for the 1967 to 1973 period as a whole. Although growing at a slightly faster pace, Brazilian imports from the U.S. followed a similar expansion path.

The rate of growth of real G.D.P. in constant dollars of 1975 slackened off in the 1973-79 period, as can be seen in Table 1. Yet the pace of the Brazilian economy was still quite vibrant. However, the data shown there makes evident that bilateral trade between the U.S. and Brazil displays a very different trend during this period. The quantity of Brazilian exports to the U.S. rises very little between 1973 and 1979, and the same pattern is shown by Brazilian imports from the U.S. Thus, a clear divorce takes place between the expansion of total production and the volume of total trade with the U.S.

No explanation for this sudden plateau in exports to the U.S. can be found in the evolution of total Brazilian exports.[1] To try another angle, the column of unit price data on exports to and imports from the U.S. was included in Table 1. This was done reluctantly as these figures resulted from very crude, unweighted calculations, directly derived from current value and volume figures. During the middle years of the period, a sudden jump in the unit values of Brazilian exports to the U.S. may help explain the volume drop that correspondingly occurred during the same time span.[2] However, Graph 3 depicts this rise as taking place in the year 1977, thus the search for another explanation is well warranted.

This may well consist of a combination of several factors. One particularly appealing strand lies in the increasing tensions that arose in the Brazilian-American relationship during the 1970's. It started with the coining of Brazil as the South American superpower and with the human rights approach to foreign policy. Trade policies on both sides may have been affected by such circumstances, which resulted in the removal of the remaining U.S. military mission in Brazil, and the rise of Western Germany as a major economic partner, through its participation in Brazilian nuclear power development.

It should be noted that the figures for imports of American products, although less erratic than their export counterparts, do also show

---

[1]See Antonio Carlos Lemgruber, Roberto Fendt, Jr., and Paulo Nogueira Batista, Jr., External Shocks and Policy Responses in Brazil During the Seventies, Centro de Estudos Monetarios e de Economia Internacional, IBRE, Fundacao Getulio Vargas and Fundacao Centro de Estudos de Comercio Exterior, mimeo, August 1980.

[2]In the unpublished Annex, section 3 shows the graphing of the terms of trade in Brazil-U.S. commerce. It can be seen that the chief culprits in the export price jump were the food and live animals and the minerals and fuels categories. The explosion of coffee prices seems to have carried most of the explanatory weight.

stagnation for the 1973–79 period as a whole. The quantity of imports grew by only 2 percent from 1977 to 1979, this being the largest expansion of any sub-period. However, in this case it is consistent with the trend of Brazilian imports from the rest of the world, which were practically held at an even keel from 1973 to 1979, if the rise in the price of fuel imports is appropriately discounted.

Sometimes graphs can support the best understanding of a situation, and it is probably useful to depict those matching the yearly values, volumes and unit values of American (A) and Brazilian (B) bilateral exports. In terms of values in current dollars the recurrent trade gap in favor of the U.S widened from 1973 to 1979, which provided the incentive for a more successful export performance by Brazil in the U.S. markets, and for a tightening of American imports into Brazil. This apparently was being accomplished by the end of the seventies.

The unit value graphs depict an interesting picture of substantial stability first, and irregular movements from 1974 on. Terms of trade jump in favor of the U.S. from 1974 to 1977, and from that year on, they are jolted in the opposite direction to suddenly improve the Brazilian position.

Table 1. Brazil: Rates of Growth of Gross Domestic Product Exports and Imports by Volume and Unit Prices in Percentages, 1967–1979

| | G.D.P.[1] | Volumes[2] of | | Unit Prices[3] of | |
		Exports to U.S.	Imports from U.S.	Exports to U.S.	Imports from U.S.
1967–1970	7.0	5.7	9.0	0.6	7.0
1970–1973	14.0	16.0	13.6	6.6	20.5
1973–1975	5.0	26.7	1.4	−9.5	27.5
1975–1977	9.0	−58.6	−0.8	134.3	−9.6
1977–1979	5.0	34.0	2.0	−8.6	1.4

Sources: For Trade Data: U.S. Dept. of Commerce/Bureau of the Census: U.S. General Imports–FT 155

U.S. Dept. of Commerce/Bureau of the Census: U.S. Foreign Trade Exports–FT 45

G.D.P. and G.D.Y. data: Kravis, Heston and Summers[4], "New Insights into the Structure of the World Economy", The Review of Income and Wealth, No. 4, December 1981.

For Population Data: United Nations Demographic Yearbook, 1980.

[1]G.D.P. in 1975 U.S. Dollars.
[2]Volume by shipping weight in thousand pounds.
[3]Unit prices in dollars per pound.
[4]Benchmark surveys were conducted in 1967, 1970, 1973 and 1975.

Graph 1

VALUES OF BILATERAL AMERICAN AND BRAZILIAN EXPORTS IN IN THOUSANDS OF DOLLARS

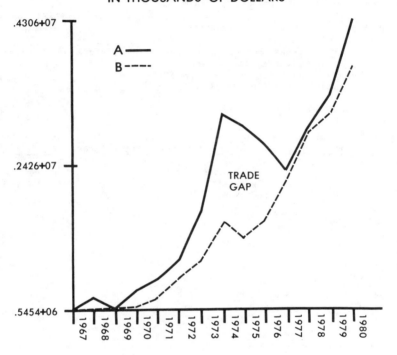

Source: **U.S. Dept. of Commerce/Bureau of the Census.**
U.S. General Imports - 155
U.S. Foreiqn Trade, Exports - FT 455

GRAPH 2. VOLUME OF BILATERAL AMERICAN AND BRAZILIAN EXPORTS IN THOUSANDS OF POUNDS.

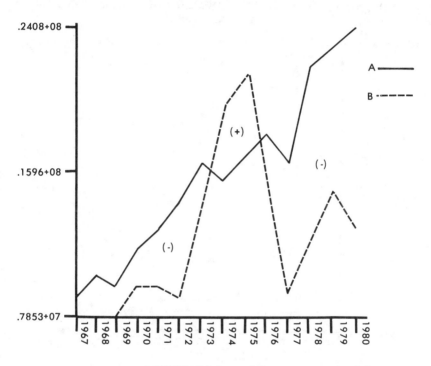

SOURCES: U.S. Dept. of Commerce/Bureau of the Census
U.S. General Imports - FT 155
U.S. Foreign Trade Exports - FT 455

Graph 3

UNIT VALUES OF BILATERAL AMERICAN AND BRAZILIAN EXPORTS, IN U S DOLLARS PER POUND.

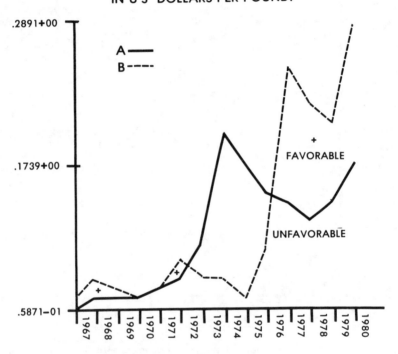

Source: **U.S. Dept. of Commerce/Bureau of the Census.**
U.S. General Imports - FT 155
U.S. Foreign Trade, Exports - FT 455

BRAZILIAN PRICE POLICIES AND THEIR EFFECTS ON TRADE

After World War II, Brazil has seldom shown rates of inflation of less than 10 percent a year. These rates have mostly been in the 10 to 30 percent range, which although unusual up to the 1970's, have been rather frequent across the world's countries in the last decade. As a result of this worldwide experience, general macroeconomic policy has come to recognize the importance of the level and structure of prices for the growth and stabilization of aggregate output. Thus, price policy has become another instrument in the macroeconomic policy arsenal, that is usually brought into play at rates of inflation that would appear moderate according to Latin American experience.

Two recent bouts of inflation in Brazil have exceeded the normal ranges, apparently being followed by a contractionary cycle. These occurred from 1962 to 1964 and 1978 to 1980, and were preceeded by an acceleration in the rates of price change. During these periods the foreign trade flows of Brazil were also significantly affected. One important policy element in these processes has been the relationship between the rates of price change and exchange rate devaluations. In Table 2, the ratio of the G.D.P. price level of Brazil to its official exchange rate, is depicted for a few benchmark years from 1962 to 1979, with the Mexican standard as a base.

The price data on which the corresponding G.D.P. aggregates are calculated, originate from a special set of surveys conducted especially in Latin America, but for other countries as well, to measure the purchasing power in their currencies. These represent independent measures of price levels for a basket of goods representing G.D.P. as a whole, and have followed a common methodology throughout.[3] They allow an inter-temporal probing of the extent to which changes in prices have been neutralized by exchange rate devaluations, within a comparative inter-country framework.

As can be seen in Table 2, the comparisons have been attempted with Mexico. The main reason for not using the U.S. as a standard is that the most recent benchmark survey for this country was conducted in 1975, which would make impossible an appropriate consideration of the recent developments in the policies determining the interrelationship between prices and exchange rates. The absolute purchasing-power-parity (P.P.P.) and the exchange rate (r) between Brazil and Mexico were practically coincident in 1962. By 1968 the PPP/r ratio indicated the Brazilian G.D.P. prices, corrected by exchange rate devaluation, were higher than those of Mexico. In other words, the Brazilian inflation in Mexican pesos had been higher than the Mexican inflation from 1962 to 1968. As the Mexican peso was fixed during those years, and was a reputable currency, this suggests a slight loss of competitiveness on the part of Brazilian exports, and of domestic products vis-à-vis imports.

---

[3]For further information on these surveys see Jorge Salazar-Carrillo, Prices and Purchasing Power Parities in Latin America 1960-72, Organization of American States/ECIEL, Washington, D.C., 1978.

Table 2. Ratios of G.D.P.: Price Levels to Official Exchange
Rates for Brazil, with Mexico as Base, 1962, 1968, 1973, 1979

1962	1968	1973	1979
1.01	1.08	1.65	1.36

Source: Jorge Salazar-Carrillo, Precios y Poder Adquisitivo en America
Latina, Ediciones SIAP, (Sociedad Interamericana de Planifica-
cion), Buenos Aires, 1980;

Jorge Salazar-Carrillo, "Comparaciones de Precios, Paridades de
Poder Adquisitivo y Producto Real en America Latina en 1973",
Trimestre Economico, Julio-Septiembre de 1982 and ECIEL,
Comparaciones de Precios, Poder Adquisitivo y Producto Real en
America Latina, Rio de Janeiro, 1982.

The deviation of exchange rates from purchasing-power-parities became more
serious from 1968 to 1973, and certainly would have affected Brazilian
exports, were it not for the export incentive policies which were
implemented during this period. The same fate, perhaps, was not deserved
by local production, which given the opening of the economy that gained in
importance during this period, probably had greater difficulty in
competing with imports. Moreover, there were reasons to believe that by
the early seventies the Mexican peso was becoming overvalued,[4] making the
internal price levels of Brazil less competitive when compared to the
dollar.

By September 1976, the Mexican peso experienced its first devaluation in
nearly 25 years. Yet, many years of overvaluation and very extraordinary
rates of inflation for Mexican standards soon again imperiled the peso.
From 1973 to 1979, the gap between the cruzeiro exchange rate with respect
to the Mexican peso, and the corresponding purchasing-power-parity, closed
significantly. Although this was counterbalanced by the factors just
mentioned, this period represented an improvement over the previous one,
as exchange rate policy appears to have reflected somewhat better the
outcome of internal policies and other events shaping internal prices.
This would have helped import substitution and export promotion during
this period, especially since they were further buoyed by stricter import
restrictions and more favorable export incentives. However, import
substitution appears, from other data,[5] to have been urged more strongly

---

[4]This was suggested in Jorge Salazar-Carrillo "Tipo de Cambio de
Paridad y Niveles de Precio y Produccion en America Latina" Memoria,
Reunion de Tecnicos de Bancos Centrales del Continente Americano, Tomo I,
Banco Central de Venezuela, Caracas, 1972.

[5]Consult Antonio Carlos Lemgruber, Robero Fendt, Jr., and Paulo
Nogueira Batista Jr., External Shocks and Policy Responses in Brazil
During the Seventies, Centro de Estudos Moneterios e de Economia
International, ISPE, Fundacao Getulio Vargas and Fundacao Centro de
Estudos de Comercio Exterior, mimeo, August 1980.

towards the early years of the 1973–79 period, while exactly the opposite seems to have occurred with regard to export promotion.

Apart from the fact that data limitations defined it, a long run comparison of the changes in price levels and exchange rates of Brazil with those of Mexico, is rather useful. Mexico is the other giant Latin American country, and has also been very successful in terms of maintaining a high rate of economic growth. However, it has traditionally kept a less protective stance, and its export promotion schemes have not been a sharp as the Brazilian ones. Because of its special conditions[6] Mexican policy has relied more on price competition with foreign goods, and it is enlightening to note that in the last two decades, Brazil has not done badly at all when measured under the long-run purchasing-power-parity criteria, with Mexico as base.[7]

---

[6]Balance of payments constraints in Mexico have been traditionally alleviated by a large influx of U.S. dollars from tourism and foreign investment.

[7]It should be noted that when compared with the Mexican, and even the international standard, the price structure of Brazil has shown relatively high prices for investment goods and public consumption, as opposed to private consumer goods, over the last two decades.

Comments by Albert Fishlow
on Roberto Fendt, Jr.'s and Jorge Salazar-Carrillo's
Brazil and the Future: Some Thoughts on the Eighties

The paper starts off this conference on the 1980s with a useful look back
to the 1973 turning point of the oil price shock. Brazilian capacity to
deal with the 1980s, does depend, in part, on the adjustment to the rise
of petroleum prices that began in 1973. However, the paper suggests an
interpretation of the Brazilian response to the oil price shock which is
based too exclusively upon the external environment with too little
attention upon the internal responses to it. In particular, it is
certainly arguable whether the oil price shock deserves all of the credit
for the more difficult economic circumstances in Brazil after 1973. There
were also certain elements associated with the very rapid expansion in
production which had begun in 1968-73 and which came to fruition in the
subsequent period, there were certain sectoral limitations leading to
(repressed) excess demand; in addition, there was an important expansion,
of external finance. Both of these developments could be identified in
advance of the oil price shock.

It is important to remember that for Brazil, being a rather closed
economy, the direct significance of the oil price shock should not be
exaggerated. Although oil imports rose as a percentage of total imports,
the latter did not amount to more than 10 percent of production. Brazil,
moreover, could and did borrow, thereby essentially nullifying the
deflationary impact of the petroleum tax. Thus the real issue is what was
done with the resources that were borrowed to facilitate adjustment to the
new international circumstances. It was not a case, in which we should
look at the 2.8% gross negative impact of the oil price increase and
decline in exports as though it were the real effect on the economy,
rather than a first round impact that was more than nullified by capital
inflow.

This distinction makes it possible to underline the importance of the lack
of direction, and the alternative targets that were followed consistently
after 1974. They arose not merely because the government was committed to
maintaining growth for political stability, but also from an initial
impression that the shock was temporary. They also derived from an
incapacity to make difficult decisions regarding changes in relative
prices. They came about as well, because of the ease with which debt was

available and the negative rates of interest that prevailed. So that borrowing, viewed as a short term process, was indeed a reasonable prospect. What went wrong is that is became a medium-term instrument.

To view 1979 as a decisive turning point, as though the return of Delfim marked the first imposition of rationality upon the adjustment process, is again a distortion. The more so, since a dispassionate analysis reveals that the policies that were followed in 1979 and the beginning of 1980 had an adverse impact on the adjustment process. This is so because the very basis of that strategy was a denial of the need to deal with imbalances. Prefixing the monetary correction as well as the exchange rate, was to depend upon expectations to contain inflation rather than monetary and fiscal policy. The government attempted not merely to satisfy new priorities in agriculture, but to satisfy all priorities simultaneously. This list included the expansion of domestic credit to the private sector, incentives to consumer durables, the investment in the alcohol program and virtually every other claim that was seen as politically valid. So to view 1979 as the beginning of the adjustment, seems to me misleading; rather it was an abortive effort to produce another miracle.

I also question the discussion of 1980 when the policy was reversed. The paper interprets the restrictive short term policy in the context of a coherent stabilization cum medium term adjustment strategy. That short term policy, however, provided the first dramatic downturn in Brazilian production since 1930, and one that continued. Its severity must be traced to earlier policy mistakes that impaired the international creditworthiness of Brazil. The 1980-81 experience in Brazil is perhaps the most classic case of liquidity crisis in recent times, dwarfed only by the later and more spectacular Mexican problem in August 1982. The short term inability to generate foreign exchange, required reduction of income as the equilibrating variable. In fact, this was not really necessary so much as a means to reduce the demand for imports, but rather as a way to try to ensure a continuous flow of capital. At that point, nothing less would have sufficed in order to persuade the international financial community that Brazil was taking its responsibilities of adjustment more seriously.

A relatively high price had to be paid at that time, an unnecessarily high price, that had less to do with the real characteristics of the Brazilian economy, than with the characteristics of international financial markets. Of course, a drastic short term adjustment of that kind complicates the longer term real adjustment process. This is so since it reduces the resources available to the government to channel to new sectors and to exports. In spite of the decline in output, there was not realignment of relative prices, nor significant advance in definining new priorities for the longer term.

The alcohol program, for example, is in considerable difficulty at the moment, in part due to the declining international price of petroleum, but also, in part, due to the rapidity of expansion, which far exceeded demand. Issues pertaining to appropriate refinery capacity, the completion of sugar cane for resources that could be applied to domestic consumption and/or exports, what is to be done with the very large automobile sector remain. They are not easier to resolve in the midst of a major downturn in aggregate production because income declines have not translated quietly into changed relative prices and real wages.

That still leaves the question of the rest of the 1980s. Again, the emphasis of the paper has been placed very substantially upon the international environment: the financial and goods markets. There is a curious inconsistency between the pessimism concerning the international climate and the general optimism with which the paper confronts the 1980s, a contradiction borne out, to some extent, by the simulations that Von Doellinger has performed in his paper contained in this volume. Rather than providing a basis for optimism, they suggest that subtantial Brazilian debt, with continuing high interest rates and continuing low rates of growth of exports, leads to disorder. Even under reasonably favorable assumptions, there is a debt service ratio on the order of magnitude of 50%–60% over a substantial part of the decade. This presumes a large deviation between the real rates of growth of exports and imports, on an order which Brazil has not sustained over any long period of time.

Brazil, by necessity, must therefore opt for a significant increase in the share of the product which is exported, an increase in the share of Brazilian world trade, and a continuing inflow of capital at a rather significant rate over a substantial part of the decade. In addition, which the paper ignores, it must achieve a large rise in domestic savings which is the counterpart of a trade surplus. These are all trend considerations, rather than short-term reactions of a temporary kind to liquidity considerations. Yet even if pursued, continuing Brazilian debt exposure means that the country is extremely vulnerable to decisions of the international banking community. Whether it is because of a Poland, a Romania, an Argentina or a Mexico, rather than Brazilian prospects, a reluctance to lend has adverse consequences.

Another possible element of undue optimism, is the position that the present political opening will move smoothly and without difficulties. There is a touching faith in the capacity of economic policy-makers to formulate all of the right decisions, however difficult they may be, over the course of the 1980's. That seems to me not only to fail to represent an accurate view of Brazil, but something close to a miraculous view of virtually any political system under these pressures. In particular, this casualness denies the reality of the populist pressures that will come to the fore with the return of the electoral franchise that has been denied. The populist pressure will take two forms. One will be an emphasis on the internal market as a means of satisfying more egalitarian income distribution as well as recuperation. The second objective will be higher wages. That again, in the context of an attempt to control inflation as well as to increase domestic savings, creates difficulties. In addition, reallocating more capital toward greater energy conservation and energy alternatives presents greater difficulties than the paper suggests.

By reason both of the international economic environment, as well as the conjunction of political circumstances, the 1980s may well be a difficult decade even for Brazilian pragmatism and ingenuity. Interestingly enough, the real grounds for optimism are not discussed in the paper. The capacity for import substitution is obviously one. It was the key element that prevented matters from getting worse in the 1970's. If one looks at the real import growth in Brazil between 1973–81, one has a remarkable result. The import elasticity falls close to zero, despite relatively rapid growth. That dramatic change from a preceding elasticity of two, that capacity to produce domestically, is a Brazilian attribute not characteristic of many other developing countries, particularly smaller ones. That clearly is very important. Export promotion is not the only ray of hope.

A second very important consideration is the increase in the production of petroleum. If one wants to examine the reasons for the significant improvement in the Brazilian balance of payments over the course of 1981 and through the beginning of 1982, it resides not merely in the lessening of price inflation in the petroleum market, but also a significant reduction in the quantity of imports owing to domestic supply. One should really explore the whole energy question in much greater detail. The alcohol program has been exaggerated as a panecea. The paper accepts favorable projections of domestic capacity without careful scrutiny.

The 1980s, as the paper correctly points out, presents a perspective that is very different from that of another earlier critical turning point in Brazilian history. In the mid-1960s, Brazil was faced with the rather pleasurable opportunity of being able to opt into an international economy that was showing unprecedented growth, in which there was room for Brazil to expand its exports relatively rapidly with favorable terms of trade. It was a period when Brazil was recovering from its own import substitution cycle of the late 1950s and early 1960s, with unutilized capcacity. It was a period when Brazilian access to new borrowing was considerable.

As we all well know, one of the characteristics of a debt-led growth process is that the early phase is easy. It is at the very beginning of indebtedness that the largest real transfer of resources occurs. In subsequent phases one is faced with the subtractions of amortization and interest, which make the large gross inflows of capital of progressively lesser stimulus to real growth. Now in the 1980s, Brazil finds itself in a much more problematic international trade setting. It finds itself with a more than $60 billion debt and less favorable circumstances for additional borrowing; even if they had continued favorable, the real transfer of resources that was possible earlier is now diminished.

In the last analysis, Brazil must contend with a series of problems that are real and difficult. It is all the more important, therefore, to understand that the political process is essentially symptomatic rather than the cause of the difficulty. It would be a mistake to assume that one could close down the political process and thereby avert the hard choices that overt politics will necessarily identify.

IMPERFECT CAPITAL MOBILITY, RISK, AND BRAZILIAN FOREIGN BORROWING

Donald V. Coes

In the past decade Brazil has emerged as one of the principal recipients of international capital flows from private lenders. Its ability to continue to finance a large current account deficit, by a continuing surplus on the capital account, without being forced to turn to official international lenders and to more severe domestic restrictions, depends in large part on the willingness of private lenders to continue a high level of capital flows to Brazil. Although the problem may be partially and possibly only temporarily alleviated by some recent improvement in the trade balance, originating primarily on the import side, the continued necessity of large service payments will require capital inflows for the foreseeable future.

The unprecedented growth of the international capital market, and the success of Brazil and other major borrowers in tapping it, might lead us to conclude that a balance of payments constraint in the traditional sense has become obsolete, or at least less serious, due to a high degree of international capital mobility. Indeed, as can be seen in the balance of payments data shown in Table 1, substantial increases in capital inflows after the 1973-74 and 1978-79 oil price shocks helped ease Brazil's painful external adjustment, despite a greater reliance on reserve loss in the latter case.

In the United States, and in other economies with relatively open and highly developed capital markets, the increase in the degrees of international capital mobility may justify a downgrading of traditional concepts of balance of payments deficit or surplus and a shift in focus to the current account, under the implicit assumption that international capital markets can finance imbalances. In the Brazilian case, however, contemporary developed economy views of international adjustment under conditions of international capital mobility must be qualified for a number of reasons. Among them are asymmetries in the ease with which capital enters or leaves Brazil, exchange and default risks, and government administration of a number of prices, including the exchange rate and "monetary correction", or inflation indexation. The major objective of this paper is to analyze some of these features of capital mobility in the Brazilian case, which do not appear to be adequately

TABLE 1: THE BRAZILIAN BALANCE OF PAYMENTS, 1971-81

(millions of US dollars)

	1971	1972	1973	1974	1975	1976	1977	1978	1979	1980	1981*
Trade Balance	-278	-98	186	-4682	-3164	-2145	7	-1208	-2506	-2829	-316
Exports	2919	4137	6325	7959	9004	10132	12031	12475	15455	20132	10855
Imports	-3197	-4235	-6189	-12641	-12169	-12278	-12023	-13683	-17961	-22962	-11171
Services	-980	-1250	-1627	-2433	-3170	-2725	-4134	-6037	-7778	-10212	-5673
Capital income	-420	-520	-618	-901	-1733	-2189	-2559	-4232	-5461	-7032	-4450
Other	-560	-730	-1009	-1532	-1437	-1536	-1536	-1597	-1805	-2317	-3180
Transfers	14	5	27	1	2	4	0	71	17	155	132
Current Account	-1244	-1343	-1464	-7114	-6332	-5866	-4127	-7174	-10267	-12886	-5857
Capital Account	1846	3492	3512	6145	6189	6651	5269	10966	6024	9804	4631
Net Foreign Direct Investment	168	318	940	887	892	962	810	1071	1505	1557	1099
Medium and Long term Financing	2037	4299	4495	6891	5933	7761	8424	13811	10924	11070	7277
Amortization	-850	-1202	-1673	-1920	-2172	-2992	-4060	-5324	-6356	-5020	-3353
Other	491	77	-251	287	1536	920	96	1407	-50	2197	-392
Errors and Omissions	-9	274	354	-68	-439	518	-602	-639	1066	-408	395
Surplus or Deficit	593	2423	2402	-1037	-581	1302	541	3153	-3178	-3490	-831

*(January through June)

SOURCE: Boletim do Banco Central do Brasil, various issues

reflected in most contemporary models of capital mobility among the major developed countries.

International economics theorists, following pioneering work by J.M. Fleming and R. Mundell, have in the last decade, thoroughly reworked theories of economic adjustment and linkages among open economies to reflect the importance of capital mobility. Moving, at first, from the no mobility case to the polar opposite of perfect mobility, contemporary macroeconomic theory for open economies has now given us a reasonably detailed analysis of the effects of an intermediate degree of capital mobility, in which assets in different countries are not perfect substitutes.[1] Despite the insights which these new developments have provided in understanding the open economies of many of the highly developments OECD or "center" countries, they are of more limited usefulness, however, in dealing with the capital receiving countries like Brazil, on the "periphery" of the international financial markets.

The approach presented here is basically microeconomic, focusing on some of the determinants of capital flows in a context like the Brazilian one. After a brief description of some of the principal features of capital flows to Brazil in Section 1, a simple model of the borrowing decision is developed in Section 2. Since exchange risk is basically borne by the borrower, this demand side model highlights the role of exchange policy and its interaction with monetary correction. In keeping with the spirit of the times, a supply side model is presented in Section 3. This model focuses on the lending decision, under the assumption that the return is uncertain. One of its features is an explanation of the way in which default risk and lender risk aversion may affect the "spread", or the difference between Brazilian borrowing rates and interest rates in the major capital markets. The paper concludes with a brief discussion of some of the implications of models of these types in identifying some of the factors which influence financial capital flows to Brazil.

IMPERFECTIONS IN CAPITAL MOBILITY
BETWEEN BRAZIL AND THE LENDING COUNTRIES

A number of features of the Brazilian case combine to produce the type of imperfect capital mobility considered here. First, and probably most important, the fact that capital can enter Brazil more easily than it can leave forces us to deal explicitly with risk. In a world of certainty or perfect foresight, any constraint on the lender or borrower which might limit the possibilities of a reverse capital flow would not be binding, since no more capital would orginally flow in than would be required by the known conditions for capital market equilibrium. In the presence of uncertainty, however, a decision which is optimal ex ante may not be optimal ex post, making the constraint on reverse capital flows from the borrowing country binding.

A second feature of the Brazilian case is the scarcity or thinness of markets which permit the transfer of different types of risk from one

---

[1]See, for example, R. Dornbusch, Open Economy Macroeconomics, Ch. 10 and 11.

party to another. Although Brazilian importers and exporters can avoid some exchange risk in a local interbank market, these operations usually cover periods for 90 to 180 days.[2] As no forward market exists, comparable to those available for a number of the major convertible currencies, the various risks inherent in financial capital flows arising from exchange rate uncertainty must be borne by the borrower or lender (or both).

Finally, throughout the last decade, financial capital flows to Brazil have been subject to a variety of restrictions which limit the extent to which capital flows have entered under the provisions of Law 4131 and Resolution 63. By the end of the decade, about two-thirds of Brazil's foreign debt, both private and public, had entered in these two catagories.[3]

Under both regulations, capital flows have been subject to a minimum term requirement before full payment of the loan, although partial repayments have been permitted sooner. During most of the last decade, the minimum term was five years; in 1978 it was raised to eight years. Among other restrictions on the capital flows are withholding taxes on the interest whose ultimate impact on the lender's earnings is partially dependent on the tax laws of the home country of the creditor. In addition, the Central Bank has at times required that part of the principal be deposited, in order to reduce the impact on the monetary base.[4] The principal difference between the two foreign borrowing regimes is that under Law 4131 there is a direct relationship between the foreign lender and the Brazilian debtor, while in the case of loans entering under Resolution 63, a local bank obtains the loan and relends to one or more local borrowers. Public borrowing by the government and state enterprises has generally been done via Law 4131, while private borrowing has occurred under both systems.

As should be clear from this brief description, conventional theoretical models which incorporate capital mobility, or even imperfect capital mobility, hardly do justice to a case like the Brazilian one. Although capital mobility between Brazil and the major lending nations might be characterized as "imperfect", it is clearly a type of imperfection different from the limited asset substitutability implicit in many models of imperfect capital mobility among the economies with more open and highly developed capital markets. Due to the absence of adequate hedging mechanisms and the asymmetry in the ease with which capital may enter or leave Brazil, with the resulting possibility that an _ex ante_ optimal decision may result in a loss _ex post_, the salient feature of the Brazilian case is the presence of risk or uncertainty in the borrowing and lending decision.

---

[2]The existence of a rudimentary forward market for the cruzeiro is discussed in E. Bacha, "The Impact of the Float on LDC's: Latin American Experience in the 1970's", in J. Williamson, ed., Exchange Rate Rules.

[3]Boletim do Banco Central do Brasil, various issues.

[4]Brazilian capital controls are discussed in T. Felsberg, Foreign Business in Brazil, and the IMF's Annual Report on Exchange Restrictions.

Both of the models which are developed in the succeeding sections emphasize the role of uncertainty in influencing the level of capital flows to Brazil. As uncertainties arise in a number of ways, a complete analysis of capital flows in this context would be a complex and possibly intractable problem. By considering, in order, several specific types of risk, which arise in part because of the Brazilian institutional arrangements described above, however, it is possible to analyze some of the factors which influence the level of capital flows to Brazil. Despite the central role which this approach assigns to uncertainty, it is not necessary to assume that either borrowers or lenders are risk averse. If we do make this highly plausible assumption, however, our results are strengthened.

THE BORROWING DECISION WITH EXCHANGE RISK

Loans which enter Brazil under the provisions of Resolution 63 or Law 4131 basically force the borrower to bear potential exchange risk, since the contractual obligation requires repayment of principal and interest in the currency of the lender. In order to focus specifically on exchange risk, we assume here that the other variables relevant to the decision to borrow or lend can be treated as given and non-stochastic, so that the potential borrower therefore faces given international capital market conditions.

As the result of an extensive system of inflation indexing, or "monetary correction" which has developed in Brazil in the past few decades most cruzeiro-denominated asset market transactions include an explicit adjustment for inflation during the holding period, based on official monetary correction indices.[5] The lender of cruzeiros therefore receives at the end of the loan period the principal and a known amount of interest, both adjusted ex post by the monetary correction index, which we denote by c.

We assume that the borrower may obtain foreign currency at r* percent via Resolution 63 or Law 4131 and convert the proceeds into cruzeiros at the current spot rate of e (we define e as cruzeiros per unit of foreign currency). We further assume that the Brazilian borrower can use the cruzeiro proceeds to earn a known return in cruzeiros of r percent, which may be either constant, or a decreasing function of the quantity of cruzeiros invested locally. The assumption that $r_q < 0$, or strictly decreasing returns, is necessary only if the borrower is risk neutral. The rate of return, r, might be thought of as the projected return from an investment, although an alternative interpretation might treat it as the return from reloaning the cruzeiros locally. Although most loans are repaid over a period of time, we assume, for simplicity, that both the principal and interest are paid to the foreign lender at the end of the period, within the minimum term set by the Banco Central. The problem thus reduces to a two period one. In the absence of any type of forward market the borrower faces a random spot rate at the end of the period, which we denote by ẽ. For given realizations of ẽ and c, the borrower's profits in real (initial period) cruzeiros are then

---

[5]Brazil's indexation system is discussed in W. Baer and P. Beckerman, "Indexing in Brazil."

$$\pi(\tilde{e},c) = \left\{ q[c(1+r) - \frac{\tilde{e}}{e}(1+r^*)] \right\}/c \tag{1}$$

where

q = the principal of the loan

c = the monetary correction index at the end of the period

(c > 1 if inflation is recognized)

r = the local rate of return, exclusive of monetary correction

$\tilde{e}$ = the random spot rate at the end of the period

e = the initial spot rate

r* = the international market rate paid by the borrower

Note that in (1) we assume that the borrower's nominal cruzeiro profits may be deflated by the monetary correction factor to determine real profits. A more realistic, but considerably more complex model, might use a different deflator, since monetary correction in Brazil does not always accompany the cost-of-living and other price indices.

We define the "real exchange rate" as x = e/c. Note that this definition is not necessarily identical to the more conventional x = e/P (or x = eP*/P if the foreign price level P* is also assumed to change). The use of c rather than P reflects the fact that in financial markets in Brazil, the appropriate index for comparing assets subject to indexation is c, and not the goods price index P.

We assume that the borrower's beliefs about likely values of x may be summarized by the subjective probability distribution F(x), where $F(x_o)$ = Prob($x < x_o$) and a<x<b. We further assume that the borrower's preferences can be characterized as a concave function of profits, or U = U(π), where U'(π)>0 and U''(π) $\le$ 0. As the notation suggests, this function might be regarded as a utility function, but this may be unnecessarily restrictive assumption, since other reasons may justify the assumption of concavity. In Brazil, for example, both corporate and individual income taxes, as well as related deductions and fiscal incentives may combine to make after-tax profits a concave function of pre-tax profits.

Under these assumptions, the borrower's decision problem is one of choosing a level of debt, q, which maximizes the expected value of a concave function of random profits, or

$$\max_{q} \int_a^b U\left\{ q[1+r(q) - x\frac{(1+r^*)}{e}] \right\} dF(x) \tag{2}$$

First order conditions for a maximum are

$$\int_a^b U'(\pi) \left\{ 1+r(q) - x\frac{(1+r^*)}{e} + qr_q \right\} dF(x) = 0 \tag{3}$$

44

The second order conditions require that

$$\int_a^b U'(\pi) \, [2r_q + r_{qq}] + U''(\pi) \, [1+r(q) - x \, \frac{(1+r^*)}{e} + qr_q]^2 dF(x) < 0 \qquad (4)$$

Sufficient conditions for (4) to hold are that $U''(\pi) < 0$ (strict concavity or risk aversion) and $r_q < 0$ (decreasing returns on the amount borrowed), but neither inequality must hold strictly, if the other one does.

Several features of (3) should be noted. First, the condition requires that there be some positive subjective probabilities of x large and small enough for the bracketed term in (3) to vary in sign over [a,b], since $U'(\pi) < 0$. This would not be the case, for example, if potential borrowers actually believed that exchange rate adjustments would be rigidly linked to monetary corrections, so that x=e/c=1. In such a case, real exchange rate uncertainty would be effectively removed, and optimal borrowing would either be zero or an amount constrained either by its decreasing return or by some limit outside our model.

Second, if we treat the local interest rate as constant (so that $r_q = 0$) and make no explicit correction for inflation (implying that c=1), then under certainty the first order condition (3) reduces to the familiar interest rate parity condition (1+r)/(1+r*) =ẽ/e, in which ẽ may be identified with the forward rate. Thus, if capital flows to and from Brazil were not restricted, equilibrium in the capital account could obtain even with domestic rates of inflation far higher than external ones, provided that both r and e reflected this expected inflation.

Finally, note from (3) that increases in r and e and decreases in r* would alter the first order condition, with a new equilibrium obtaining only if q is increased. Thus, the model preserves the result from conventional deterministic models that capital flows would respond positively, ceteris paribus, to the interest rate differential (r-r*). Note, however, that even if E(ẽ) = e and c = 1, our assumption of risk aversion implies that r does not have to equal r*.

We turn now to the question of how changes in the subjective distribution of x might affect the borrower's ex ante determination of the optimal level of borrowing. One such change of interest arises from the minimum term restrictions on foreign loans imposed by the Banco Central. If we view the future value of the real exchange rate, x, as in part the outcome of series of random shocks, then the uncertainty about x increases as the time period lengthens. Under reasonable assumptions, for example, we might represent the time path of x(t) as a simple random walk, or perhaps more appropriately, as a random walk with drift, depending on the exchange and inflation indexation policies followed by the monetary authorities.[6] If the random shocks are u_t each period, then the error variance of a forecast of x for a time k periods ahead is simply $k \, \sigma_u^2$.

---

[6] See, for example, R. Pindyck and D. Rubinfeld, Econometric Models and Economic Forecasts, 2nd ed., Ch. 16.

Since the central bank regulations impose a minimum, but not a maximum term, we assume that the borrower may choose to maintain the loan if it is profitable to do so beyond the minimum term. As may be seen from (1), however, if the real exchange rate has depreciated considerably, with the ex post realization of x relatively large, profits from the borrowing will be small or negative. In such circumstances, the sooner the loan may be terminated, the less the loss from the exchange movement.

There are a number of ways in which these considerations might be represented. One convenient and analytically tractable way, however, is to represent the reduction in the minimum term, or a similar relaxation on the outflow of financial capital as permitting the borrower to reduce the upper limit of the subjective distribution of x, the real rate at which foreign currency to repay the loan must be acquired. The change in the probability density might then be represented as a "piling up" of the upper tail of the original density at some maximum point $x'<b$. This is shown graphically in Figure 1.

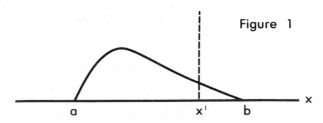

Figure 1

The change in the subjective distribution induced by the relaxation of the restriction then alters the first order conditions for the borrower, which becomes,

$$\int_a^{x'} U'(\pi) \ \{1+r(q) - x\frac{(1+r*)}{e} + qr_q\} \ dF(x) \ +$$

$$U'(\pi_{x'}) \ \{1+r(q) - x'\frac{(1+r*)}{e} + qr_q\} \ (1-F(x')) = 0 \qquad (5)$$

This may be expressed more succinctly as the implicit function $\phi(q,x') = 0$, which implies that

$$\frac{dq}{dx'} = \frac{-1}{\phi_q} \ \phi_{x'} \qquad (6)$$

By the second order conditions $\phi_q < 0$, so that dq/dx' will have the sign of $\phi_{x'}$. Evaluating this term, we have

$$\phi_{x'} = U'(\pi_{x'}) \ \{1 + r(q) - x\frac{(1+r*)}{c} + qr_q\} \quad f(x')$$

$$- \ U'(\pi_{x'}) \ \{1 + r(q) - x\frac{(1+r*)}{c} + qr_q\} \quad f(x')$$

$$+ \ U'(\pi_{x'})\{\frac{-(1+r*)}{e} \ (1-F(x')) + U''(\pi_{x'}) \ \frac{-(1+r*)}{e}\}^2 \quad (1-F(x')) \ (7)$$

As the first two term cancel, and the last two are unambiguously negative, we have

$$\frac{dq}{dx'} < 0 \qquad (8)$$

46

Hence, a lowering of the borrower's estimate of the maximun value of the random real future price for foreign exchange, which he will face at the end of the loan period, will unambiguously raise the optimal level of the initial loan.

There are a number of ways in which to interpret the change in the borrower's ex ante subjective distribution of x which leads to our result. One obvious way would be to view the fixing of a maximum value for x as the result of a guarantee that foreign exchange would be available for repayment of the loan at a cruzeiro price no greater than x'. As a practical matter, such guarantees do not appear to have been used in Brazil, but a "two-tier" exchange regime might permit this type of policy.[7]

Our interpretation of the change in the subjective distribution, as the result of a reduction by the Banco Central, in the minimum term of the foreign loan is less straightforward, since it rests on several additional implicit assumptions. Among them is the idea that the distribution of x below x' is unchanged by the elimination of the possibilities of x greater than x'. If the risks of a large exchange loss are attenuated or eliminated by a reduction in the minimum term, it is clearly possible that the prospects of a large gain, if x turns out to be much lower than initially expected, may also be reduced. This is clearly a more complex change in the distribution, but if we restrict the change to one in which the expectation of x is unchanged, but the probabilities of high or low values of x reduced or eliminated, then the response of the borrower may be analyzed in terms of a mean-preserving spread (MPS), a concept developed by M. Rothschild and J. Stiglitz. Although in the interests of brevity we do not present the results here, it is possible to show that this kind of reduction in uncertainty would increase the optimal level of borrowing even if E(x) is unchanged by the policy. This result, moreover, holds if the borrower is risk averse, and does not require any additional assumptions about the utility function, other than concavity.

The latter case is of some interest in a Brazilian context. The policy of "minidesvalorizacoes" or crawling peg adopted in 1968 maybe interpreted as a narrowing in the range of possible outcomes for e about a relatively unchanged expectation. In such a case, the above results suggest there would be a strong presumption that the level of borrowing would increase, even if the conditions under which the supply of financial capital to Brazil were unchanged, due to increased demand by risk averse borrowers. Whether or not this effect was a significant element in the increase in financial capital flows to Brazil in the late 60's and early 70's is unclear, but in principle the effect could be strong, if the degree of risk aversion were high.

DEFAULT RISK AND THE LENDING DECISION

Although a loan to a Brazilian borrower payable in dollars (or in another foreign currency) in effect forces the borrower to bear the exchange risk,

---

[7]M. Castello Branco, O Dilema da Politica Cambial no Brasil: Origens e Debate no Inicio dos Anos 80, discusses two tier possibilities.

the lender must still face the possibility that the loan may not be repaid or may yield a net return lower than that expected at the time the loan was negotiated. In practice, it is possible to imagine a wide range of outcomes between complete default of both interest and principal, and repayment of the loan at the negotiated terms. In this section we develop a general model involving repayment risk and then examine the specific case of full repayment versus complete default.

Suppose that a lender, for example a New York bank, must decide what proportion k of a given initial loan portfolio W_0 be allocated to loans to Brazilian borrowers. We denote its opportunity cost, or the rate available on loans made to other borrowers, by r_{NY} and that on loans to Brazilian borrowers by r_B, and assume for analytical convenience that r_{NY} is regarded by the bank as known or risk free. In this case, the bank's problem is a straightforward portfolio problem of choosing k to maximize the expected value of a concave function of end-period wealth, W , or

$$\max_{k} E\{U(W_1)\} = {}_c\int^d U\{(1-K)W_0(1+r_{NY}) + kW_0(1+r_B)\}\, dG(r_B) \qquad (9)$$

As was the case with the lending decision model of the preceding section, U(W) may be regarded as a utility function, but need not be, since tax laws and other factors in the home country could make its objective function concave. First order conditions require that

$$_c\int^d U'(W_1)\,(r_B - r_{NY})\, dG(r_B) = 0 \qquad (10)$$

where we have used the fact that initial wealth W_0 is non-stochastic.

The first order condition (10) has several important implications. First, for equilibrium to hold, there must be positive probabilities of r_B both greater than and less than the opportunity cost return r_{NY}. If this is not the case, there would be no internal maximum for k, leading to k = 0 (if $r_B < r_{NY}$ in all cases) or k = 1 (if $r_B > r_{NY}$). The economic intuition of this case is that Brazilian loans would either be eliminated from or completely dominate the bank's portfolio, even if we assume risk aversion.

Second, unless $U'(W_1)$ is constant, as would be the case if the bank were risk neutral, there is no reason for $E(r_B)$ to equal r_{NY}. Indeed, if the bank is risk averse, $E(r_B) > r_{NY}$. This can be seen as follows. Let $U'(W)$ be marginal utility when $r_b = r_{NY}$ Then by concavity ($U''(W) < 0$), $U'(W) < U'(\bar{W})$ if $r_B > r_{NY}$, with the inequality reversed if $r_B < r_{NY}$. Hence the inequality $U'(W)(r_B - r_{NY}) \leq U'(\bar{W})(r_B - r_{NY})$ holds for all r_B. Integrating both sides over $G(r_B)$, we have

$$_c\int^d U'(W)(r_B - r_{NY})\, dG(r_B) \leq {}_c\int^d U'(\bar{W})(r_B - r_{NY})\, dG(r_B) \qquad (11)$$

By (10), the LHS is zero, and since $U'(\bar{W})$ is non-stochastic and positive,

$$_c\int^d (r_B - r_{NY})\, dG(r_B) > 0$$

or

$_c\int^d r_B\, dG(r_B) = E(r_B) > r_{NY}$. Hence, the expected value of the return on

the Brazilian loan must exceed the rate available in the home country if the bank is to be in portfolio equilibrium, assuming some degree of risk aversion.

Although it is possible to use (10) to analyze rather general types of changes in distributions on the optimal level of k, such as an MPS of the Rothschild-Stiglitz type in the distribution of r_B about a given expectation, the simpler case of a two point distribution of r_B, corresponding to complete default or normal repayment provides a number of interesting insights. Let the probability of default ($r_B = -1$) be p, and the probability that the loan will be repaid at the negotiated rate r′ therefore be (1-p). In this case the first order condition (10) simplifies to

$$-p \ U'\{W_1(-1)\} \ (1+r_{NY}) + (1-p) \ U' \ \{W_1(r')\} \ (r'-r_{NY}) = 0 \qquad (10')$$

since the return in the case of total default is the loss of the principal, or -1. If we define the "spread" as the difference between the negotiated rate on the loan r′ and the opportunity cost in the New York capital market r_{NY}, we may rewrite (10′) as

$$(r'-r_{NY}) = \frac{p}{1-p} \ \frac{U'\{W_1(-1)\}}{U'\{W_1(r')\}} \ (1 + r_{NY}) \qquad (12)$$

Equation (12) shows clearly how for a given share k of the bank's portfolio allocated to Brazilian loans the spread paid by the Brazilian borrower would be affected by the probability of default, risk aversion on the part of the lender, and changes in the interest rate in the home country capital market. As the probability of default decreases toward zero, the spread disappears, while the spread would in theory become infinite as p tends to one. It should be noted that this relationship is highly non-linear, so that small increases in p have a much more than proportional effect on the spread.

If the lender is risk neutral, then the middle term on the RHS of (12) is unity, since marginal utility is constant. In the presence of either risk aversion or some other factor making the bank's objective function of end-period wealth concave, $U'(W) < 0$. Hence $U'\{W_1(-1)\} > U'\{W_1(r')\}$, implying that the middle term exceeds one. Thus, the amount of the spread will increase as the degree of risk aversion by the lender increases. Finally, note that an increase in the rate of interest in the home country will, ceteris paribus, result in an increase in the spread itself.

CONCLUSION

The common element in both of the models of international capital movements examined in this paper is the idea that the borrowing and lending decisions are made in the presence of uncertainty. Although only two specific types of uncertainty, exchange risk and default risk, are considered here, it is clear that a number of other types of uncertainty may affect capital flows. Much of Brazil's foreign borrowing has been in the form of variable rate loans, in which the spread, but not the underlying rate (r_{NY} in the model of the preceding section, or a rate like the LIBOR, in reality) is known ex ante. Thus, the borrower would face not only real exchange rate uncertainty, but foreign rate uncertainty as well. Similarly, the lender in our second model faces an uncertain world rate r_{NY}, as well as uncertainty as to whether r′ will actually be paid. Other types of uncertainty not considered explicitly in the models developed here, arise from the variability in the rate of return by the

lender and from government policies affecting realized after--tax
earnings.

One can question how important the different types of uncertainty
considered here may actually have been in Brazil in the past decade. With
the development of a widespread indexing system for financial assets and
for many other transactions, as well as the extension of indexing to the
exchange rate with the adoption of a crawling peg policy in 1968, many
types of real uncertainty caused by unknown future rates of inflation have
been substantially reduced. Indeed, our model of the lending decision
suggests that the reduction in real exchange rate uncertainty after 1968,
could have had a positive effect on capital flows to Brazil, independently
of any change in the international-domestic interest rate differential.

Real exchange rate uncertainty was reduced, but not eliminated by the
adoption of the crawling peg. Table 2 shows the nominal cruzeiro/dollar
rate (the selling rate of the Banco Central), the monetary correction
factor (the index adjustment for ORTN's, or national treasury obligations), and a 1968 base index of the ratio of the two year-end series for
the 1964-82 period. As is clear from Column c, there have been large
variations in the real exchange rate since 1964, even after the adoption
of the crawling peg in 1968. The tendency for the cruzeiro to appreciate
in real terms, which prevailed during most of the 1970's, was abruptly
reversed with the devaluation in late 1979. Only in the past few years,
when the monetary authorities have explicitly linked exchange rate
adjustments to monetary correction, have changes in the real rate been
negligible. It should be noted, moreover, that from the viewpoint of our
theoretical models, it is the subjective distribution of the future rate,
rather than the actual distribution of the rate in the past, which is
relevant to the lending decision. One interesting implication of our
model is that if real exchange rate uncertainty is more or less
eliminated, as would be the consequence of a continuous and credible
policy linking the exchange rate to the monetary correction index, then
the first order conditions (3) may not be satisfied. In this case, the
demand for foreign loans might become considerably more sensitive to the
internal-external interest rate differential, than would be the case if
real exchange rate uncertainty were greater.

Although the models developed in this paper do show the importance of a
number of factors which are normally not made explicit in the analysis of
capital flows to a country like Brazil, it would be asking too much of
them to expect them to capture much of the complexity of financial capital
flows to Brazil. Both models are partial equilibrium models, looking at
one side of the capital flow, and treating as exogenous a number of
variables which in a larger context would be endogenous. The major
difficulty which arises in constructing a larger and more macro-
economically oriented model, arises from the fact that many of the random
variables of interest, for example the external interest rate and the
exchange rate, cannot reasonably be treated as distributed independently.

A number of empirically relevant and policy oriented insights nevertheless
do emerge from the approach adopted here. On the lending side, our model
suggests that the availability of capital to Brazil may be highly
sensitive to small changes in the subjective probability lenders attach to
default. Alternatively, if Brazil's share of the loans available in the
international capital market is not to fall, small changes in default
probabilities can have magnified effects on the spread it must pay.

TABLE 2: THE EXCHANGE RATE AND MONETARY CORRECTION

End of year	(a) Exchange Rate (Cr$/US$)	(b) Monetary Correction	(c) Index
1964	1.850	10.00	168.8
1965	2.220	16.30	124.3
1966	2.220	22.69	89.3
1967	2.710	27.96	88.4
1968	3.830	34.95	100.0
1969	4.350	41.42	95.8
1970	4.950	49.54	91.2
1971	5.635	60.77	84.6
1972	6.215	70.07	80.9
1973	6.220	70.07	71.8
1974	7.435	105.41	64.4
1975	9.070	130.93	63.2
1976	12.345	179.68	62.7
1977	16.050	233.74	62.7
1978	20.920	318.44	59.9
1979	42.530	468.71	82.8
1980	65.500	706.70	84.6
1981	127.800	1382.09	84.4
1982 (March)	148.210	1602.99	84.4

SOURCE: Boletim do Banco Central do Brasil, various issues

On the borrowing side, the approach highlights the importance of the exchange rate regime followed, and its link to the domestic price level. As the degree of uncertainty itself is partially dependent on the restrictions on return capital flows. The model suggests that other potential tools besides the exchange rate and domestic interest rates may be avialable to policy makers. Finally, at a more general level, the approach suggests that policies which affect the level of uncertainty about the future values of relevant variables may have an impact on capital flows, which is independent of any change in the interest rate differential, a factor so central to deterministic models of capital mobility.

References

Baer, W. and Beckerman, P., "Indexing in Brazil", World Development, Dec. 1974.

Banco Central do Brasil, Boletim, various issues.

Castello Branco, M., O Dilema de Politica Cambial no Brasil: Origens e Debate no Inicio dos Anos 80, Master's Thesis, Pontifica Universidade Catolica do Rio de Janeiro, 1981.

Dornbusch, R., Open Economy Macroeconomics, New York, Basic Books, 1981.

Felsberg, T., Foreign Business in Brazil, 2nd ed., Sao Paulo, Interinvest Editora e Distribuidora Ltda., 1976.

Fleming, J.M., "Domestic Financial Policies under Fixed and under Floating Exchange Rates", IMF Staff Papers, 1962.

International Monetary Fund, Annual Report on Exchange Restrictions, various issues.

Mundell, R., International Economics, New York, MacMillian, 1968.

Pindyck, R. and Rubinfeld, D., Econometric Models and Economic Forecasts, 2nd ed., New York, McGraw-Hill, 1981.

Rothschild, M., and Stiglitz, J., "Increasing Risk II: Its Economic Consequences", Journal of Economic Theory, Jan. 1971.

Williamson, J., Exchange Rate Rules, London, MacMillan, 1981.

Comments by Rudiger Dornbusch on Don Coes' "Imperfect Capital Mobility,
Exchange Risk and Brazilian Foreign Borrowing"

Don Coes' paper offers a valuable and interesting analysis of
international capital mobility under conditions of capital controls. He
rightly singles out the minimum borrowing term constraint as an important
modification of standard analysis and draws interesting policy
implications. In my comments I will go over the same issues, discussing
some of the special features of Coes' model.

A GENERAL MODEL

The general setting we present is that of a firm that borrows in the home
and foreign market and with the proceeds makes real investment that
generate payoffs in the next period. Thus with the random real value of
payoffs (in terms of consumption) denoted by y we have the problem of
maximizing expected utility.

(1) Maximize $EU = EU(y)$
     subject to the constraint:

(2) $y = p\sigma(I+I*) - vI - v*I*$; $I, I* > 0$

where p, v and v* are the random real prices of output and real costs of
domestic and foreign debt service and $\sigma > 1$ is the given productivity of
investment.

The real price of output the firm produces is random and so are, because
of uncertain monetary correction and depreciation policy, the real costs
of domestic and foreign debt. Suppose, to simplify matters, that U can be
approximated by a quadratic function, then we can solve for the optimal
levels of domestic and foreign borrowing, I and I*. The ratio is given
by:

(3) $$I/I* = \frac{\sigma(s_p^2 - 2v_{pv*}) + s_{v*}^2 - k[s_{vv*} + \sigma(s_p^2 - s_{pv*})]}{k[\sigma(s_p^2 - 2s_{pv}) + s_v^2] - s_{vv*} - \sigma(s_p^2 - s_{pv} - s_{pv*})}$$

with

$$k \equiv (\bar{p}\sigma - \bar{v}*)/(\bar{p}\sigma - \bar{v})$$

and where a bar denotes a mean, while s_{ij} is the covariance between i and j.

Coes in his analysis focuses on exchange rate risk, that is uncertainty about the real cost of external debt service compared to the real cost of domestic finance. He treats the real payoff, $\tilde{p}$, as deterministic and that, of course, simplifies matters quite a bit. In that event (3) reduces to:

$$(3') \quad I/I* = \frac{s_{v*}/s_v - k\rho}{k\sigma(s_v/s_{v*}) - \rho}$$

where ρ is the correlation coefficient of v and v*. Equation (3)' draws attention to the correlation between the internal and external real cost of finance, ρ, as one of the determinants of the borrowing pattern. Other determinants are the relative mean real returns as captured in the term k, the productivity of investment and the relative standard deivations.

Equation (3)' immediately brings out one of Coes' results: Increased variability, as measured by the standard deviation, of foreign relative to domestic finance costs will raise the fraction of finance secured domestically. That result assumes, however, an unchanging correlation coefficient. The effect of increased correlation, by contrast, is ambiguous.

A point worth noting is that Coes, in imposing the assumption that the real price ρ is non-stochastic, really simplifies matters too much. It is entirely plausible that for some industries the real price and the real cost of external finance are highly correlated. This would surely be the case for foreign trade firms. Indeed, the correlation might conceivably be as high or higher than that between external finance and monetary correction. Consider the example where k=1 and where monetary correction is non-stochastic, $s_{iv} = 0$. In this event the share of foreign borrowing in total investment becomes:

$$(4) \quad I*/(I+I*) = \sigma\delta\frac{s_p}{s_{v*}}$$

where δ is the correlation coefficient between the real price and the real cost of external finance.

Equation (4) shows that the firm will always finance part of its projects externally. The external finance share is higher the higher the correlation between the real price and the real exchange rate and the lower the standard deviation of the cost of external finance relative to domestic real price variation. Equation (4), too, shows Coes' point that increased variability of the real exchange rate reduces external financing, given correlation and the variability of the real price.

In Coes' formulation the minimum investment term leads to the notion that the real exchange, because its stochastic behavior is modeled as a random walk, has a variance that increases with the investment term. Such a model of the real exchange rate is not really acceptable. A variable that follows a random walk will pass any limit in finite time with probability one. Clearly we do not believe that the real exchange rate could be a couple of hundred percent of its present level with probability one, given just enough time. Moreover, if this were the case for the real exchange rate it would similarly have to be the case for other real variables, including certainly the real price in some sectors. Thus a strong argument can be made that there is no such thing as "real exchange rate uncertainty" taken by itself, without correlation to other key variables that have an impact on investment decisions. Given such correlation the impact of increased uncertainty needs to be studied with more attention to the precise details of the stochastic structure. Even so, one suspects that the basic message of Coes' paper will stand.

REAL EXCHANGE RATES AND REAL INTEREST RATES

One of the striking features of Brazilian macroeconomics in the period since 1979 is the mismanagement of the internal-external balance relationship. The double oil shocks have deteriorated the full employment external balance, reinforced by the increased burden of world real interest on the already expanded real debt. Figure 1 shows the dilemma. The IS schedule shows the full employment in the goods market depending on the real interest rate, r, and the real exchange rate, θ. Increased real interest rates create unemployment that requires relief via a real depreciation. Thus points above IS respond to unemployment. The schedule CC shows current account balance. Points above the schedule, given external debt and world real interest rates, show surpluses, points below deficits. Internal and external balance prevail at point Q.

Actual policy has been to maintain the real exchange rate approximately constant at a level θ.' Given the overvaluation, the full employment deficit would be beyond hope of financing. Therefore, the government has raised home real interest rates to extraordinary levels--40% <u>real</u> interest rates charged for corporate loans--maintaining an equilibrium at a point like Q'. Even at Q' there is a deficit in the external balance requiring financing. This leads to the argument that further increases in interest rates are required to secure external financing.

It is quite apparent that the Brazilian case is <u>the</u> standard case where policy assignments are handled in exactly the wrong fashion. Real interest rates should be lowered and the real exchange rate should be depreciated. The magnitude of <u>real</u> depreciation required may be of the order of 20% to 25%. Such a depreciation would, of course, lower the standard of living of those now employed, but would also restore high employment and an economy less on the brink of disaster.[1] Overvalued exchange rates and the concomitant need for close attention to external finance have become symptomatic of the Latin American experience in 1979-82. They bring with them a very undesirable feature: financial considerations, especially foreign exchange speculation, come to dominate real activity as the chief concern. Enterprises are increasingly persuaded to invest in financial assets, not real assets and management attention is

---

[1]Needless to say real depreciation would be effective if at the same time wage indexation were suspended and the monetary budget was brought under control. See Cardoso (1982) and Dornbusch (1982).

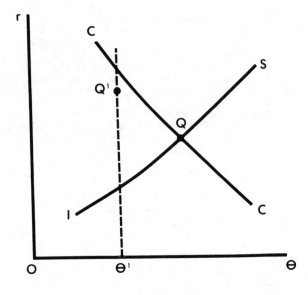

Figure 1

devoted to finance, not production. The overvaluation ultimately leads to a speculative crises that breaks economic activity. This has already been the case in Chile, Mexico and Argentina. It is no doubt around the corner for Brazil. The reason it is around the corner is that high unemployment cannot persist and therefore, with import substitution largely exhausted and controls in the long run infeasible, the real exchange rate must go, and by a lot. With that being common knowledge the door is open to speculation.

The issue of overvaluation is closely related to the topic of Coes' paper. In the early post-oil shock discussions it used to be argued that access of LDCs to the world capital market, in conjunction with recycling, was a major advantage. It is now clear that access to capital markets has delayed real depreciations that were required, as in the case of Brazil. Ironically, the longstanding policy of mini-devaluations invented to provide more macroeconomic stability proved the source of trouble once real depreciation became inevitable. Now, with external capital drying up the likelihood of real depreciation is much higher and, therefore, external borrowing is declining. The government responds by raising real interest rates still further, rather than implementing depreciation to restore exchange rate confidence, employment and capital inflows.

References

Cardoso, E., "Inflacao, Emprego e Balanco de Pagamentos," Revista de Economia Politica, Vol. 2, No. 4.

Dornbusch, R., "Stabilization Policy in Developing Countries," World Development, September, 1982

EXPORTS AND FOREIGN DEBT IN BRAZIL:
FORECASTING THE EIGHTIES

Carlos Von Doellinger

There is a remarkable distinction to be made when analyzing Brazilian trade policy before and after the mid-sixties. From the late forties until 1964, a clear downward trend in export performance prevailed. While world trade expanded by an average of six percent annually between 1953 and 1963, Brazilian exports declined by an average of 0.9% percent per year despite successive exchange rate depreciations.

Hence, in 1953 Brazilian exports rose to US$ 1,539 million, or about 2.1 percent of the world exports (excluding socialist countries). In 1964, after ten years of growth of the Brazilian economy at a rate of 7 percent per year, exports declined to US$ 1,430 million, or about 0.9 percent of the world trade. As a corollary, the Brazilian economy experienced a huge reduction in its "degree of openness" to international trade.

After 1964 this trend was reversed by a new foreign trade policy. A combination of exchange, fiscal and financial incentives provided the conditions necessary for a sustained export growth at average rates higher than those for Brazilian domestic economic growth and international trade growth. Between 1964 and 1980, Brazilian exports increased about 17.9 percent annually, while world exports increased 16.9 percent, industrialized countries´ exports increased 16.5 percent and Latin Americans´ increased 15.9 percent. Therefore, the Brazilian share in the international trade jumped from 0.9 percent in 1964 to 1.1 percent in 1980.

This performance had been particularly outstanding prior to the 1973 oil crisis. Hence, between 1964 and 1973, the annual average growth of Brazilian exports was 18.5 percent, while world exports grew at 15.5 percent per year, industrialized countries´ at 15.6 per cent and Latin American exports at 13.5 percent. In 1973 the Brazilian share of world trade was 1.2 percent.

The key to this outstanding growth has been the permanent search for new markets and products, as is shown in Tables 1 and 2; even in the presence of major difficulties in the world economy.

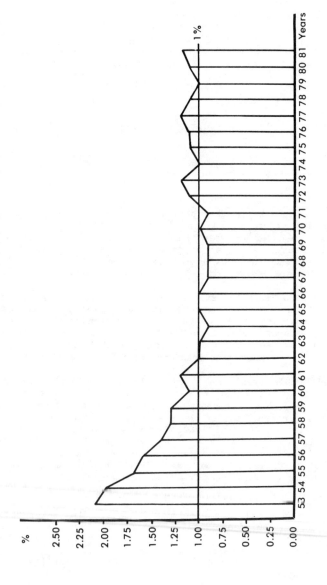

BRAZILIAN SHARE IN WORLD TRADE

Table 1 shows the relatively high degree of market diversification already
attained by Brazilian exports: A comparison between 1970 and 1980 shows a
sharp decrease in the share of such traditional markets as the USA and
EEC, and an increase in the participation of the developing nations (Latin
America, Africa, and OPEC countries).

Also the efforts made since 1964 to diversify the composition of Brazilian
foreign sales have achieved notable results. In 1980 industrial products
accounted for 51.8 percent of total exports, as compared to 22.4 percent
in 1970, while coffee--still the major primary product--was responsible
for 35.8 percent of overall 1970 export revenues, as compared to 13.8
percent in 1980.

At present, Brazilian exports encompass seven thousand products, placed on
the markets of one hundred fifty nations. In accordance with this policy
of trade diversification and with the increased development of export
facilities, the Brazilian government intends to further expand the already
significant increase of the foreign sector.

The growth potential of Brazilian exports in the coming years can be seen
through a comparison between export value and the GDP in recent years. In
the latest years exports accounted for something between 8 and 9 percent
of the GDP, a very low ratio when compared to other countries. Brazilian
share in overall trade is in the range of one percent. Therefore, all
indications are that the export sector possesses the potential for
significant future growth.

On the other hand, it is well known that the key to the adjustment process
of the Brazilian balance of payments lies in its export performance, and
that there exists huge current account deficits resulting from the trade
deficits brought about by two oil crises (1974 and 1979/80).

The growth of import expenditures after 1974 was caused by the pronounced
increase of the oil account (more than 50 percent of total imports).
Brazil depends on imported oil to provide 80 percent of total domestic
consumption. Also, the increase of the international interest rates after
1980 caused the balance of payments deficits to worsen, given the high
level of Brazilian foreign debt. The foreign debt increased about 20
percent annually between 1974 and 1981, or 9.1 percent in real terms. This
rate is higher than the export growth rate (about eight percent in real
terms) and GDP growth rate. In 1981 the foreign debt reached US$ 61,411
million, which is about 24 percent of the Brazilian GDP and 2.64 times the
export revenue of 1981.

Despite this apparently unfavourable picture, we strongly believe that the
continuation of the positive performance attained by Brazilian exports
during the last 15 years, will lead to a gradual adjustment of the current
account, reversing the growth intensity of the foreign debt. This result
is possible, even in the presence of an import recovery (which is supposed
to follow the expected industrial recovery this year) and of the expected
average annual growth of five percent for the coming years.

To demonstrate this statement, a simplified mathematical model was
developed. It attempts to reproduce the Brazilian foreign debt process as
an outcome of current deficits in the Brazilian balance of payments.
Throughout this model we try to simulate alternative growth patterns for
the foreign debt, mainly as a function of the export performance. All

the foreign debt, mainly as a function of the export performance. All simulations assume a set of realistic hypothesis about the behavior patterns of the main accounts.

In what follows, this working paper presents the description of the model, the hypothesis assumed and the simulation results. We will start from a basic simulation, which is considered the most desirable. Besides different export growth rates, we have also simulated different alternatives for interest rates. This is also a crucial parameter, though it is not within the control of the country's economic policy. The different results we derived from all simulations, indicate the sensitivity of the balance of payments and debt levels to export performance and interest rates.

Table 1. Market Distribution of Brazilian Exports

Countries	(%) 1970	(%) 1973	(%) 1980
United States	24.7	18.1	17.4
European Economic Community	28.1	37.1	26.6
European Free Trade Association	12.1	4.6	3.2
Japan	5.3	6.4	6.1
Latin America	11.1	9.0	17.2
OPEC Countries	0.1	3.2	7.5
COMECON	4.5	5.5	6.5
Africa	2.1	3.0	5.7
Other Countries	12.0	12.7	9.7
Total	100.0	100.0	100.0

Source: Banco do Brasil S/A, CACEX.

Table 2. Exports - Main Products

Item	(%) 1970	(%) 1975	(%) 1980
1. Primary products	76.7	62.7	46.8
Coffee	35.8	10.8	13.8
Soya	2.6	13.3	9.2
Sugar	4.6	12.7	6.4
Iron Ore	7.7	10.6	7.7
Others	26.0	15.3	9.7
2. Industrialized products	22.4	34.9	51.8
Semimanufactured	9.0	7.4	10.0
Manufactured	13.4	27.5	41.8
3. Others	0.9	2.4	1.4
T O T A L	100.0	100.0	100.0

Source: Banco do Brasil S/A, CACEX

THE MODEL

The simulation of the growth pattern for the Brazilian foreign debt was possible to be implemented in a model designed to reproduce the balance of payments.

The variables, parameters and relations are defined as follows:

Let:

X_t = Total exports (FOB) in the t year, at current dollars;

X_o = Exports (FOB) in the initial year of the simulation, at current dollars;

r_x = Annual growth rate of exports, at current prices.

Hence:

$$X_t = X_o (1 + r_x)^t$$

M_t = Total imports (FOB) in the t year, at current dollars;

M_o = Total imports (FOB) in the initial year of the simulation;

r_m = Annual import growth rate, current prices.

Hence:

$$M_t = M_0 (1 + r_m)^t$$

$S^n_{nf_t}$ = Net "non-factor service" expenditures, in the _t_ year, at current dollars. Includes: transportation, insurance, international travels, government expenditures and other services;

R^n_t = Net payment of interests, in year _t_;

r = Average interest rate on foreign debt;

D_t = Gross foreign debt at year end (_t_ year).

Hence:

$$R^n_t = r \cdot D_{t-1}$$

P^n_t = Net profit remittances, in _t_ year;

K_t = Stock of foreign capital at year end;

γ = Profit rate (net) on foreign investment in Brazil (excludes reinvested profits).

So:

$$P^n_t = \gamma \cdot K_{t-1}$$

I_t = Net inflow of foreign investment in the country, in _t_ year.

i = Annual growth rate of foreign investments in the country.

Hence:

$$I_t = I_0 (1 + i)^t$$

ΔRs_t = Required annual increase in international reserves of the country, in _t_ year

Df_t = Balance of payments current account deficit, in the t year.
Hence, from the definition of the balance of payments in current account we've got:

$$Df_t = M_t + S^n_{nf_t} + R^n_t + P^n_t - X_t,$$ excluding net transfers. We may also define foreign debt (D_t) as follows:

$$D_t = D_{t-1} + Df_t - I_t + \Delta Rs_t$$

Hence:

$$D = D_{t-1} + M_t + S^n_{nf_t} + R^n_t + P^n_t - X_t - I_t + \Delta Rs_t$$

Consider also the following relations:

i. $\quad S^n_{nf_t} = \alpha \cdot M_t$, with α = constant

In a simplified way, this relation defines the net payments of "non-factor services" as a fixed proportion of total imports. This simplification is justified by the predominance of transportation and other service expenditures that depend on the import level.

ii. $K_t = K_{t-1} + I_t = K_{t-1} + I_o(1+i)^t$

Where I_o is the net inflow of foreign investment in the initial year of the simulation. The relation defines the stock of foreign capital in the country (excludes reinvestments of profits).

iii. $\Delta \ Rs_t = 0.4 \ (M_t - M_{t-1})$

This relation defines a minimum requirement for the annual increase of foreign reserves. The proportion between Rs_t and M_t was 0.34 in 1981. Hence this restriction provides for better liquidity conditions of the country.

Using these relations the debt equation can be rewritten as follows:

$$D_t = (1+r)D_{t-1} + M_o(1.4+\alpha)(1+r_m)^t + \gamma[K_{t-2} + I_o(1+i)^{t-1}] - I_o(1+i)^t - X_o(1+r_x)^t - 0.4 \cdot M_o(1+r_m)^{t-1}$$

Using the 1981 initial conditions, the equation was solved in order to simulate values of D_t for the period 1982-1990. In 1981 we've got:

X_{1981} = US\$ 23,293 million
M_{1981} = US\$ 22,080 million
D_{1981} = US\$ 61,411 million
I_{1981} = US\$ 1,569 million
K_{1981} = US\$ 13,533 million

Besides α = 0.13, a profit rate of γ = 0.03 was admitted. This rate is slightly above the average for the last two years, but still below the average for the 70's (0.04). It was also assumed a growth rate of ten percent annually for the net inflow of foreign investment (the historical rate of the 70's had been 19 percent).

All the variables are shown in current values. An average world inflation rate of eight percent is assumed during the period. Imports and exports prices are supposed to grow at the same proportion. That means stable terms of trade.

BASIC SIMULATION

The first simulation (basic hypothesis) was made under the assumption of an average interest rate of 14 percent, which conforms to a real rate of 5.0 percent, throughout the period. It refers to an apparently high level, according to historical records. Though it seems to fit better the present situation in the world economy. Alternative simulations were performed to evaluate the debt growth sensitiveness as a result of different interest rates within given conditions of export performance.

The basic simulation assumes a real export growth of eight percent, so, r_x = 16.6 percent, and a real import growth of five percent, so r_m = 13.4 percent.

The 16.6 percent growth of exports is below the average rate of the 1964/80 period (17.9 percent), but very close to that verified in the 1974/80 period (16.8), after the oil crisis. Considering this growth path, and assuming an increase in world trade of 11.2 percent (real of 3%), the Brazilian share in overall world trade goes from 1.2 percent in 1981 up to 1.8 percent in 1985, reaching the proportion of the early fifties. Alternative simulations show the consequences (on the indebtedness process) of less favourable export performances.

The import growth rate was kept constant at the real level of five percent annually (hence r_m = 13.4 percent). Behind this assumption there is a minimum requirement for economic growth measured by a GDP growth rate of five percent. This minimum level is considered crucial to the economic and social stability of the country, given the labor force growth at about 3 to 3.5 percent per year. Therefore, a constant and unitary import elasticity (income elasticity) in relation to the GDP (historical relation) is assumed.

Table 3 shows the main results we have derived from the assumptions and initial conditions of 1981--the "basic simulation".

The figures for the balance of payments lead to the set of liquidity coefficients shown in Table 4, which indicates a pattern of smooth adjustment of the foreign sector. The relative figures for 1990 are very close to those of 1973. At that year the Brazilian balance of payments showed the best results of the post-war period.

This outcome depends almost solely on the level of export growth, provided realistic assumptions for import growth and interest rate levels. Nevertheless, we recognize the difficulties to keep the system of export incentives in the future. These difficulties point to the strong necessity to improve the trade policy.

In alternative simulations, lower export rates were tried. The results are not optimistic. As a matter of fact, some are hardly acceptable, leading to a deep concern about the real possibility of a balance of payments crisis. Still considering the basic simulation, Table 5 presents some additional results. For example, the foreign saving ratio in 1987 reaches the level of the early seventies, while the proportion of exports to GDP seems more suitable to the economic pattern of the country (the level of industrialization).

In 1985 the debt growth still seems abnormally high, at about 13.9 percent per year. It leads to a slight increase in the Debt/GDP ratio. Nevertheless, in the second half of the eighties we obtained a less pronounced growth rate (7.4 percent per year). This level is below the world inflation rate. As a consequence, Brazilian debt increases in real terms until it reaches a maximum level in 1987. From 1987 on, a downward trend prevails, leading to a figure for 1990 close to that of 1984.

Table 3. Basic Simulation

$$r = 0.14$$
$$r_m = 0.134$$
$$r_x = 0.166$$

(U.S.$ millions)

Item	1981	1982	1990
Exports FOB (X_t)	23,293	43,055	92,792
Imports FOB (M_t)	22,080	36,513	68,473
Net Interest Payments (R_t)	9,179	12,887	19,948
"Non-Factor Services" (net) ($S^n_{nf_t}$)	3,207	4,747	8,901
Net Profits (P_t)	370	577	998
Current Account Deficit (Df_t)	10,976	11,669	5,528
Gross Debt (D_t)	61,411	103,149	147,553
Reserves (Rs_t)	7,500	13,273	26,057

Source: Supplied by author.

Table 4. Main Coefficients

Item	1981	1982	1983	1984	1985	1986	1987	1988	1989	1990
D_t / X_t	2.64	2.61	2.57	2.49	2.40	2.28	2.13	1.97	1.79	1.59
D_t / GDP_t (%)	23.6	24.1	24.2	24.3	24.3	23.4	22.6	2.15	20.0	18.3
$D_t - Rs_t / X_t$	2.31	2.29	2.25	2.18	2.09	1.97	1.83	1.68	1.50	1.31
Debt Service$_t$ (*/X_t) (%)	65.0	61.0	60.5	59.4	57.7	55.5	52.7	49.4	45.7	41.5

Source: Supplied by author.
(*)Interest and amortization.

Table 5. Export/GDP and Foreign Savings Ratios

Years	Deficit/GDP (Foreign Savings Ratio)	Exports/GDP	Foreign Debt (Gross) ($)	Debt in 1981 Dollars
1981	4.2	8.6	61,411	(61,411)
1982	3.4	9.2	71,006	(65,746)
1983	3.2	9.5	81,265	(69,672)
1984	3.0	9.7	92,050	(73,072)
1985	2.7	10.0	103,149	(75,818)
1986	2.4	10.3	114,253	(77,759)
1987	2.0	10.5	124,934	(78,730)
1988	1.7	10.9	134,606	(78,542)
1989	1.2	11.2	142,488	(76,982)
1990	0.7	11.5	147,553	(73,813)

Source: Supplied by author.

ALTERNATIVE SIMULATIONS

The Effects of Lower Rates of Export Growth
Three alternative rates of export growth were considered:

a) The same rate of import growth (13.4 percent annually);
b) The average rate assumed for world trade growth (11.2 percent, or 3 percent real);
c) A nominal rate of eight percent per year, which implies zero real growth.

The results are shown in Table 6. For a comparison, the figures of the basic simulation are also presented. These results suggest a high sensitivity of the balance of payments and foreign debt to the export performance. The 11.2 percent and 8.0 percent growth alternatives seem to lead to unthinkable results in 1990, as shown in Table 7. The main coefficients for the foreign sector indicate absurd levels in 1990.

We also observe that, even at the average growth of 13.4 percent per year (real five percent), the results for 1990 are hardly acceptable, since it would imply the debt service representing almost 80 percent of total exports (69 percent in 1985). The same coefficients for the 11.2 percent default. Hence, this conclusion would hardly be acceptable in the long run, neither for the country nor for the international economy.

The Effects of Higher Interest Rates

The deficit configuration seems also to indicate some sensitivity to the level of interest rates. The reason is the overwhelming burden of interest payments. In 1981, for instance, the net interest payments accounted for 83 percent of the current deficit. Hence, this second alternative simulation with three different levels of interest rates: 13 percent, 15 percent, and 16 percent. Export and import growth rates were assumed as in the basic simulation. The results we got are shown in Tables 8 and 9. This simulation showed no relevant alterations in the main coefficients, provided export and import growth rates are kept in the basic simulation.

Provided this is a realistic range of variation for interest rates, the conclusion that arises is that the debt growth pattern depends much more on the export performance rather than on the average cost of debt itself. According to this conclusion the economic policy (export policy) seems to play the main role in the foreign debt control.

Table 6. Alternative Simulation - 1

$$r_x = \begin{matrix} 0.166 \\ 0.134 \\ 0.112 \\ 0.080 \end{matrix}$$

Item	1981	1985				1990			
		$r_x=0.166$	$r_x=0.134$	$r_x=0.112$	$r_x=0.080$	$r_x=0.166$	$r_x=0.134$	$r_x=0.112$	$r_x=0.080$
Exports FOB (X_t)	23,293	43,055	38,519	35,616	31,690	92,792	72,234	60,558	46,563
Imports FOB (M_t)	22,080	36,513	36,513	36,513	36,513	68,473	68,473	68,473	68,473
Interest (net)	9,179	12,887	13,710	14,259	15,031	19,948	29,748	35,778	43,630
"Non-Factor Services"($S^n_{nf_t}$)	3,207	4,747	4,747	4,747	4,474	8,901	8,901	8,901	8,901
Net Profits (P_t)	370	577	577	577	577	998	998	998	998
Current Account Deficit (Df_t)	10,976	11,669	17,028	20,480	25,178	5,528	35,886	53,590	75,439
Gross Debt (D_t)	61,411	103,149	114,388	121,757	131,973	147,553	247,907	308,638	386,618
Reserves (Rs_t)	7,500	13,273	13,273	13,273	13,273	26,057	26,057	26,057	26,057

Source: Supplied by author.

Table 7. Main Coefficients Alternative Simulation - 1

$$r_x = \begin{array}{l} 0.166 \\ 0.134 \\ 0.112 \\ 0.080 \end{array}$$

Item	1981	1985				1990			
		$r_x=0.166$	$r_x=0.134$	$r_x=0.112$	$r_x=0.080$	$r_x=0.166$	$r_x=0.134$	$r_x=0.112$	$r_x=0.080$
D_t / X_t	2.64	2.40	2.97	3.41	4.16	1.59	3.43	5.09	8.30
D_t / GDP_t (%)	23.6	24.3	26.6	28.3	30.7	18.3	30.8	38.3	48.0
$D_t - Rs_t / X_t$	2.31	2.09	2.63	3.05	3.75	1.31	3.07	4.67	7.74
Debt Service(*) / X_t(%)	65.0	57.7	68.6	77.2	91.5	41.5	79.4	113.9	180.1
Df_t / GDP_t (%)	4.2	2.7	4.0	4.7	5.9	0.7	4.5	6.6	9.4

Source: Supplied by author.
(*) Interest and amortization.

Table 8. Alternative Simulation – 2

$$r = \begin{array}{l} 0.13 \\ 0.14 \\ 0.15 \\ 0.16 \end{array}$$

Item	1981	1985				1990			
		r=0.13	r=0.14	r=0.15	r=0.16	r=0.13	r=0.14	r=0.15	r=0.16
Exports FOB (X_t)	23,293	43,055	43,055	43,055	43,055	92,792	92,792	92,792	92,792
Imports FOB (M_t)	22,080	36,513	36,513	36,513	36,513	68,473	68,473	68,473	68,473
Interest (net)	9,179	12,551	12,887	13,229	13,577	18,321	19,948	21,682	23,527
"Non-Factor Services" ($S^n_{nf_t}$)	3,207	4,747	4,747	4,747	4,747	8,901	8,901	8,901	8,901
Net Profits (P_t)	370	577	577	577	577	998	998	998	998
Current Account Deficit (Df_t)	10,976	11,333	11,669	12,011	12,359	3,901	5,528	7,262	9,107
Gross Debt (D_t)	61,411	99,517	103,149	106,877	110,703	132,991	147,553	163,219	180,057
Reserves (Rs_t)	7,500	13,273	13,273	13,273	13,273	26,057	26,057	26,057	26,057

Source: Supplied by author.

Table 9. Main Coefficients Alternative Simulation – 2

			r =	0.13 0.14 0.15 0.16					

Item	1981	1985				1990			
		r=0.13	r=0.14	r=0.15	r=0.16	r=0.13	r=0.14	r=0.15	r–0.16
D_t / X_t	2.64	2.31	2.40	2.48	2.57	1.43	1.59	1.75	1.94
D_t / GDP_t (%)	23.6	23.1	24.3	24.9	25.7	16.5	18.3	20.3	22.3
$D_t - Rs_t / X_t$	2.31	2.00	2.09	2.17	2.26	1.15	1.31	1.48	1.65
Debt Service (*) / X_t (%)	65.0	54.1	57.7	61.5	65.3	36.7	41.5	46.7	52.5
Df_t / GDP_t (%)	4.2	2.6	2.7	2.8	2.9	0.5	0.7	0.9	1.1

Source: Supplied by author.
(*) Interest and amortization.

BRAZILIAN FOREIGN DEBT
(Forecasting for 1982 - 1990 with r = 0.14)

Debt 1 (rx = 0.134 • rm = 0.134)
Debt 2 (rx = 0.112 • rm = 0.134)
Debt 3 (rx = 0.08 • rm = 0.134)
Debt 4 (rx= 0.166 • rm = 0.134)

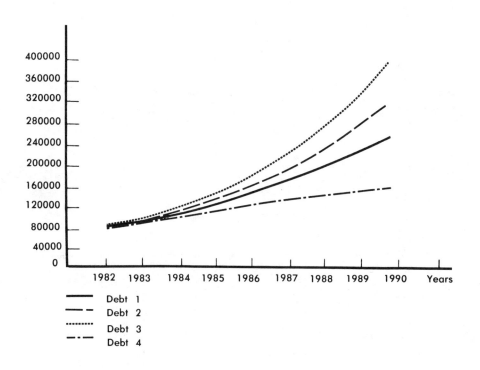

Debt 1
Debt 2
Debt 3
Debt 4

BRAZILIAN FOREIGN DEBT
(Forecasting for 1982 - 1990 with rm= 0.134 rx= 0.1661=0.10)

Debt 1 (r =0.134)
Debt 2 (r = 0.14)
Debt 3 (r = 0.15)
Debt 4 (r = 0.16)

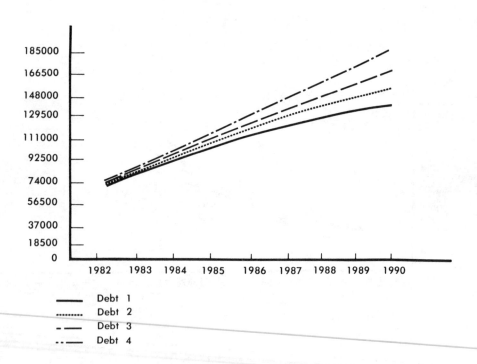

Debt 1
Debt 2
Debt 3
Debt 4

Comments by William G. Tyler on Carlos von Doellinger's,
"Exports and Foreign Debt in Brazil: Forecasting the Eighties"

Carlos von Doellinger has provided us with a timely, useful, and practical paper. The core of the paper represents an attempt to project the Brazilian balance of payments through the 1980s, with changes in the stock of the country's external debt being determined rather passively from the flow items in the balance of payments. The question is what will the Brazilian balance of payments and debt picture look like in 1990. This is obviously a very important question, but one which is difficult to address in a satisfactory manner. Dr. von Doellinger makes a valiant effort. His base case projections are rather optimistic, showing substantial reductions in the current account deficit, the debt service ratio, and the relative size of the external debt.

A major value of the paper is that it focuses our attention on two critical dimensions. First it is evident from von Doellinger's paper, along with other work, that export growth is crucial for the Brazilian economy. Second, the paper focuses our attention on the nature and importance of the parameter estimates and assumptions in the projection exercise. Accordingly, I will divide my comments in two parts, initially looking at export behavior and the external sector, in keeping with von Doellinger's analysis in the first part of his paper. Then I will proceed to make some comments about the projections themselves.

EXPORT PERFORMANCE AND THE EXTERNAL SECTOR

It is commonly thought that export growth in Brazil has been enormous. It is of course a relative concept. Relative to the Brazilian past, i.e., the postwar period prior to the mid-sixties, the country's export growth has indeed been enormous. But such growth does not appear overly impressive when compared to that of a number of other countries. Moreover, export growth in more recent years has not been dramatic. One should not, I think, treat the years from the mid-sixties until the present as one rather homogeneous period with regard to export performance. Two very different periods are discernible, with the break occurring in the mid-1970s. Accordingly, to make projections on the basis of observed export performance in the entire period since the mid-1960s appears misleading.

From the mid-1960s until the mid-1970s Brazilian exports grew very rapidly. Adjusting for dollar inflation, total and manufactured exports grew at real rates of 13 and 25 percent, respectively for the 1964-74 period. Following this period, however, there was a substantial slowdown in export growth. Real growth rates for total and manufactured exports were 5 and 12 percent, respectively, from 1974 to 1978. During this later period the Brazilian share of total world exports actually declined. The last three years have not altered the general picture of slackened Brazilian export growth since the mid-1970s.

To take a better look at what the future might hold one might strive for a better understanding of the past. Understanding the reasons for the decline in Brazilian export growth, especially of manufactures, seems to be relevant. One commonly accepted argument involves the demand side. World recession in the mid-1970s and an increase in protectionism are frequently presented as explanations. Yet, if so, how is relative success of some other countries to be explained in this same period? Were they immune to adverse world demand conditions and protectionism? Obviously not. Also, one has to bear in mind that Brazilian exports represent only about one percent of total world exports, and only in a couple of products (especially coffee and soybeans) is Brazil able to affect the level of international prices. While international demand conditions did most likely contribute to Brazil's reduced export growth rate, especially in the case of primary products, such conditions alone are an unconvincing explanation. One should look, therefore, at the supply side, and particularly at Brazilian economic policies, as well.

To cope with the terms of trade shock imposed by the increase in petroleum prices in the mid-1970s, the Brazilian Government increased import restrictions, expanded external borrowing, and failed to appreciably adjust the exchange rate, i.e., to depreciate. One important effect in this delay in macroeconomic adjustment was to effectively terminate the cautious trade policy liberalization that had been occuring in the late 1960s and early 1970s. In fact, renewed import substitution became a policy objective. Accordingly, an increase in the anti-export biases in Brazilian commercial policies was brought about, in effect discriminating against export activity. A recent study has presented econometric evidence linking the reduction of export growth rates for manufacturing industries to the increases in the anti-export biases imposed, in fact, by the exercise of commercial policies in the aftermath of the first petroleum shock.[1]

The situation in early 1982 is substantially different from that which existed in the mid-1970s. In goods markets, Brazil has become much more of a closed economy. Effective domestic market protection for manufacturing averages some 46 percent, with very high rates observed in a number of industries. Brazilian commercial policies have in effect rendered many ostensibly tradable goods into de facto nontradables. Opportunities for trade have simply been cut off, although the evidence points to

---

[1]William G. Tyler, "The Anti-Export Bias in Commercial Policies and Export Performance: Some Evidence from the Recent Brazilian Experience," Welwirtschaftliches Archiv, March 1983.

considerable international competitiveness in many industries.[2] The result is that Brazil is now one of the world's most closed economies. Only a handful of countries—Uganda, India, Turkey, and China—possess smaller ratios of exports to GDP.

If in the goods sphere Brazil has become, and remains, a very closed economy, this is not true in the financial sphere. The accumulation of external debt, dating most dramatically from the mid-1970s, has placed Brazil in a position of enormous dependence, and to that extent openness, with respect to international financial markets. It must continually rollover and service its external debt, not to mention the need to obtain new credits. As such, the international financial exigencies imposed by the debt do much to dictate domestic macroeconomic demand management, and especially financial, policies. In view of this international financial vulnerability, on the one hand, and the relatively closed nature of the economy in goods markets, on the other, it can be argued that Brazil has the worst of both worlds. Its international financial dependence means that it must undertake painful domestic economic measures to satisfy its international obligations. Yet, the closed nature of the economy means that Brazil cannot take adequate advantage of export opportunities, which would make servicing its debt much easier.

THE BALANCE OF PAYMENTS PROJECTIONS

Turning to the balance of payments projections presented in the paper, I have indicated that I believe these exercises are very useful. They try to paint possible pictures of the future under alternative assumptions. Having some appreciation of possible future scenarios appears to me to be essential. Yet, economists are very reluctant to engage in crystal ball gazing or the type of projection exercises presented in this paper. Perhaps it is because such efforts are very difficult or perhaps because they are so easy for others to criticize. Rather than dwell on the weak points that any exercise such as von Doellinger's, commendable as it is, is bound to possess, I would instead like to offer three principal suggestions for future work along these lines.

First, I think it might be possible to endogenize some of the more interesting elements in the exercise. The model, as presented in the paper, is not really a model but rather a set of identities. There is no emphasis on behavioral relationships. Moreover, most of the important things, the really interesting things, are essentially exogenous. The parameter values are given, and it is they, along with central exogenous variables, that drive the projections. These given values include such things as the growth rate of exports and the growth rate of GDP. The aggregate import demand elasticity with respect to income is given as one, despite evidence of its considerable fluctuation over time. At the same time, any reformulation of the model must nevertheless leave some crucial variables exogenous, such as petroleum prices and the Libor.

---

[2]See William G. Tyler, "Incentivos Efetivos para Vendas no Mercado Domestico e para Exportacao: Uma Visao dos Vieses Anti-Exportacao e a Politica Comercial no Brasil, 1980-81." Pesquisa e Planejamento Economico, 1983.

Second, the exercise would be benefitted if it were carried out in the context of a larger macro model framework. There seems to be a lack of integration of the projection exercise with the rest of the economy. Ideally one would like to examine the consistency of the balance of payments with domestic savings and resource availability.

Third, one might gain from a disaggregation of exports and imports. On the export side, a few primary commodity exports should be examined and projected separately, as should an aggregate of manufacturing exports. The most important disaggregation on the import side would involve petroleum. Domestic demand and production should be projected, with imports, valued at an exogenously determined international price, being determined as a residual. For non-petroleum imports a better econometric appreciation of the effects of import restrictions and income changes appears to be desirable.[3]

No matter how well formulated the projection's model may be, any exercise of this type is bound to be fraught with considerable uncertainty. While being useful for focusing our attention on key parameters and policy variables and presenting plausible scenarios under different circumstances, any projections must be qualified and necessarily accepted for what they are. The enormous degree of uncertainty prevailing in the world today precludes any precise picture of the future. Domestic political circumstances in Brazil, and as a result economic policies are not predictable in the medium term. Nor are international circumstances, affecting such key exogenous variables as the international petroleum price and the Libor.

Finally, some doubt must be raised concerning the functioning of international financial markets themselves. Dr. von Doellinger implicitly assumes that Brazil will continue to have ready access to those markets, as it has in fact had over the past twenty years. Brazil's external debt size is derived in the projections as a residual. Yet, can one reasonably expect that international financial markets will function in the future as smoothly as they have functioned in the past? Maybe not. The current Falklands War in the South Atlantic has sent tremors through the international banking system, and a crisis of confidence may be brewing, entailing substantial repercussions for Brazil as well as for the international financial system itself. A refusal of the international banks to continue the rollover of Brazil's international debt, for whatever reason, would generate a crisis. Under such circumstances it is obvious that all bets are off on the type of projections exercise presented in von Doellinger's careful and useful paper.

---

[3]For a first approximation of some continuing work along these lines, the reader is referred to Milton Assis, Um Modelo Macroeconometrico de Politica a Curto Prazo para o Brasil (Rio de Janeiro: IPEA/INPES, 1981).

COMMERCIAL POLICY IN BRAZIL: AN OVERVIEW

Jose L. Carvalho

The purpose of this paper is to describe and, in some sense, to evaluate the commercial policies adopted by Brazil since World War II. This overview is necessary for understanding Brazil's present situation. The commercial policies are specifically evaluated in terms of protection of domestic production and, in terms of the cost of domestic resources utilized for every dollar of export revenue realized. We also consider how the commercial policies affected Brazilian trade and their impact upon the use of factors of production.

In Section 1 we describe all commercial policies adopted by Brazil. In Section 2, the policy instruments used by the Brazilian authorities to implement her commercial policies are briefly described and then, inferences about the impact of such measures are made based on previous studies. Section 3 summarizes our findings and presents a prospective view of the most likely trends for Brazilian commercial policy.

BRAZILIAN COMMERCIAL POLICIES: AN OVERVIEW

Brazilian commercial policies have been described and analyzed by several authors. The summary we present draws heavily on Carvalho-Haddad (1980). The description that follows, is divided into periods that display some marked characteristics. They are presented in chronological order and the major events are briefly described. When we considered it advisable, some comments were added in order to point out the main features of each period.

The Pre-War Period

The industrialization through import substitution process (ISI) in Brazil is generally said to have begun after World War II, but in fact it started long before. Since the end of the nineteenth century, tariffs were already high by world standards and industry began to grow at a rapid pace. Nevertheless, this early import substitution process differed from the post-war process in two important aspects. First, there was no conscious industrialization policy, properly speaking, since tariffs were raised primarily for revenue purposes. Second, the process was carried out, at least until the 1930's, in a quite liberal environment with a minimum of government intervention (coffee being an exception), general flexibility of prices (including the exchange rate) and the absence of selective controls or incentives.

With that particular political and economic climate, coupled with tariff barriers which would be considered high for that time (although low by today's standards), it is not surprising to find that the industrial sectors which grew faster were the ones in which we would expect, a priori, that Brazil had strong comparative advantages. These included textiles (the most important Brazilian industry during the first half on the 20th century), footwear, beverages and food products. In fact, the growth rates were high. It is estimated that industry grew at an average, annual compound rate of 6 percent in the period between 1900-02 and 1945-47.[1]

After 1930, liberalism was gradually abandoned and the government started to intervene in the economy directly through state enterprises and indirectly through increased utilization of control schemes and selective policies. However, it was not until after World War II that such policies, especially those connected with the trade sector, were vigorously pursued.

The Early Years, 1946-1952

The major characteristic of this period was a highly overvalued exchange rate. (See Table A.1.) In order to have kept the 1937-38 parity, in real terms, the government should have devalued the cruzeiro by 42 percent immediately after the second world war. It is interesting to note that although the exchange rate was highly overvalued in terms of the 1937-38 parity, it remained fairly constant in real terms until 1951, falling significantly only in 1952.

The consequence of the overvaluation of the exchange rate was a sharp increase in imports as soon as the war restrictions were lifted. Even the tremendous rise in coffee prices (which more than doubled from 1948 to 1951) was not sufficient, with the exception of 1950, to equilibrate the current account.

Instead of devaluing the cruzeiro, the authorities chose to impose a licensing system on imports, starting in 1947. Foreign exchange was allocated according to the "essentiality" of the product and to its potential as a competitor to domestic production.

Three reasons may be advanced to explain the preference for import controls devaluations. First, the demand for Brazilian exports was said to be inelastic and, in the case of coffee, foreign demand was considered inelastic such that a devaluation would result either in rents to exports, or in a fall in foreign prices that would more than compensate for the devalution, generating no additional incentives to exports. Second, following the interventionist trend of the 1930's there was a clear preference for discretionary controls over reliance on market forces, a

---

[1]Haddad, Cláudio L.S., "Crescimento do Produto Real Brasileiro 1900/1947," Revista Brasileira de Economia 29, 1975.

preference that remains pervasive today. Third, there is still a myth held by policy makers and the general public, that the level of the exchange rate was a thermometer of the country's health. In addition to that, the recent Bretton Woods agreement, in a sense, ratified that view, thus imposing political costs on policy makers as far as devaluations were concerned.

The burden of the policy fell unequivocally upon exports. Although exports increased in value terms from 1946 to 1951 this was due exclusively to the boom in coffee prices. In terms of quantum, the exports of coffee remained fairly constant during that period, while non-coffee exports fell, from 1946 to 1952 by 50 percent.

The abrupt fall in the real exchange rate in 1952, coupled with expansionary domestic policies and the stabilization of coffee prices, produced a trade account deficit of 286 million dollars. In that same year the overall balance of payments deficit reached 615 million, which represented 43 percent of total exports. That deficit paved the way for important policy changes as far as the balance of payments was concerned.

1953-57: Multiple Exchange Rates and the Auction System

The changes in the exchange rate policy were marked. On the export side, exporters were, at first, permitted to transact part of their earnings (as much as 50 percent) in the free market. But later in 1953, this permission was rescinded and a system of multiple exchange rates was implemented. On the import side, available amounts of foreign exchange were divided into five categories and auctioned. Some commodities, like wheat, petroleum products and newsprint, were excluded from the auctioned and negotiated at custo de câmbio, approximately equal to the average export rate. The share of those particular imports in the total was around 30 percent.

The official exchange rate had been kept at 18.7 cruzeiros per dollar from 1947 to 1952. Although in 1953 there were devaluations in all categories, they differed markedly according to the end use to which the foreign exchange was put. They were extremely high for finished consumer goods, lower for foodstuffs, and so on, presenting, therefore, that "cascade" structure characteristic of tariff barriers. Since the importer is indifferent to whether the exchange rate or the tariff is higher, it is apparent (see Table A.2) that the system of multiple exchange rates laid a firm basis for import substitution that would progress according to the degree of final processing of the products.

On the other hand, the bias against exports is also evident (see Table A.2). The non-coffee export rate stays below all the import rates, being close to custo de câmbio, the privileged rate used for imports of petroleum of products and wheat. In fact, compared with the official rate in 1952, the devaluation of the export rate in 1953 was about 30 percent in real terms, which was not sufficient to restore the 1947-48 parity. Thus, exports were implicity taxed even more heavily in the period 1953-57 than in the previous one (1947-52).

The coffee rate was kept below other rates based on the idea that foreign demand for Brazilian coffee was still inelastic and, therefore, the gain in the terms of trade would more than compensate the loss to the producers.

We also note that the import rates devalued slowly, in real terms, from 1953 to 1956, while the export rate remained fairly constant. On the other hand, all rates appreciated in real terms in 1957. The free market rate in 1957 was 21.5 percent below the 1953 parity in real terms.

When we examine the behavior of the average import rate (total imports in cruzeiros divided by their dollar value), we can see that the overall devaluation was not very large, even on the import side. In fact, the average import exchange rate devalues very slowly, in real terms, from 1953 to 1956, being a trifle above the non-coffee rate. The reasons were, first that many important items were imported at <u>custo de câmbio</u> (petroleum products, wheat), and second that the majority of the remaining items fell into categories I to III, which absorbed about 80 percent of total exchange available for auction. Since the rates for categories I to III were much below the ones for categories IV and V, the average import rate was in fact quite low. This fact rather than implying an "easy" aspect of the policy, shows how distorted the system was. The average rate was low because imports of goods in high categories were prohibitive. This generated enormous incentives for the inflow of direct foreign investment in Brazil, aimed mainly at the production of final durable goods.

Another reason, connected with the inflow of foreign investments, was Instruction 113 (January 1955) which enabled foreign firms to import capital goods without exchange cover. The payment was made through the acquisition of equity in existing or newly established firms. Since the exchange rate for finanacial transfers was low, this tended to push down the average import rate.

Instruction 113, together with other government facilities for capital transfers, the prohibitive rate for imports of durable consumer goods and other quantitative barriers, induced a large amount of direct investment, especially in those areas. The automobile industry, for instance, was created during this time.

1957-60: From Multiple Exchange Rates to High Ad-Valorem Tariffs

The auction of exchange was completely modified in August, 1957. Items such as petroleum products, wheat, newsprint and fertilizers remained on the most favored list, imported at a very low exchange rate, approximately equal to the export rate. The five other categories were reduced to two: a "general" category and a "special" one. In the latter were included finished consumer goods and other goods which competed with domestic production. Both rates were set by auction, with the rate for the "special" category being around two or three times the one for the "general" category,

On the other hand, a set of ad-valorem tariffs was introduced. The tariff rates were usually high. They varied between 0 percent and 10 percent for goods whose supply source was completely external; between 10 percent to 60 percent for goods which were mildly competitive with domestic production; and between 60 percent to 150 percent for products which were largely available from domestic sources.

In addition to the tariffs other restrictions were imposed. A government council, Conselho de Politica Aduaneira (CPA) was created and empowered to lower or to raise tariffs when deemed necessary. The criterion followed, was, generally, availability from domestic sources. The Law of Similars, under which imports of products that could be available from domestic sources could be prohibited, was activated.

According to Fishlow, however, the number of products classified as "similars" did not show, in the period 1958-63, an increase with respect to the previous five years.[2] This fact, coupled with other evidence, suggests that the Law of Similars did not impose significant quantitative restrictions on imports.

With regard to exports, the change from multiple exchange rates to just a few categories coupled with more devaluations increased the average real exchange rate paid to exporters (see Table A.1).

From 1957 to 1960, the real non-coffee export exchange rate was devalued by 43 percent. However, this was not sufficient to increase non-coffee exports significantly. The reasons were many. First, although the real exchange rate improved when compared with the 1951 parity, we can recall that this parity was already highly overvalued when compared with the level in 1938-39. In fact, the devaluation, in real terms, from 1957 to 1960 was not even sufficient to compensate for the loss in purchasing power during World War II. Second, the import substitution policy implied a heavy tax on exports, by directing resources and investments to industries that would compete with exports and, consequently, pulled resources away from the export sector. Third, the terms of trade deteriorated for Brazil between 1957 and 1960. Not only did coffee prices fall, but also the prices of other export products. In fact, non-coffee exports increased 15.8 percent in terms of quantum between 1955-57 and 1958-60, although the increase in value was just 5.3 percent. Fourth, although the devaluations were occasional they were in large amounts which increased the risk to businessmen engaging in export activities.

Unfortunately, the poor performance of exports during this period and the deterioration of the terms of trade "confirmed", to some policy makers, the theories advanced by ECLA of "inelasticity" of exports and the need for industrialization via import substitution. At least, in what concerns the "inelasticity" of exports, those theories would prove to be completely false in the period after 1965.

1961-64: An Interlude
The period 1961-64 was a difficult one for the Brazilian economy. The "industrailization at any cost" program of the period 1955-60, coupled with other ambitious projects like the construction of Brasilia, generated large government deficits. They were mainly financed by borrowings from the monetary authorities, thereby substantially increasing the money supply. Inflation gained momentum in 1958 and, in 1959 prices increased by 39.5 percent. In 1960, the increase was 30.5 percent, but the growth in money supply was 38.8 percent.

The newly elected President, Janio Quadros, responded to the imbalance with orthodox measures. In March 1961, there was a devaluation of 40 percent coupled with the abolition of the auction system and the special

---

[2]Fishlow, A. Foreign Trade Regime and Economic Development: Brazil, Report to NBER April 1975 (mimeographed).

exchange rates for petroleum products, newsprint, wheat and other privileged imports. The movement, in fact, unified all exchange rates. Prior deposits, in the full value of the contracts for 150 days with 6 percent interest to the depositor, were imposed being regarded as a temporary measure.

Prior deposits had, of course, two objectives: first, the 6 percent interest represented a substantial implicit tariff, since inflation ran at a rate above 30 percent; second, the deposits were intended to reduce the monetary base. In fact, this second objective was realized. Despite larger fiscal deficits than in the previous year, the growth of the money supply between December 1960 and June 1961 was just 12 percent.

However, due to the well known long lags of monetary policy, inflation continued at a high rate in the first half of 1961. In August, President Janio Quadros resigned and the country entered into a period of political turmoil, in which it was difficult to sustain sound, or even coherent, economic policies.

The contractionary monetary policy was abandoned in the last quarter of 1961, when the money supply increased by 21 percent.[3] Thereafter, it increased by 64.1 percent in 1962, 64.4 percent in 1963, and 81.6 percent in 1964. The inflation rates were, respectively, 51.3 percent, 81.3 percent and 91.9 percent. However, the exchange rate remained fixed until May 1962, being devalued in that month by just 15 percent. Petroleum products and wheat were again imported at a very low subsidized rate. Therefore, not only was domestic policy unsuited for equilibrium in the balance of payments, but also the exchange rate policy was completely unrealistic.

The real exchange rate appreciated sharply from 1961 to 1964 (see Table A.1) being devalued, in a substantial way, only in the year after the military takeover.

But, in any event, the period 1961-64 marked an end to autarkic policies aimed at import substitution with hidden, but important, disincentive to exports. From 1965 on, an active policy of export promotion started to be implemented and economic policy, in general, was changed in important respects.

1964-74: From Autarkic Policies to Trade Promotion

After World War II until 1963, the growth of Brazilian real output proceeded at a rapid pace measured by world standards. From 1950 to 1962, the average rate of growth of real GDP was about 7 percent per year, which, in spite of the fact that population increased substantially as well, produced a 58 percent rise in real per capita income. The level of exports, however, did not follow that steep upward trend. As one can see from Table 1, exports remained fairly constant during that period, even displaying a slight downward trend.

---

[3]This increase in money supply, if maintained, would correspond to an annual rate of 114 percent. However, the increase in the money supply in the fourth quarter is seasonally large compared to the other quarters. Thus, this annual rate is overstated.

TABLE 1: BRAZILIAN EXPORTS

(in current U.S.$ millions)

YEARS	EXPORTS (FOB)		
	NRB GOODS*	MANUFACTURES	T O T A L
1950			1355
1951			1769
1952			1418
1953			1539
1954			1562
1955			1423
1956			1482
1957			1392
1958			1243
1959			1282
1960			1269
1961			1403
1962			1214
1963			1406
1964	581	89	1430
1965	758	130	1595
1966	816	152	1741
1967	725	196	1654
1968	912	202	1881
1969	1181	284	2311
1970	1341	416	2739
1971	1509	573	2904
1972	2306	898	3991
1973	3421	1434	6199
1974	4709	2263	7951
1975	5152	2584	8670
1976	4954	2776	10128
1977	5655	3840	12120
1978	5629	5083	12659
1979	6273	6645	15244
1980	8331	9028	20132
1981**	10410	11924	23293

SOURCE: CACEX

    *NRB= Natural Resource Based Goods = Total non-coffee
    Exports - Manufactures.
    **January-November 1981.

Which were the factors responsible for that poor performance of exports?
One such factor was undoubtedly the import substitution policy of the
fifties. It had not been adequately recognized by Brazilian policy makers
that, due to the general equilibrium nature of the problem, import
restriction implied a tax on exports. The tax comes indirectly through
the effect of the restrictions on the production and, on the consumption
side of the economy. By raising the prices of importables, the
restrictions stimulate their domestic production. In order to expand, the
import substitution industries bid resources away from the rest of the
economy, increasing their relative prices and hindering the production of
exportables. On the other hand, imports become relatively more expensive
to consumers who tend to substitute other goods for them, thereby
increasing their comsumption of exportables. However small any of those
two effects might be, they together imply a lower volume of goods
available for exports, as if the latter were taxed. What the conclusion
means is that although the real exchange rate paid by importers increases,
the one received by exporters falls. Assuming international prices to be
fixed,[4] this adjustment can come either through appreciation of the
nominal exchange rate, in case it is flexible, or through a rise in the
domestic price level, in case the country operates on a fixed exchange
rate regime.

The fact that Brazil was under a fixed rate system during 1950/68,
however, also played a key role in the poor performance of exports. This
happened because in that period inflation accelerated, attaining the
record of 88 percent in 1964, prices increasing more than a hundred and
twenty fold from 1950 to 1968. Furthermore, even if, on the average, the
occasional massive devaluations kept the real exchange rate received by
exporters and consequently their average profitability constant, its
coefficient of variation was high enough to add a great deal of
uncertainty and undesired fluctuations in the export business to
discourage the growth of such activities.

Finally, since no rebate was granted for domestic indirect taxes connected
with the production and commercialization of the export goods, they were
in fact subjected to double taxation, since they were also taxed in the
countries of destination according to their fiscal laws.

All those disincentives to exports, besides accounting for the slight
downward trend in their level until 1964, had the effect of basing their
composition in a few primary goods. This was so, as they were the only
products for which Brazil's comparative advantage was strong enough to
permit exportation at a profit. In 1964, for instance, the exports of
coffee, sugar, cotton and cocoa accounted for 65.5 percent of the total.
If we add to that the exports of the other primary products we would reach
85.3 percent of the total. (For more details, see Table A.3.)

The inward strategy adopted in the fifties produced, then, a decline in
both imports and exports. On the other hand, the rapid growth of real
income during the same period and the industrialization pattern that

---

[4]The basic assumption throughout the analysis is the "small country
hypothesis" under which the country is considered to be price taker in
international markets.

developed in Brazil placed growing demands on industrial raw materials, semi-manufactured goods and on machinery and equipment. All products for which Brazil had become increasingly dependent upon foreign suppliers. (See Table 2.)

By 1963, the balance of payments had become one of the most important bottlenecks to the country's further development. Indeed, a moratorium on all payments of interest and amortization of the foreign debt was even considered, after efforts at renegotiation proved unsuccessful.[5]

Policies were drastically changed after 1964, however. Starting in 1965 and especially after 1967, an active policy of export promotion was followed, in regard to the fiscal treatment of exports, credit and the exchange rate.

The export promotion measures will be analyzed below. Let us mention, briefly, the changes as far as imports are concerned. Exchange premiums and prior deposits were eliminated for general category imports and the premiums were substantially reduced on "special" category imports. In March 1967, the special category was eliminated and there was a general tariff reform that lowered nominal and effective tariffs. Finally, from 1964 to 1967 the real exchange rate appreciated by 20 percent. We can also notice that the real exchange rate does not return to the original value of 1964, and it remains almost constant from 1969 to 1974, after adoption of the crawling peg system in 1968 (see Table A.1.).

Of course, and this is an important point, the appreciation of the exchange rate and the reduction of import controls were made possible by the rightward shifts of the supply of exports in response to new incentives. In other words, instead of an import substitution strategy which taxed exports heavily, the export promotion policies after 1965 also generated, incentives to import. Therefore, one can safely divide Brazilian commercial policy into two distinct periods: anti-trade, i.e., autarkic policies from 1945 until 1964, and pro-trade policies thereafter.

The list of fiscal incentives granted to exports is, undoubtedly, impressive. However, on many occasions, in recent years, governmental policies regarding the trade area implied substantial taxes on exports of some food products. In order to protect the internal market, restrictions in the form of tariffs and quotas were placed on exports of meat and soybeans in 1973, following an increase in the international prices of those products. In 1974, the exports of sugar were taxed in a subtle way. Although the international price of sugar increased almost three-fold, the domestic price was allowed to rise only a trifle in real terms. This policy implicity entailed a substantial tax on production and a substantial subsidy on consumption, and was thus equivalent to an export tariff.

---

[5]Simonsen advances another deterrant to exports motivated by non-economic reasons. For instance, the reluctance to export raw materials because of the fear that our resources would be forever depleted, and so on. See M.H. Simonsen, Brasil 2002 (Rio: APEC, 1972), pp. 97–112.

TABLE 2 - BRAZILIAN IMPORTS

(in current U.S.$ millions)

YEARS	IMPORTS (FOB)					
	CONSUMER GOODS	RAW MATERIALS	CAPITAL GOODS	PETROLEUM*	TOTAL EXCEPT PETROLEUM	TOTAL
1950				136	798	934
1951				200	1503	1703
1952				238	1464	1702
1953				231	1088	1319
1954				252	1382	1634
1955				203	1104	1307
1956				214	1020	1234
1957				200	1289	1489
1958				219	1134	1353
1959				199	1175	1374
1960				202	1260	1462
1961				200	1260	1460
1962				196	1279	1475
1963				195	1292	1487
1964		240	288	180	1083	1263
1965		209	229	157	939	1096
1966		236	357	166	1330	1496
1967		229	447	154	1513	1667
1968		312	622	204	1928	2132
1969		291	731	204	2061	2265
1970		370	938	236	2613	2849
1971		499	1225	327	3374	3701
1972	417	1567	1734	409	4374	4783
1973	649	2563	2109	711	6288	6999
1974	875	5593	3107	2840	11328	14168
1975	822	4354	3934	2875	10717	13592
1976	862	4060	3556	3613	10113	13726
1977	930	3911	3074	3814	9443	13257
1978	1113	4535	3553	4196	10858	15054
1979	1582	5954	3775	6434	13370	19804
1980	1313	7061	4381	9844	13116	22960
1981**	987	5740	4013	10600	11486	22086

SOURCE: MINISTRY OF FINANCE
*Crude oil and sub-products
**January-November 1981

Finally, a fact that has certainly been influential in the export growth of recent years was the new exchange rate policy adopted in 1968. Under this "mini-devaluation" policy, the exchange rate is periodically devalued in small amounts (generally not exceeding 2 percent), the guiding principle being to keep the exchange rate fairly constant in real terms (i.e., corrected for both domestic and foreign inflation.)

That policy had two major effects. First, it eliminated the uncertainty of abrupt changes caused by the previous policy of infrequent, but massive devaluations. Second, by keeping the real exchange rate approximately constant in light of the whole battery of fiscal incentives granted to exports, it allowed the rightward shifts in the supply of exports to manifest themselves in a rapid expansion of export receipts. We will come back to the mini-devaluation policy later on, but there is no doubt that until 1974 the policy was highly favorable to export growth.

The inward development strategy adopted after World War II was thus drastically changed from 1965 on. In the following decade, Brazil followed an outward looking strategy with a rapid incrase both in the volume of exports and of imports. From 1965 to 1975 exports increased more than five times in nominal value. Their annual compound rate of growth for that period was 29.5 percent.

Besides the large expansion in the total value of exports, there was also a gradual change in their product mix. The share of primary products in the total declined from 91.1 percent in the period 1964/68 to 64.4 percent in 1974, while the share of industrialized products rose from 8.9 percent to 35.6 percent during the same period. Within the primary products category, one can discern a continuous fall in the relative importance of coffee and, a marked increase in the share of sugar and soybeans in total exports, largely due to the dramatic rise in the international prices of the latter commodities in recent years.

1974-79: The Oil Crisis and the Return to the Import Substitution Strategy

With the sharp increase in the world price of petroleum and the high proportion of imports for domestic consumption, Brazil had to adjust to this situation. Although Brazil had no way of substituting for petroleum, in the short run, there were several ways of adjusting to this new reality. Nonetheless, the policy makers adopted a rather peculiar solution: subsidize domestic consumption of oil and; to cope with the balance of payments difficulties, borrow from abroad, reduce imports other than petroleum and engage in a new import substitution program directed towards capital goods.

With this strategy, inflation gained momentum. The crawling peg exchange rate system did not follow the inflation path after 1974. It lagged behind, inducing residents to borrow from abroad at negative real interest rates. Part of the appreciation of the cruzeiro, with respect to the dollar (about 30 percent by 1979), was compensated by subsidies given to exports and by strong controls on the import side. These import restrictions were mainly comprised of: a general increase in tariffs, expecially for capital goods, a slow down in the import licensing procedure and; prior deposits in the full value of imports, for 360 days, bearing no interest.The main result of this strategy was a tremendous growth in the Brazilian foreign debt (see Table A.4.).

Although inflation was increasing and the accumulation of foreign debt had been accelerated, Brazil managed to maintain high rates of growth for GDP (see Table A.5). But, the fragility of such strategy would emerge when the international interest rates (in real terms) turned positive. This, would destabilize the financial scheme adopted by Brazil, in the international market and, together with the new increase in the petroleum price (1979) would produce a very significant restriction on the country's ability to both maintain growth and inilation.

1979 to date: The Balance of Payments Constraint

The year of 1979 was a very peculiar one. A new government took power in March, but from August on there were various changes in the ministries of the economic domain. Since 1978, there was a major restriction on Brazilian manufactured exports to the U.S. due to the tax credit premium given by Brazil to those exports. Pressures by the U.S. and by the GATT produced, in January 1979, a phase out scheme for this export subsidy—as follows: reduction of 10 percentage points in the first and second quarters of 1979 and from then until the second quarter of 1983, a constant reduction of 5 percentage points per quarter.

Nevertheless, in December 1979, a maxi-devaluation of the cruzeiro (30 percent) with respect to the US$ was decided upon by the government and export subsidies were completely abolished. This measure was in fact a mistake. The main source of Brazilian problems in the balance of payments was in the capital account, that is, the service of the foreign debt which in 1979 amounted to US$ 6.2 billion, compared with US$ 2.7 billion of commercial debt. Once the subsidies to exports were eliminated and the maxi-devaluation was sufficient to compensate the exports for both this and for the appreciation of the cruzeiro with respect to the dollar, the maxi-devaluation had an almost neutral effect upon Brazilian exports of manufactures. However, it represented a benefit to the export of goods not subjected to subsidies. The main beneficiaries, the natural resource based goods were, though, taxed on their exports. Some of these goods, had, later on, their taxes abolished as was the case for iron ore. Coffee and sugar are still subject to confisco cambial (export tax).

The maxi-devaluation generated a capital loss to those who borrowed from abroad. This loss, though, could have been compensated by maintaining governmental bonds denominated in U.S. dollars. Despite the possibility of maintaining an asset as hedge against new maxi-devaluations, there was a strong reaction to borrow from abroad. Quantitative restrictions for credit expansion based on domestic resources were imposed, later on, to induce residents to borrow abroad.

Soon enough, domestic inflation accelerated. Indexation and the mini-devaluation of the cruzeiro were announced for the following twelve months to be 50 percent and 45 percent, while inflation was running at the 70 percent level.

To cope with the appreciation of the cruzeiro during the previous year, in April 1981 the government adopted, once again, the tax credit premium to manufactured exports in agreement with the GATT; a flat benefit to all manufactures as percentage of their FOB value as follows: 15 percent up to

December 31, 1981; 9 percent up to December 31, 1982; and 3 percent up to June 30, 1983.[6]

Indexation and the cruzeiro devaluation followed quite closely the inflation path in 1981, thus keeping the domestic interest rates at very high levels in real terms (20 percent to 30 percent).

The necessity of exporting more and more, in order to keep the balance of payments situation manageable, led the government to increase the export subsidies via low interest rate credit (the real rates were in fact negative) as this was the only alternative available, since the new phase out agreement was already established.

Together with the maxi-devaluation of 1979, several other measures were put into practice. In terms of the balance of payments, the most important was the adoption of a more realistic policy for setting the domestic price of petroleum and its subproducts. This decision restrained oil imports from growing as rapidly as before (see Table 2).

Table 3 summarizes the Brazilian commercial policies presenting, for each period, the main policy instruments used, the exchange rate regime and the purpose of such policies.

THE POLICY INSTRUMENTS

In this section, we will describe the policy instruments used by the Brazilian authorities to implement her commercial policies. We will also, briefly discuss the impact of those measures.

Government controls are generally spread throughout Brazilian society and, as one should expect, they have been permanently present on the adopted commercial policies. We will not bother to stress the specific costs associated with those controls, nor the ways people have used to avoid them. We are interested in their overall effects. Only eventually, we will call attention to some particularities associated with some specific controls.

In order to comment on the policy instruments used by Brazil to implement her commercial policies, we will consider separately the import controls and the export promotion measures. Before describing these policies, let us comment briefly on the exchange rate strategy adopted by Brazil.

As is clear from the previous section, the exchange rate has been controlled by the Brazilian government since the pre-war period. Until 1953, Brazil had one official exchange rate, and devalued from time to time. These time intervals, though, were very large, thus inducing a strong speculation, a very active black market and, all sorts of falsified invoicing on exports associated with complementary payments not registered

---

[6]This phase out has been changed by Brazilian authorities as follows: 15 percent up to 3/30/1982; 14 percent up to 6/29/1982; 12.5 percent up to 9/29/1982; 11 percent up to 12/20/1982; 3 percent up to 6/30/1982.

TABLE 3: THE BRAZILIAN COMMERICAL POLICIES: AN OVERVIEW

	Main Policy Instruments	Exchange rate regime	Objective
1 - Pre-War	Fiscal - specific tariffs and export taxes.	Fixed exchange rate with large devaluation from time to time.	Treasury revenue.
2 - 1946-1953	Fiscal - tariff and export taxes. Import controls: licensing system on imports favoring products considered essentials.	Same as before with substantial appreciation of the cruzeiro in real terms.	Import substitution.
3 - 1953-1957	Fiscal - same as before. Import controls - same as before. Products were categorized according to their essentiality. Foreign investments on imported equipment could be made without monetary transaction (SUMOC Instruction 113).	Multiple exchange rates established for different categories of improted products through an auction system. Several rates were fixed for export products.	Import substitution.
4 - 1957-60	Fiscal - ad-valorem tariffs and export taxes Council was created with power to either lower or to raise tariffs. Law of Similars - to protect domestic production from imports.	Same as before with less product categories.	Import substitution.

TABLE 3 Continued

	Main Policy Instruments	Exchange rate regime	Objective
5- 1961-1964	Fiscal - Same as before. Prior deposit in the full value of imports for 150 days bearing an interest of 6% a year.	One fixed exchange rate. Cruzeiro appreciated up to 1963. A sharp devaluation in 1964.	Control balance of payments deficit.
6 - 1964-1974	Fiscal - Substantial reduction of internal taxes on exports; tax credit premium to manufacture exports; reduction or elimination of tariffs on imported products used in the production of exported goods; income tax reduction on exports. Subsidised credit to export. Low premium insurance on exports. Elimination of imports prior deposits.	One exchange rate devalued at short intervals on small proportions (crawling peg) after 1968. Until then, same as before with the cruzeiro being appreciated (20%) in real terms with respect to the US$. The crawling peg kept the real value of the cruzeiro about the same up to 1974.	Balance of payments control. Trade promotion with emphasis on export.
7 - 1974-1979	Fiscal - All incentives to export were kept; restrictions to import, especially capital goods; a general increase in tariffs; strong quantitative controls to imports through slow down on import licensing. Prior deposit in the full value of the imports for 360 days bearing no interest.	Crawling peg with the cruzeiro being appreciated (30%) in real terms with respect to the US$.	Import substitution for capital goods to reduce domestic impact of the oil crisis.

TABLE 3 Continued

	Main Policy Instruments	Exchange rate regime	Objective
8 - 1979-to date	Fiscal – due to reaction of partners a phase out of the tax credit premium to export was established. They were completely eliminated after a maxi-devaluation, but they were restored once more. Prior deposits on imports also phased out and were replaced in 1980 by an ad-valorem tax of 15% on any excahnge transac-tion. Later on, in 1981 this rate was raised to 25%. Subsidies to export through credit was increased. General facilities for exporters entering new markets was granted.	To devalue the cruzeiro (25%) in real terms with respect to the US$ a 4.5% per year devaluation above the parity rule was established. A maxi-devaluation of 30% (Dec. 1979) interrupted the gradual adjustment but since then, the cruzeiro appreciated in real terms with respect to the US$ due to the abandonment of the parity rule devaluation: the cruzeiro devaluation was pre-fixed under some very optimistic hypothesis about 1980 inflation.	To control balance of of payments deficit.

officially. Given the illegal nature of the majority of these activities, no information on them was registered, but the existence and the consensual operation of an active dollar black market, in the main Brazilian cities, is strong evidence of the frequency with which these illegal transactions were made.

In 1953, an exchange rate reform was enacted and a multiple exchange rate regime was adopted. This regime would be subject to major reform in 1957, but its multiple exchange rate nature would remain until 1960. From 1961 on, Brazil adopted one official exchange rate to the U.S. dollar, as in the period prior to the 1953 reform. Finally, in 1968 a crawling peg system was adopted. Most unfortunately, after 1974, this system was not properly administered in the sense of sustaining a real devaluation of the cruzeiro sufficient to restrain the trade balance deficits that emerged with the oil shock. Thus, the dollar black market in Brazil grew once more.

Today, there is a spread of about 30 percent between the official exchange rate and the dollar black market.

No doubt, these exchange regimes had strong effects on Brazilian trade, as we indicated in the previous section. Let us make some remarks on the recent history.

As we mentioned before, in December 1979 Brazil devalued the cruzeiro with respect to the U.S. dollar by 30 percent. The month to month cruzeiro real exchange rate index is reported on Table 3.A.

From December 1979 to December 1981 there was no significant real devaluation of the cruzeiro with respect to the U.S. dollar. Nevertheless, during this same period, the cruzeiro appreciated about 12 percent with respect to an average of domestic currencies of Brazil's main trade partners (including U.S.). Since the relative importance of the U.S. dollar has been declining in Brazilian trade (see Table A.3), this devaluation scheme discriminates against exports and cannot be justified on the basis of Brazil's foreign debt, once a majority of it is in U.S. dollars.

Let us now turn to the commercial policies and their internal effects.

The Import Substitution Strategy

To promote internal industrial production as a substitute for imports, Brazil adopted a highly protective posture using tariffs (especially after 1953), and selective import policies which generally penalized consumer goods and favored capital goods and raw materials (this was the main reason for having multiple exchange rate in the 50's).

The barriers to imports attracted foreign investments producing a large capital inflow to Brazil, not only by the high protection, but also, by relatively liberal regulations on profit remittances and, internal subsidies to capital.[7] This environment produced a huge transformation in

---

[7]Novaes R.F., Investimentos Estrangeiros no Brasil, Rio de Janeiro: EXPED, 1975.

TABLE 3A: CRUZEIRO REAL EXCHANGE RATE INDEX

(Base Dec. 1979=100)

Period	To[a] a weighted average[b]	To the US$
Dec. 1979	100.0	10.0
1980		
Jan.	103.7	103.0
Feb.	103.6	103.6
Mar.	101.2	103.4
Apr.	101.7	104.3
May	102.9	102.8
Jun.	103.2	101.9
Jul	101.3	99.1
Aug.	100.1	98.7
Sep.	99.2	97.2
Oct.	97.0	95.2
Nov.	92.8	92.6
Dec.	90.5	91.0
1981		
Jan.	91.4	91.1
Feb.	88.8	91.4
Mar.	89.3	92.0
Apr.	88.6	93.3
May	86.5	93.3
Jun	84.8	95.5
Jul.	83.3	96.7
Aug.	82.2	96.9
Sep.	84.5	97.2
Oct.	86.6	99.3
Nov.	86.6	100.0
Dec.	88.2	101.3

SOURCE: CECEX

Notes: a) Deflated by consumer prices indexes.

b) Weighted average of nominal exchange rates of the cruzeiro with respect to the currencies of main Brazilian trade partners. The weights are given by export shares of each individual partner. The U.S. dollar is included in the weighted average.

the structure of the Brazilian industrial sector (see Table 6). It also produced a highly protected, dependent industrial sector.

The main argument for protection is perhaps the infant industry argument. The idea behind this argument, is that new industrial ventures need, initially, to be protected from foreign competition, due to high installation costs and the necessity of a learning by doing period, after which production costs would decline due to their "mature" level. The weakness of such an idea is that in general, the infant industry never reaches maturity and therefore the protection is maintained forever.

A general and valid accepted definition of protection, although its application requires some controversial adjustments relevant for inferring the degree of protection, is based on the concept of effective protection.[8] Although the tariff reflects, in part, the degree of protection, it does not allow us to compare, in an unequivocal way, different products and to comment on their relative protection. This is due to the fact that a simple tariff on a final product does not reflect how protected this product is. To produce a final good one needs raw materials and production factors which are subject to different taxes and subsidies. Thus, the apparent protection reflected by a high tariff can be compensated by other taxes on raw materials or on factor use. Therefore, in order to have a good idea about the degree of protection, we should consider not only the final product tariff, but also all tariffs, taxes or subsidies levied on all materials and factors involved in this final good production. Hence, the concept of effective protection should reflect the difference between the value added generated by the production of a good at domestic prices and the value added generated by the production of this very same good, at the international prices which are free from the tariffs, taxes and subsidies reflected in the domestic prices.

Table 4 summarizes the results of several studies on effective protection to Brazilian manufactures. The rates presented in this table are given in percentage by:

$$ERP = \frac{V - V^*}{V^*} \times 100, \text{ where,}$$

ERP = effective rate of protection;
V   = domestic value added;
V* = value added computed at international prices under free trade conditions.

From Table 4 we can see how uneven the protection is and how it appears to be declining from 1958 to 1967.[9] Take for example the average for manufactures. In 1958 the protection afforded this sector was 106 percent, that is, on average Brazil was allowing domestic production of manufactures 106 percent more expense in terms of factor use, than their

---

[8]For details on the methodological problems, see Bergsman (1970) Appendix 3.

[9]The reader should note that the differences on the ERP's calculated for the same year by authors, result from some methodological differences emergent from the particular method used by each author or from differences in the basic information (e.g. Fishlow, 1967).

imported counterpart. This was made possible by imposing tariffs on final imported goods, subsidies on imported raw materials, and subsidies on the domestic use of capital, compensated in part by some domestic taxes.

As we can see, the rates in 1958 (a year situated in the heart of the ISI process) were already very high by world standards. The bias against agriculture is reflected in a negative protection rate of 47 percent for primary vegetable products. Also, the wide range within manufacturing is apparent. The lowest rates are found in pharmaceuticals, machinery, chemicals and metallurgy, while the highest are the ones for food, tobacco, textiles and clothing, perfume and plastics. Thus, for the manufacturing sector, the effective tariff rate ranges from 17 percent (pharmaceuticals) to 52 percent (food).

Also illustrated in Table 4 is the sharp increase in protection from 1958 to 1963. The rates go up in all sectors and the general average more than doubles. By 1966, they were again reduced. Although the general average in 1963, according to Fishlow, was still higher than in 1958, the picture in manufactures was very similar to the one in that latter year. In 1967, however, there was a substantial reduction in protection. In spite of the fact that Bergsman's rates in 1967 still indicate relatively high effective tariff barriers, the relative reduction in his rates between 1963 and 1967, are similar to those found by Fishlow. Whichever rate structure we choose, there is no doubt that trade liberalization was very extensive by 1967.

The de-protection trend that continued during the period 1968–73 was characterized by a pro-trade strategy. In 1973 the level of protection to the Brazilian manufacturing sector was 27 percent, as computed by CECEX. During this pro-trade period, tax exemption was quite common and, therefore, it is no surprise that the ERP declined during those years. With the onset of the oil price shock, import restriction policies were implemented and a new wave of import substitution, this time for capital goods, gained momentum. From CECEX calculations, the manufacturing protection in 1975 was 30 percent and the indications we have are that this rate has been increasing since.

The "cascade" aspect of the structure of protection is well reflected in the averages, calculated by Fishlow, for three sub-groups of products: consumer, intermediate and capital goods. The averages are shown below in Table 5.

Until 1966 there was a clear distinction among the rates, which were very high for consumer goods, much lower for intermediate goods, and even lower for capital goods. In 1966 and 1967 the rates for capital goods are higher than the ones for intermediate goods, although the result might be due to the fact that some consumer durables are included in the group of capital goods. Since raw materials and agricultural products were imported with zero or very low tariffs, we can see how strong the "cascade" effect really was.

However, we can notice that starting in 1963 and especially in 1967 the "cascade" structure was reduced in relative terms. While in 1958 the average rate for consumer goods was equal to almost five times the rate for capital goods, by 1963 this ratio was reduced to about three and by 1967 to two. One of the main causes of distortion from the protection rates come from the variation in the rates, rather than from its average

TABLE 4: EFFECTIVE RATES OF PROTECTION IN BRAZIL
(percentage)

SECTOR	1958[a] (F)*	1963[a] (F)*	(B)[b]	(F)[a]	(B)[b]	(F I*)[a]	(F II*)[c]	1973 CECEX[d]	1975 CECEX[d]
I. Primary Vegetable Products	-47	-15	35	-13	8	-14	-14	na	na
II. Primary Animal Products	24	12	164	16	17	18	--	na	na
III. Mining	-5	34	25	24	13	13	9	-8	-8
IV. Manufacturing (Average)	106	184	254	108	117	63	48	27	30
1. Non-Metallic Minerals	73	103	86	72	39	45	48	21	26
2. Metallurgy	61	124	58	63	36	35	33	18	17
3. Machinery	22	68	41	30	32	32	31	9	13
4. Electrical Equipments	83	169	215	112	97	67	57	19	22
5. Transportation	82	147	151	103	75	64	81	30	37
6. Wood	138	176	45	120	25	81	44	19	24
7. Furniture	221	367	239	251	124	90	92	44	42
8. Paper	86	169	118	91	59	43	42	24	32
9. Rubber	139	221	136	158	116	126	182	56	54
10. Leather and Hides	248	405	117	174	85	127	84	26	36
11. Chemicals	56	146	59	56	42	29	20	28	22
12. Pharmaceuticals	17	60	39	1	35	10	10	28	18
13. Perfumery	279	453	8480	281	3670	121	70	33	40
14. Plastic	281	489	183	332	58	133	117	99	111
15. Textiles	239	298	379	232	162	162	88	36	58
16. Clothing	264	481	337	321	142	107	154	26	37
17. Food	502	678	87	423	40	252	71	33	37
18. Beverages	171	243	447	183	173	104	76	143	139
19. Tobacco	273	469	313	299	124	114	79	-6	-6
20. Printing and Publishing	139	305	142	142	678	4	8	10	13
21. Miscellaneous	88	175	128	95	72	47	45	17	21
V. General Average	30	75	181	44	76	24	14	25	29

SOURCE: Carvalho-Haddad (1980) and Neuhaus-Lobato (1978)

NOTES: [a]Computed with input-output coefficients from the 1959 matrix deflated by 1959 tariffs. *Fishlow.
[b]Computed with input-output coefficients from the 1959 matrix, unadjusted. **Bergsman.
[b]Computed with input-output coefficients from the 1971 matrix deflated by 1967 tariffs.
[c]Computed with input-output coefficients from the IBGE 1970 matrix deflated by 1973 tariffs.
[d]Computed with input-output coefficients from the 1959 adjusted for tariffs with
All the Fishlow's totals and sub-totals were weighted by the structure of value added in 1959 adjusted for tariffs with
vegetable products assumed to have zero tax. The Bergsman's totals and sub-totals were weighted by doemstic value added in
1964.

level. We can infer from Table 5 that the tariff structure became much
less distortive after 1966 than previously, since after that year, not
only is the average level of protection substantially reduced, but the
tariff structure becomes much more homogeneous.

One interesting question concerns the relationship between the effective
tariff rates and some variables relevant to Brazilian industry. What
would explain or be correlated with the effective tariff structure? How
about the relationship between the tariff structure and labor
requirements, skill content or the degree of concentration in each sector?

To answer these questions Carvalho-Haddad examined the relationship
between the structure of protection (in 1958 and 1967) and certain other
variables for Brazilian industry, cross-sectionally. The structure for
1967 was taken at Fishlow's rates, computed as in version II. It is
apparent, though, by looking at Table 4, that the two sets of rates are
very close to one another, with the exception of textiles, clothing and
food. Their results, summarized below, are based on partial correlations
obtained in two regression analyses on the dependent variable using the
ERP's for each sector as is found in Table 4.The results obtained by
Carvalho-Haddad are:

a) As far as labor requirements in industry are concerned, it was found
   that in 1958 there was a significant negative association between
   that variable and the effective tariff structure. That is, sectors
   that absorbed less labor per output value received higher
   protection. The relationship vanishes in 1967, although the labor
   requirements and other independent variables are computed for 1970,
   i.e., three years later. Note that the total labor requirements,
   adopted by the authors, include only direct and indirect labor in
   the industrial sectors. Due to data difficulties, the linkages with
   agriculture and services are not taken into account. There can be
   no doubt, that this measure of labor requirements could give
   misleading results for some sectors.

TABLE 5: EFFECTIVE RATES OF PROTECTION BY GROUPS OF PRODUCTS

(percentage)

Year	Consumer Goods	Intermediate Goods	Capital Goods
1958	242	65	53
1963	360	131	113
1966	230	68	69
1967-I	122	40	56
1967-II	66	39	52

SOURCE: Fishlow (1975), p. 58a.

b) With respect to industrial concentration,[10] a positive (and statistically significant) relationship with the effective tariff structure was found. That is, the more concentrated the sectors, the higher the protection received. But we must be careful, since causation may run the other way: the high protection barriers may have fostered concentration. In fact, as the authors call attention to, they were not estimating, with their regressions, any explanatory model of the tariff structure. They were simply using a statistical device to determine the sign and significance of the partial correlation coefficients between the effective protection rates and the independent variables.

c) With regard to skill, they found a negative and significant relation between the effective tariff rates and the skill content of the labor force. From Table 4 we can get a clue as to why this is so. While skill-intensive sectors, like chemicals and machinery, received below-average protection, sectors such as textiles, wood and furniture, which are intensive in unskilled labor, received much higher than average protection.

What conclusions can we draw from these results? Concerning factor proportions the picture is not clear. We can say that in the middle of the ISI process (1958) the effective rates of protection were negatively related to labor requirements, but in 1967 they were neutral with regard to that variable (no correlation could be detected). On the other hand, sectors that were less skill intensive received higher protection, which is a somewhat surprising result. But can we infer from this that the effective structure favored the absorption of unskilled labor to the detriment of skilled labor? Not at all. The problem we face is one of redundancy. True, effective tariff rates were always high for textiles, wood, furniture, clothing and other "traditional" sectors, but in those sectors import substitution had taken place long ago. Actually, most items produced in those sectors were classified by the authors as either export or home goods, and not as import substitutes. The share of imports in total consumption for the traditional sectors was already low in 1955. Therefore, the high protection afforded those sectors in the 50's and in the 60's was largely redundant.

The novelty in the 50's was the enormous increase in protection for the durable goods industries, like transportation and electrical equipment, which are relatively skill intensive. Therefore, although the gross effect still points towards a positive correlation between the effective tariff rates and the absorption of unskilled labor, the net effect in the 50's and 60's was certainly against unskilled labor absorption. This proportion refers just to the effects of protection on products. It is reinforced by the many subsidies that were granted to capital, which we would expect, a priori, to be complementary to skilled labor and the taxes that have been imposed on labor.

With regard to industrial concentration we can just say that, on average, the higher the protection the higher the degree of concentration. This

---

[10]Industrial concentration was measured by the percentage sales of the four largest establishments in total sectoral sales.

result is valid in 1958 and in 1967. The direction of causation is uncertain, however. Also, we again call attention to the high level of aggregation employed in the computation of the effective tariff rates and of the other sectoral variables. Rates computed at the 2-digit level can really disguise much of what it is going on and, therefore, our conclusions have to be viewed as tentative until further tests can be performed once better data are available.

How did this protection affect domestic industrial production? Carvalho-Haddad, classified these goods into four categories and calculated their share of total production in 1959 and 1970 using census data. Their results are reported on Table 6.

With regard to importables, we see that their shares are the smallest of the four. The share of importables in total production is even reduced from 1959 to 1970. Actually, except for the share of the import substitutes, all the others are reduced from 1959 to 1970. In 1970 the largest volume of manufactures consisted of import substitutes, as contrasted with 1959, when home goods absorbed the largest share of total production. It is interesting to notice that although the volume of exports of manufactures increased substantially from 1959 to 1970, the share of exportables in total production of manufactures fell during that period. This means that domestic consumption of those products did not keep pace with industrial production. Since the exportable goods were produced mainly in the "traditional" sectors, and since the income elasticity of demand for products in those sectors should, generally, be less than one, the above result is not surprising.

TABLE 6 – DISTRIBUTION ACCORDING TO TRADE STATUS
OF BRAZILIAN MANUFACTURES, 1959 AND 1970

(Values in current US$1000)

ITEM	1959		1970	
	Value of Production	%	Value of Production	%
Import Substitutes	1,702,644	31.47	8,609,760	41.01
Importables	63,086	1.17	205,308	0.98
Home Goods	2,335,593	43.17	8,101,190	38.58
Exportables	1,308,684	24.19	4,079,463	19.43
TOTAL	5,414,227	100.00	20,973,775	100.0

Source: the author.

The fact that the share of import substitutes in total production increased from 1959 to 1970 to the detriment of the others has a double meaning: it shows that the import substitution process had progressed a great deal from 1959, but it also reflects the higher degree of openness in the Brazilian economy in 1970 as compared with 1959. This latter conclusion follows from the fact that the share of home goods in total production decreased between the two benchmarks. Since one way to transform import substitutes into home goods is to impose prohibitive tariffs, the fall in the share of home goods during the period 1959/70 is testimony to the decrease in effective protection in the same period, as we saw from ERP's of Table 4.

The Export Promotion Drive
The export promotion strategy in Brazil began in 1965, but it was vigorously pursued from 1968 on. The strategy was based on three main instruments: the trade liberalization measures of 1966 and 1967 discussed in section 1, fiscal incentives and; the mini-devaluation (crawling peg) policy mentioned above.

Let us now take a deeper look at the export promotion policy, analyzing and measuring the impact of the fiscal instruments and of other factors in the growth of Brazilian exports. Fiscal incentives for exports are based on three instruments: tax exemption, subsidies and other benefits of a general nature. Our main concern here is with those instruments whose impact on exports has been quantitatively important.

Before turning to these instruments, we will describe briefly the workings of the IPI, a tax on industrial production, and the ICM, a turn-over tax on merchandise. This will be helpful in understanding the mechanics of the export incentives, which are mainly based on those two taxes.

The IPI, a federal tax on all industrial products, varies among products according to its "essentiality". Thus the rate on cigarettes, alcoholic beverages is 365 percent, on cars it is 30 percent, while foodstuffs are subject to only six percent on average.

The ICM is a state tax on all traded products. The ICM tax rate is unique to each state, as its level is established by state authorities.

Although the IPI and the ICM have been treated as valued added taxes, this is not exactly correct as can be seen from the description of how they are applied and how they are collected. Since the main purpose of the tax reform which generated these two taxes was to avoid cascading taxation, a complete independent tax accounting system is necessary and each firm has an accounting book for each tax.

Suppose that the IPI and ICM tax rates are 10 percent and 13 percent respectively. Consider a firm which buys materials in the value of Cr$50.00, ICM included, but paid a total of Cr$55.00, IPI included. Thus, this firm will register a credit of Cr$6.50 (0.13 x 50) in its ICM book and a credit of Cr$5.00 (0.10 x 50) on its IPI book. Note that for tax accounting purposes the ICM is calculated as a percentage of total payment including ICM taxes. This implies that in this case, the ICM tax rate is $\frac{0.13}{1 - 0.13}$, which is approximately 15 percent, of the input costs (50-6.50 = 43.50). We should also note that the IPI tax rate is applied to a base that includes the ICM tax.

Consider now that this firm produces a product whose value is Cr$100.00. Adding the IPI tax (10 percent) the firm will sell it for Cr$110.00. The accounting will be as follows: debit of Cr$13.000 on its ICM book and a debit of Cr$10.00 on its IPI book. Thus, the net result of these operations will be: a net payment to the state government of Cr$6.50 due to ICM and a net payment to the federal government of Cr$5.00 due to IPI. Note that the net ICM payment is 13 percent and the net IPI payment is 10 percent of the value added produced by the firm: Cr$50.00 (100-50). Nevertheless, this does not imply that the IPI is a true value added tax. Had this firm bought Cr$50.00 of agricultural inputs, there would be no IPI credit. The net debt in the IPI book would be Cr$10.00 which is 20 percent of the value added and not 10 percent, as in the previous case. In the ICM case, if the inputs were exempted from this tax there would be no credit registered in the ICM book and therefore Cr$13.00 would be paid, corresponding to a 26 percent tax on value added and not 13 percent as before. Let us now describe the main fiscal instruments used in promoting exports.

Tax Exemption

a) Rebates of IPI tax by the Law 4502 (1964) and regulated by Decree-Law 61514 (1967).

b) Rebates of ICM tax on manufactured products (Constitution of 1967 and Decree-Law 406, 1968). Pressed by the Federal Government, some states extended the rebates to primary product exports as well.

c) Drawback of import duties on all intermediate products entering in the production of an exported good. Decree-Law 53967 (1964), extended by Decree-Law 37 (1968) and Decree-Law 68904 (1971).

d) Rebates of other less important taxes on inputs, in the production and commercialization processes of exports, like the tax on financial operation (IOF) and the tax on fuel and lubricants (CL).

e) Exemption of import tariffs and otehr indirect taxes on machinery and equipment bought by firms that had an obligation with CACEX to export.

f) Exemption of the income tax corresponding to the export activities (Law 4663, 1965 regulated by the Decree-Law 56967 (1965)). This exemption was intended to be temporary (until 1968), but it has been kept effective. We should also note that not all exporting activities can benefit from this exemption. A list of beneficiaries is determined by the Ministry of Finance and primary products are usually not included. Several expenditures related to exports such as marketing, maintenance of offices abroad etc., are considered as cost for income tax purposes. We should note that the income tax exemption and other benefits associated with the income tax, in fact, favor capital and in this aspect it has an allocative effect on factor use in the economy. Also note that they are excluded from GATT agreements.

Subsidies

a) IPI and ICM tax credit premia--Fiscal credits in the amount of IPI are given, up to the limit of 15 percent and in some cases, depending on the state, a similar fiscal credit is given based on ICM. The ICM fiscal credit rate is equal to the IPI rate up to the limit of 13 percent. The fiscal credits are granted to the export manufacturers and can be used for other IPI or ICM debts. Eventually, the positive balance in favor of the firm can be paid in cruzeiros by the government (Federal or State). We should note that if the drawback of tariffs on imported inputs is undertaken, the fiscal credits will be applied to the exporting price net of the imported inputs. The firm has the option of deciding to benefit from the drawback or to obtain these subsidies applied to the full exporting price. As we mention in section one, these subsidies will phase out by March 1983.

b) Credit incentives are available in the form of subsidized interest rates for loans linked to exporting activities. Some sectors can also benefit from existing programs under which loans are awarded, under very special conditions. The principal source of subsidy to the exporting sector via credit is the Resolucão 71 (1967) of the Central Bank. Under the Resolucão 71, any commercial bank which operates with foreign currencies can obtain resources from the discount window at low rates (4 percent per year) as long as they lend to the export sector. The exporting firm obtains from CACEX a certificate indicating the firm will export (Certificado de Habilitacão) and with this certificate the firm can obtain funds up to 80 percent of the exporting value for 120 days at an interest rate of 8 percent per year. Credit can be obtained under these same conditions based on previous exports for which no borrowing was undertaken earlier. In Table 7, we summarize the main elements of export credit program. Note that the same product can be financed, at these special interest rates both while being produced and later on when exported.

Other Benefits
Several other benefits are given to exporting firms. They are associated with the simplification of the exporting procedures, marketing of Brazilian products by the federal government, insurance against client bankruptcies, special benefits to trading companies, sectoral programs, special incentives to the transfer of corporations operating abroad to Brazil if they mainly produce to export, etc.

One of these programs that has been particularly important in recent years is the one coordinated by BEFIEX (Comissão de Beneficios Fiscais a Programas Especiais de Exportacão). BEFIEX is a commission with a total of six representatives, one each from a bureau of ministry connected with exports. The incentives, which are granted to national or foreign firms operating or not in the country, which agree to fulfill an export program to obtain basically the following benefits:

Exemption of tariffs and IPI on imports approved by the program: The annual imports so benefitted cannot exceed 1/3 of the net value of the yearly average value of exports during the length of the program. The Decree-Law 71-278 exempted from the 1/3 restriction mentioned above the initial imports of machinery and equipment approved by BEFIEX. The exemptions can only be granted to imports, if they, added to other imports under the "draw-back" regime, do not amount to more than 50 percent of the total value (FOB) exported.

The imports under the program are not subjected to the Law of Similars, and can consist of either new or old equipment.

Together with other decrees regulating the program, the provisions of the BEFIEX programs imply that the restriction of 1/3 of the net value

TABLE 7: SUBSIDIZED CREDIT PROGRAMS TO BRAZILIAN EXPORTS ON INTERNATIONALLY CONVERTIBLE CURRENCIES

Legal instrument and Financial Agent	Beneficiaries	Financing Conditions		
		Value	Terms	Costs
1 - Resolução BACEN 674 All commercial banks that operate with money exchange.	Producer registered with CACEX.	12%, 20%, 30%, 40% of exporting FOB value	Maximum 360 days	Semesterly at a rate of 40% a year.
2 - FINEX-Resolução CONCEX 68 Banco do Brasil	Producer and exporting agent including trading companies.	85% of exporting FOB value. If insurance and freight are provided by Brazilians, the limit of 85% if on CIF value.	Not less than 180 days	To exporter: semesterly interest rates of 7.5% to 8.5% a year. To producer: semesterly interest rate of 35% a year. To support activities: rates of 60% a year.
3 - Resolução BACEN 643 Same as in (1)	Trading companies in operation for: a) more than a year b) less than a year.	a) 25%, 40% or 60% of exporting FOB value b) 10% to 20% of FOB value	Up to 180 days	Semesterly interest at a rate of 40% a year.
4 - Resolução BACEN 330 same as in (1)	Goods on customs warehouse.	a) 80%; b) 70% and c) 60% of FOB value	a) 90 days; b) 90 to 180 days and c) above 181 days	Yearly interest at a rate of 40% a year.
5 - Banco do Bazsil -CIC - GRECE-14-11 Banco do Brasil	Exporting goods.	To be defined by CACEX-BB	180 to 360 days	Quarterly interest at a rate not superior to 45% a year.

TABLE 7 (continued)

Legal instrument and Financial Agent	Beneficiaries	Financing Conditions		
		Value	Terms	Costs
6 - Communicado GECON 331 same as in (1)	Exporting agent with closed contracts.	a) 100% of the contract's value b) 80% of the contract's value.	a) 90 days b) 90-180 days	Monthly interest at rates of 0.5% to 2.5% a year.
7 - FUNDECE - Decree-Law 54105 Banco de Brasil	Producer engaged in a program.	To be defined by CREAI-36 productivity improvement.	6 to 36 months	Semesterly interest at a rate of 12% a year plus 10% of monetary connection.
8 - Resoluções BACEN 509 and 637 same as (1)	a) Capital goods and consumer durable goods; b) Research and technicals projects; c) Expenditures abroad.	a) Same as in (2); 100% of FOB value if loan refers to more than 24 months. b) To be defined by CACEX. c) Up to 20% of the revenue produced by those expenditures.	a) 6 months to 8 years b) 3, 5 or 8 years c) To be defined by CACEX.	Same as in (2). In this case, the commercial bank obtains resources from abroad to lend at FINEX subsidized rates, receiving from FINEX the necessary subsidy.

exported, mentioned previously, apply only to imports of raw materials directly used in the production process.

The BEFIEX programs have been utilized extensively by foreign firms that make new investments in Brazil and by the automobile industry. These programs became extensively utilized after 1973, when the BEFIEX trade deficit (imports-exports) was US$232.5 million. This deficit declined to US$67.0 million in 1976, turning to a surplus (exports-imports = US$323.6 million) from 1977 on. In that year, the BEFIEX exports amounted to US$761.7 million, compared to the US$135.3 million of exports in 1973.

We should recall that all the incentives described above refer to manufactures. This implies that the exports of agricultural and mining products have been implicitly taxed by subsidizing manufactured exports. In fact, some agricultural goods have been explicitly taxed, as is frequently the case with coffee, cocoa, sugar and soybeans. Aside from penalizing non-manufactured goods, what were the main results of this export drive? No doubt the exports of manufactured goods increased rapidly after 1968, but at what cost? Let us consider this question on only the following two grounds. Was there any alternative way to promote exports? Did Brazil promote the exportation of manufactured goods that cost her less, in terms of domestic resources, per exported dollar?

The alternative to all these incentives is the exchange rate. Carvalho-Haddad (1980) concluded that exports grow twice as much as a consequence of a dollar obtained from a devaluation of the cruzeiro than from a dollar obtained from the above described subsidy scheme. Note that an active exchange rate policy seems to produce twice as much manufactured exports as the subsidies, and does so without all its costs, bureaucratic inconveniencies and without discriminating against other exported goods. Although this policy could easily have been implemented in 1968 (note that from 1968 to 1978 the real exchange rate Cr$/US$ devalued about four percent (see Table A.1)) due to the actual foreign debt that Brazil has to manage at present, promoting export via exchange rate devaluation is quite difficult, unless a multiple exchange rate regime is implemented. This latter alternative, we think, is out of consideration. Thus, actually the Brazilian authorities, facing the phase-out scheme for the export subsidies, have to work out new artificial ways to promote exports and consequently will be generating a greater dependence of the private sector on the public sector.

Since the purpose of exporting is to obtain foreign currency to pay for imports and reduce foreign debts, exports are, in this sense, a way of transforming domestic resources into foreign currency, specifically US dollars. In this way, we should expect that a rational export promotion policy would promote more intensively the exportation of goods that can generate more dollars per unit of domestic resources. Savasini-Kume (1979) did a study to compute the costs, in terms of domestic resources of Brazilian exports. Their principal results are summarized in Table 8 below.

Savasini-Kume classified Brazilian exports into three categories: a) exports that generate net benefits to the country if their costs in terms of domestic resources were less than US$ 1.25 to produce an export revenue of US$1.00; b) those with indeterminate net benefit if for each dollar of export revenue, Brazil expended to produce them from US$ 1.25 to US$ 1.35 in domestic resources; c) those with negative net benefit, that is, their exports represent a loss to the country, if for each dollar exported, the domestic cost was equal or above US$1.35.

Two results emerge from Table 8. First, the benefits of commercial policies adopted to promote exports have been mainly appropriated by those manufacturers which are producing a net gain, to the country, per dollars worth of export. Second, and perhaps more importantly, this export drive is costing Brazil more as the share of the products with negative net benefits is growing through time. Note, that as we should expect, the subsidy to the manufactures with indeterminate or negative net benefits are quite high compared to the 3.01 percent or 9.01 percent (mining excluded) appropriated by those manufactures that, under this classification, generate a net benefit to Brazil.

TABLE 8:
DOMESTIC RESOURCE COSTS (c), EXPORTING SHARE AND EXPORTING SUBSIDY
FOR BRAZILIAN EXPORTING GROUPS OF MANUFACTURES

Groups of Manufactures with exporting net benefits	Exporting Share		Nominal subsidy (%) per exported cruzeiro
	1970	1975	
Positive ($c \leq 1.25$)	79.62	71.23	3.01
Positive (excluding mining)	59.76	51.67	9.01
Indeterminate ($1.25 < c < 1.35$)	8.51	9.85	27.96
Negative ($c \geq 1.35$)	11.87	18.93	33.76

SOURCE: Savasini-Kume (1979) p. 81.

On the other hand, since the majority of the Brazilian exports receive a small subsidy, the phase-out scheme adopted for the tax credit, which is only a part of it, might have a minor impact on Brazilian exports.

It is also interesting to mention that, despite all the distortions produced by the export incentives, about half of the exported manufactures (mining excluded) are probably in conformity with Brazil's international comparative advantages.

The strong drive to export, aside from producing a diversification of Brazilian exports, has also produced (as one should expect) a marked change in the direction of trade (see Table A.3). In 1975, about 42 percent of Brazilian exports were to the U.S. (Puerto Rico included), but by the beginning of the 80's this fraction had dropped to about 17 percent. Most of the new products exported by Brazil went to LAFTA countries and to new trading partners in Asia, the Middle-East and

Africa. In this way, with the increase in the export of manufactured goods, the U.S. share declined, since Brazil had little or no comparative advantage to export those goods to U.S.; the European Economic Community maintained its relative share of 25 percent; the LAFTA share went up from about 10 percent in 1955 to about 18 percent in the early 80's; while Asia (China excluded) Middle-East and Africa, the main new trade partners, imported in 1955 about 5.5 percent of Brazilian exports and in the early 80's, their share went up to about 22 percent. We should also note that the strong changes in the direction of exports occurred after 1975, when exports to the Middle-East increased substantially. The latter results much more from the sharp increase in Brazilian imports from this region, due to the oil price increase, than from any commercial policy measure adopted by Brazil.

Finally, after considering the protection generated by the import substitution strategy and the pitfalls of the export drive, let us consider the commercial policies under a more broad and general view, that is, under the Heckscher-Ohlin proposition.

The Heckscher-Ohlin theorem occupies center stage in discussion concerning the origins and patterns of trade between countries. According to that theorem, a country exports those commodities which are relatively intensive in the use of the country's relatively abundant factor. However, in 1954 Leontief showed that the United States exported labor intensive and imported capital intensive commodities, a pattern which does not conform with the obvious fact that the United States is relatively more highly endowed with capital than any other country. This finding, called the Leontief paradox, led to a deeper study of the Heckscher-Ohlin theorem which was substantially qualified with respect to their theoretical implications, and simultaneously broadened to account for a more disaggregated view of the concept of factor production, treating natural resources as distinct from reproducible capital and dividing labor into different skill categories.

This question of relative intensities is not merely academic. It has important implications for the choice of trade policies that take into account the labor market. If exports are more labor intensive than import substitutes, a policy of export promotion with imports held fixed would generate a larger increase in the demand for labor than a policy of import substitution with exports held fixed, although the effects of both policies on the balance of payments could be the same. If the supply of labor in Brazil is perfectly elastic, at the going wage rate, the policy of export promotion would simply absorb more labor, under the above hypothesis, than the equivalent policy of import substitution. If the supply of labor is not perfectly elastic, in addition to the employment effect we would have a greater redistribution of income more toward labor in the case of export promotion than in the case of import substitution. If, however, the economy is already at full employment, all effects of the trade policies will fall on the distribution of income and, there will be no net employment effects. Looking at the high rates of economic growth experienced by the Brazilian economy after 1968, we would tend to discard the simple hypothesis of a perfectly elastic supply of labor, especially when we take differences of skill into account. It is important to bear these qualifications in mind when we discuss, later on, some implications with regard to labor "absorption".

Carvalho/Haddad (1980) tested the Heckscher-Ohlin theorem for Brazil, determining relative factor intensities of her exports and of her import competing goods. To avoid problems with comparative advantages coming from the availability of natural resources the test was made only with regard to manufactures.

According to previous introspection, Brazil's exports of manufactures should be more labor intensive than her manufactures which compete with imports. And, as far as the skill content of the work force is concerned, the reverse should be true: exports of manufactures should require less skill in their production than import substitutes made in Brazil. The results obtained by the authors are in agreement with these theoretical propositions for Brazil.

SUMMARY AND CONCLUSIONS

Brazil has had both import substitution and export promotion phases in her trade regime. Although import substitution policy was successful in increasing domestic industrial output, employment did not grow accordingly and protection substantially increased from 1955 to 1965.

Protection was decreased and its cascade structure reduced from 1966 to 1974, when a new import substitution drive was re-established due to the oil shock. In this same period, an export promotion strategy led Brazil to reduce import restriction and subsidize manufactured exports. To protect domestic consumption from international price increases some export taxes were levied on agriculture products such as sugar, cocoa and soybeans, aside from the traditional control on coffee exports. Employment growth in the export promotion period has been more substantial as Brazil's exports have been found to be labor-intensive.

Despite all subsidies given to exports, the majority of Brazilian exports receive about nine percent per exported cruzeiro as subsidy (about three percent if mining is included). This, together with the fact that the exportation of these products can be considered as generating a net gain to the country, implies that Brazil is exporting in accordance with her comparative advantages. The results described here, also imply that in the process of exporting more, Brazil has been subsidizing products which in generating US\$1.00 of export revenue use at least US\$1.35 of domestic resources.

After the petroleum price increase in 1973, Brazil adopted an adjustment strategy based on borrowing from abroad to cover the commercial debt contracted due to oil imports. The accumulation of a large and growing foreign debt has been imposing strong limitations on Brazilian commercial policies. The short run objective has been to generate international reserves, at any cost. This has been producing some strong controls on imports and a variety of incentives for exporting.

The foreign debt has been managed by heavily borrowing from abroad. Due to the increases in international interest rates, domestic monetary policy has been used to maintain the domestic interest rate above the international rate in equivalent cruzeiros, in order to induce residents to borrow from abroad. The devaluation of the cruzeiro has been kept in line with the purchasing power parity rule, except for the US dollar inflation, that is, it is following the domestic inflation in order to induce a real devaluation to promote exports. Therefore, Brazil's exchange rate policy depends on inflation in other countries, mainly that of US.

In this manner, domestic monetary policy is conditioned to the international interest rates and therefore, has been used to peg the internal interest rate at a level that will induce people to borrow from abroad. Also, the real devaluation of the cruzeiro is conditioned to exogenous facts, mainly US inflation, which declining, imposes a limit on the impact on exports as the real devaluation will be smaller.

The US and the GATT restrictions on Brazilian export subsidies constitute another exogenous constraint on Brazil's commercial policies. The phase-out scheme adopted for the export subsidies, will have a small impact on the bulk of Brazil's exports (recall that about 79 percent of her exports obtain about 3 percent of subsidy) at the moment but, it will impose a severe constraint on its increase. In this manner, subsidized credit is the way out to promote exports. It is estimated that exports will need about Cr$600 billion compared to a monetary base of Cr$1200 billion. This, dramatically illustrates the trade off between more credit (subsidized) to exports and the goal of reducing domestic inflation which presently is about 100 percent per year.

References

Carvalho, José L. and Haddad, Cláudio L.S. Estratégias Comerciais e Absorcão de Mão-de-Obra no Brasil, Rio de Janeiro: Fundaçao Getulio Vargas, 1980.

Fishlow, A. Foreign Trade Regimes and Economic Development: Brazil. Report to NBER April 1975 (mimeographed).

Haddad, Cláudio L.S. "Crescimento do Produto Real Brasileiro 1900/1947" Revista Brasileira de Economia 29, pp. 3-26; 1975.

Neuhaus, P. and Lobato, H. "Proteção Efetiva à Indústria no Brasil 1973-75," Fundaçao Centro de Estudos do Comercio Exterior - (CECEX) 1978, (mimeographed).

Novaes, R.F. Investimentos Estrangeiros no Brasil, Rio de Janeiro: EXPED, 1975.

Savasini, J.A.A. and Kume, H. Custo dos Recursos Domésticos das Exportações Brasileiras, Rio de Janeiro: Fundaçao Centro de Estudos do Comércio Exterior, Serie Estudos no. 3, 1979.

Simonsen, M.H. Brasil 2002, Rio de Janeiro: APEC 1972.

Skidmore, T.E. Politics in Brazil 1930-64, London: Oxford University Press, 1967.

TABLE A.1 - NOMINAL AND REAL EXCHANGE RATES

1946-1981

(Nominal rates: Cr$/US$)

	Nominal Rate[a]	Real Rate Index[b] (1951=100)
1938-1939	0.0169	153.6
1946	0.0196	108.8
1947	0.0187	116.4
1948	0.0187	117.3
1949	0.0187	107.3
1950	0.0187	108.8
1951	0.0187	100.0
1952	0.0187	86.4
1953	0.0284	n.a[c]
1954	0.0363	n.a[c]
1955	0.0430	100.7[c]
1956	0.0500	109.6[c]
1957	0.0530	77.3[c]
1958	0.0654	117.1
1959	0.114	143.2
1960	0.160	152.6
1961	0.268	182.0
1962	0.390	176.3
1963	0.575	148.1
1964	1.284	181.8
1965	1.900	178.3
1966	2.220	152.5
1967	2.660	145.3
1968	3.390	154.0
1969	4.070	161.6
1970	4.590	158.2
1971	5.290	154.7
1972	5.930	154.0
1973	6.130	156.0
1974	6.790	159.4
1975	8.126	163.0
1976	10.670	161.3
1977	14.138	161.9
1978	18.063	160.1
1979	26.870	170.5
1980	52.699	181.4
1981	93.015	183.6

SOURCE: Carvalho/Haddad (1980)

NOTE: [a]For non-coffee exports during the years of multiple exchange rates.
[b]Real rates are the product of nominal rates multiplied by the ratio of United States wholesale prices to Brazilian wholesale prices.
[c]See Table A.2.

TABLE A.2 – EXCHANGE RATES – NOMINAL AND REAL BY
CATEGORIES (1953–57)

(Old Cr$/US$)

C A T E G O R Y		1953 (Oct.-Dec.)	1954	1955	1956	1957 (Jan.-Aug.)
A. Imports						
I	Nominal	31.2	41.8	63.8	73.8	58.3
	Real	31.2	33.9	42.7	42.1	29.7
II	Nominal	37.8	44.9	66.0	81.3	74.5
	Real	37.8	36.4	44.2	46.3	38.0
III	Nominal	44.0	57.8	82.4	103.2	100.6
	Real	44.0	46.8	55.2	58.8	51.3
IV	Nominal	48.8	68.3	86.3	115.6	138.3
	Real	48.8	55.3	57.8	65.9	70.5
V	Nominal	81.5	110.8	17.16	222.4	299.1
	Real	81.5	89.7	115.0	126.8	152.5
Average[a]						
	Nominal	33.8	46.1	58.0	n.a.	
	Real	n.a.	27.4	30.9	33.1	n.a.
B. Exports						
Coffee	Nominal	23.4	27.4	36.4	36.7	38.8
	Real	23.4	22.2	24.4	20.9	19.8
Non-Coffee[b]	Nominal	28.4	36.3	43.0	50.0	55.0
	Real	28.4	29.4	28.8	28.5	28.1
Free Market	Nominal	49.2	62.2	73.5	73.6	7.57[c]
	Real	49.2	50.4	49.2	42.0	38.6

SOURCE: Carvalho-Haddad (1980)
Real rates were calculated as the product of nominal rates by an index of
wholesale prices in the U.S. divided by a similar index for Brazil (IPA).

NOTES: Key to categories:
          I: Chemicals and pharmaceuticals, capital equipment for basic
            industries.
       II: Essential raw materials and spare parts.
     III: Raw materials, spare parts and machinery for consumption goods
            industries.
     IV: Foodstuffs and all other imports.
      V: Finished consumer goods.
     [a] Total imports in dollars divided by value in cruzeiros.
     [b] Arithmetic average of three different rates.
     [c] Average for the whole year.

TABLE A.3 - BRAZILIAN EXPORTS BY ECONOMIC REGIONS, 1955-1981

(Percentage share)

	1955	1960	1965	1970	1975	1976	1977	1978	1979	1980	1981*
Latin American Free Trade Association (LAFTA)	10.26	6.95	12.64	11.06	13.81	11.87	11.00	12.48	16.23	17.18	18.43
Central American Common Market (SIECA)	0.00	0.01	0.03	0.05	0.21	0.21	0.29	0.50	0.36	0.34	0.29
Other Countries in Latin America	0.01	0.05	0.02	0.17	0.44	0.60	0.35	0.52	0.32	0.23	0.27
Caribbean Free Trade Association	0.00	0.08	0.05	0.19	0.20	0.16	0.16	0.12	0.13	0.21	0.26
Canada	1.06	1.31	1.56	1.48	1.57	1.35	1.18	1.20	1.31	1.21	1.27
United States (Puerto Rico included)	42.28	44.42	32.61	24.68	15.42	18.20	17.73	22.67	19.29	17.43	17.60
Other American Countries	0.01	0.85	0.03	0.28	1.14	0.52	0.16	0.18	0.25	0.17	0.27
Eastern Europe	2.95	5.59	5.60	4.51	8.79	8.99	7.08	5.76	6.40	6.49	7.29
European Economic Community (EEC)	25.08	26.67	32.22	34.93	27.82	30.42	32.07	29.51	29.55	26.56	25.68
European Association for Free Trade	6.35	5.69	5.79	5.42	3.58	4.49	4.62	3.95	3.34	3.25	2.34
Other Countries in West Europe	5.93	3.46	4.06	5.93	6.00	7.48	6.33	4.02	3.76	4.29	2.25
China	0.32	0.04	0.02	0.05	0.78	0.09	1.34	1.02	0.78	0.36	0.42
Asia (China excluded)	4.52	3.30	3.00	8.20	9.11	7.78	8.23	8.20	9.15	9.51	9.39
Middle East	0.39	0.38	0.81	0.64	5.14	2.69	2.74	2.82	3.40	5.16	5.37
Africa (Middle East excluded)	0.66	0.95	1.40	2.15	4.61	3.78	4.42	5.02	4.27	5.73	7.25
Oceania	0.18	0.25	0.16	0.11	0.32	0.43	0.29	0.60	0.51	0.58	0.67
Others	0.0	0.0	0.0	0.15	1.06	0.94	2.01	1.43	0.95	1.30	0.95
T O T A L	100.00	100.00	100.00	100.00	100.00	100.00	100.00	100.00	100.00	100.00	100.00

SOURCE: CACEX
*January to November 1981.

TABLE A.4 – BRAZILIAN CURRENT ACCOUNT DEFICIT, EXTERNAL DEBT AND
FOREIGN RESERVES

(in current US$ millions)

Y E A R S	CURRENT ACCOUNT DEFICIT	EXTERNAL DEBT ON DEC. 31	FOREIGN RESERVES ON DEC. 31
1968	508		257
1969	281	4403	655
1970	562	5295	1187
1971	1307	6622	1723
1972	1489	9521	4183
1973	1688	12571	6416
1974	7122	17166	5269
1975	6700	21171	4040
1976	6013	25985	6543
1977	4037	32037	7256
1978	5927	43510	18895
1979	10760	49904	9669
1980	12807	53847	6913
1981	11717	61411	7507

SOURCE: Central Bank Bulletin, several issues

TABLE A.5 – BRAZIL: SOME ECONOMIC INDICES 1970–1981

	Average Rate of Change (%)				
YEAR	Net Domestic Product (1)	General Price Index (2)	Exchange Rate Cr$/US$ (3)	Foreign Debt Exports (4)	Average export incentives(%) for manu- factures (5)
1970	8.8	19.3	12.7	1.500	28.2
1971	13.3	19.5	15.1	1.687	36.5
1972	11.7	15.8	12.3	1.338	39.8
1973	14.0	15.5	3.2	0.993	39.8
1974	9.8	34.6	10.8	1.496	41.2
1975	5.6	29.4	19.7	1.976	44.3
1976	9.0	46.2	31.3	1.920	49.5
1977	4.7	38.8	32.5	2.045	45.3
1978	6.0	40.8	27.8	2.498	44.2
1979	6.4	77.2	48.7	2.638	41.7
1980	7.9	110.2	96.1	2.675	
1981	-3.6	95.2	76.5	2.636	

SOURCE: 1 and 2 – Getulio Vargas Foundation.
3 – Central Bank of Brazil. Yearly average rate of change.
4 – Table A.4 and Table 1.
5 – As percentage of the real exchange rate subsidy included, for manufactured exports. Carvalho-Haddad (1980).

Comments by Larry A. Sjaastad on Jose L. Carvalho's,
"Commercial Policy in Brazil: An Overview"

My comments will concern four topics dealt with in the Carvalho paper,
which is, in my opinion, an excellent and useful summary of the current
state of Brazilian commercial policy and its evolution. Those topics are
(a) the objectives of commercial policy, (b) the relationship between
commercial and exchange rate policy, (c) the internal consistency of
Brazilian commercial policy, and (d) the degree of protection actually
prevailing in Brazil at the current time.

OBJECTIVES OF COMMERCIAL POLICY

According to Carvalho, and I have no reason to dispute his judgment,
commercial policy in Brazil prior to World War II was aimed largely at
raising revenue for the government but, since 1946, the objectives have
oscillated between that of import substitution (or domestic
industrialization) and balance of payments control. If I interpret
Carvalho correctly, that policy began its last balance-of-payments control
phase in 1980. While it is widely recognized that commercial policy can
influence the volume and composition of trade, and thus import-
substitution goals, it is less obvious that it can influence the current
account of the balance of payments, unless it is accompanied by
expenditure in influencing policies. By its effects on relative prices, a
restrictive commercial policy affects both imports and exports in the same
direction, "elasticities" arguments notwithstanding. It is only to the
extent that some time may be required for relative prices to adjust that
one would attempt to use commercial policy in this way. The only
exception could be the extent to which exercise of commercial policy has
fiscal implications, but those apparently have not been the objective in
Brazil since World War II.

COMMERCIAL AND EXCHANGE RATE POLICY

It is also recognized that commercial policy, as is usually exercised,
influences the equilibrium real exchange rate. Departing from free trade,

for example, the imposition of, say, a uniform 20 percent tariff will increase the domestic price of importables by 20 percent and the prices of non-traded goods by some fraction of 20 percent, if the exchange rate remains fixed. If the latter is flexible, and if other policies are aimed at stabilizing the prices of non-traded goods, real equilibrium can be restored only by an appreciation. In either case, the real exchange rate will have fallen. Thus exchange rate policy must be consistent with commercial policy, or internal markets will become distorted. The possibility of this consequence is particularly marked in the case of Brazil, where so many policies, each of which really consists of a numeraire, are simultaneously in force.

On a more practical level, the external instability of exchange rates makes it difficult to conduct exchange rate policy in Brazil. When the dollar appreciates 25 percent against other major currencies, the Cruzeiro is also appreciated. But if the authorities attempt a constant "real" exchange rate (defined against the dollar and some U.S. price index), clearly a disequilibrium is created. Add to that an official wage indexation policy, and you have robbed the economy of flexibility of prices of labor-intensive non-traded goods <u>vis à vis</u> those of traded goods, thereby eliminating the only relevant degree of freedom inherent to the real side of the economy. This problem might be simplified by the choice of a simple "basket" against which to peg; it could be that because the bulk of Brazilian trade (at least on the export side) is roughly evenly divided between the dollar bloc and Western Europe, a simple 50-50 dollar-DM basket might be sufficient to eliminate much of the effects of external exchange rate instability. Of course, more comprehensive baskets such as the SDR are available.

CONSISTENCY OF COMMERCIAL POLICY

It is elementary that an import substitution policy, which is trade reducing, and an export promotion policy, which is trade increasing are grossly inconsistent at the macro level. Until recently, of course, these policies were not simultaneously implemented. The export promotion associated with the trade liberalization of the post-1965 period can be interpreted as a manner to effectively reduce protection without appearing to do so, and as such, the political problems were much less severe. Thus I would not argue that the pre-1972 export subsidies were inconsistent with the import tariffs except in the superficial sense that they were intended to reduce the "bite" of those tariffs. From the Lerner symmetry theorem, we know that such a result is possible.

More recently, however, it seems that both policies are being pursued with some considerable vigor. As such, both must fail.

Upon examination of Brazilian policy in general, however, one suspects that the aim is as much to maintain effective control at the micro level as it is to influence macro variables such as the volume of trade. The key characteristic of Brazilian economic policy is the high degree of discretion that it provides the administrators of that policy. If that is the objective, it is not, of course, inconsistent from the viewpoint of the policymakers to pursue policies whose macro implications are in conflict.

DEGREE OF PROTECTION

The most recent estimates of effective protection in Brazil as presented in the Carvalho paper indicate the (weighted) average protection was of the order of magnitude of 30 percent in 1975. The paper also suggests that export subsidies are currently of the order of magnitude of 11 percent of FOB value of exports. The dispersions are enormous, of course, but the implication is that the average rate of protection in Brazil may be relatively low at the present, and that several sectors are not protected at all.

Obviously, the effect of export subsidies is to reduce the degree of protection offered by any given collection of tariffs and other import barriers. The mechanism might be thought of as nominal wages; "protecting" exports increase the demand for labor in that sector, and the implied higher domestic prices of exportables shift demand towards non-traded goods and hence put upward pressure on wages in that (labor-intensive) sector. If the export subsidies were uniform at 11 percent and the import protection were also uniform at 30 percent, the wage effect would reduce the degree of protection to 30-11=19 percent. That this is so can be seen by noting that this combination of tariff and subsidy is equivalent to an 11 percent devaluation coupled with a 19 percent uniform tariff insofar as its effects on internal equilibrium relative prices are concerned.

But the story does not stop there. A devaluation of 11 percent coupled with the imposition of a uniform tariff of 19 percent would increase equilibrium wages, relative to the exchange rate, by more than 11 percent because the tariff would shift demand towards and supply away from non-traded goods, creating an excess demand to be resolved by an increase in the prices of those goods, and hence wages. Recent work by Roberto Fendt indicates that the (partial) elasticity of the price of non-traded goods with respect to that of importables is about 0.7. Applying that coefficient to the 19 percent tariff, we predict another 13 percent increase in non-traded goods prices, and hence wages. Thus the "true" protection arising from this scheme, that is, the rise in internal prices of importables relative to wages, would be only about 6 percent (30 minus 11 minus 13).

It would be heroic to extrapolate these results to the actual Brazilian protection scheme, as both the import duties and the export subsidies are highly variable. If one were to do that, however, one would conclude that any sector with (effective) protection less than 24 percent is really being disprotected. Note that 11 of the 23 sectors appearing in the final column of Table 4 of the Carvalho paper are in that category. This result is quite speculative, but it surely suggests that true protection in Brazil is highly exaggerated by the conventional measures of effective protection.

FOREIGN INVESTMENTS IN BRAZIL:
THEIR BENEFITS AND COSTS

Werner Baer

Foreign capital has played an important role in Brazil's economy since the
country became politically independent. For almost as long a period of
time, controversy existed about the impact of such capital. Did it
promote or stifle or distort the development of the country? The main
purpose of this article is to consider this question for present-day
Brazil in the light of available evidence. I shall first briefly review
foreign capital's historical role in Brazil's development. This will be
followed by a summary of arguments establishing its benefits and costs,
given its present structure. Finally, I shall review the evidence
available for each side of the argument.

HISTORICAL PERSPECTIVE

In the early post-independence era, foreign capital (mostly of British
origin) was mainly concentrated in finance and trade. While the
production of export products (coffee, sugar) was dominated by Brazilians,
shipping and financing of exports and also the importation of manufactured
products was in the hands of foreigners. The easy access of British goods
to the Brazilian market was the result of the political pressures of
England (a quid-pro-quo for the political support of the country's
independence) and contributed to maintaining the country as a primary
export economy until the 20th century.[1]

During the second half of the 19th century large amounts of foreign
capital flowed into Brazil to build up the economic infrastructure--
railroads, ports, urban public utilities--much of which was designed to

---

[1]Graham, in his classic study, states that "...The grip which the
British held upon the railroad, the exporting firm, the import business,
the shipping company, the insurance agency, the financial bank, and even
the government treasury...tended to choke off any efforts to reduce
reliance on British imports," in Richard Graham, Britain and the Onset of
Modernization in Brazil, 1850-1914 (Cambridge University Press, 1968), p.
73.

more effectively integrate Brazil into the world trading network as a supplier of primary products. This capital consisted of both direct investments and of the financing of projects through the sale of bonds. In 1880, the total stock of foreign capital was estimated at US$ 190 million; this expanded to US $1.9 billion in 1914 and to US $2.6 billion in 1930. Before the thirties, Britain dominated foreign investments in Brazil, though the share of the United States increased in importance by the turn of the century. In 1930, half of foreign capital was British and one quarter was of U.S. origin.[2]

Although foreign capital contributed resources and technology to the growth of the Brazilian economy prior to the 1930's, many observers of that period have had misgivings about the impact of such capital on the nature of the development it helped to produce and its cost to the country.[3] The issues most frequently cited in criticizing foreign capital in the pre-1930 era are: (1) The railways and ports built were meant to integrate the country more effectively into the international economy, i.e. to more efficiently ship primary products from the interior to overseas markets and to distribute more efficiently imported manufactures. They did not integrate the various regions of the country into a larger national market. (2) The cost of foreign capital was excessive, as foreign companies were granted guaranteed rates of return on their investments and, as loan capital was extremely expensive, either due to high interest rates and/or due to the large discount at which bonds

---

[2]Eric N. Baklanoff, "Brazilian Development and the International Economy," in Modern Brazil: New Patterns and Development, edited by John Saunders, (Gainesville: University of Florida Press, 1971), p. 191.

[3]In 1854 the Brazilian minister to Great Britain stated that "...the commerce between the two countries is carried on with English capital, on English ships, by English companies. The profits,...the interest on capital,...the payments for insurance, the commissions, and the dividends from the business, everything goes into the pockets of Englishmen." Quoted by Graham, op. cit., p. 73. Cottrell observes that British dominance "...over the Brazilian export sector was increased by inter-company links. English export merchants had financial interests in the shipping and railways, and consequently exerted pressure for better port facilities, the construction of which was financed by British capital. The bulk of the liabilities of the British-owned banks were local deposits, but they were lent primarily to the alien companies and contractors. The majority of Brazil's imports came from Britain and were handled by English export-import houses..." P.L. Cottrell, British Overseas Investment in the Nineteenth Century (London: The Macmillan Press Ltd., 1975), p. 42. A classic description of British influence on the Brazilian economy can be found in: Alan K. Manchester, British Preeminence in Brazil (Chapel Hill, NC: University of North Carolina Press, 1933).

were sold in international financial markets by underwriters.[4] (3)
Tariffs of foreign-owned public utilities were often very high in order to
insure a quick return on investments, and services were often
inadequate. Since the 1930's, increased state controls of the tariffs of
public utilities gradually led to a decline of foreign investments in that
sector, and ultimately to the nationalization of most foreign-owned public
utility enterprises, since controls were applied in such a way as to
substantially decrease the profitability of the sector.[5]

Foreign investments continued to flow to Brazil in the 1920's, though at a
reduced rate when compared to the pre-World War I period. Some went to
expand public utilities and financial and commercial operations, and a
certain amount even went to new industrial ventures (though manufacturing
was dominated by domestic capital prior to World War II).[6] With the Great
Depression, inflows came to a virtual standstill.

The 1950-1982 Period
Since the early 1950's, when Brazil adopted the strategy of Import Substitution Industrialization (ISI) to promote economic growth and development,
foreign investments have shifted to the manufacturing sector, and their
share in the infrastructure has gradually declined. This was the result
of various incentives given to foreign capital, as it was felt that rapid
ISI was only possible with a heavy contribution of foreign funds and know-
how. The decline of foreign investment in the infrastructure was the
result of both government controls, which made returns to investment in
that sector unattractive, and the fear of nationalist reaction against the
foreign control of strategic sectors.[7]

As can be seen in Table 1, foreign investments prior to World War II were
concentrated primarily in public utilities, trade, finance and petroleum

---

[4]The burden of guaranteeing a minimum rate of return to foreign-owned
railways became so onerous that the state began to borrow money abroad
after the turn of the century to gradually buy them. By 1929 almost half
were in government hands, growing to 68 percent in 1932, 72 percent in
1945 and 94 percent in 1953. See: Annibal V. Villela and Wilson Suzigan,
Politica do Governo e Crescimento da Economia Brasileira, 1889-1945 (Rio
de Janeiro: IPEA/INPES, 1973), pp. 397-99.

[5]Villela and Suzigan, op. cit. pp. 381-82; Werner Baer, The Brazilian
Economy: Its Growth and Development (Columbus, Ohio: Grid Publishing,
Inc., 1979), p. 138.

[6]While private direct investment from abroad increased from US $1.2
billion in 1914 to US $1.4 billion in 1930, there was a notable change in
its geographical origin: direct French investment declined from US $391
million to US $138 million, British investments changed from US $609 to US
$590, while U.S. direct investments rose from US $50 million to US $194
million. See: Eric N. Baklanoff, "External Factors in the Economic
Development of Brazil's Heartland: The Center-South, 1850-1930," in The
Shaping of Modern Brazil, Edited by Eric N. Baklanoff (Baton Rouge:
Louisiana State University Press, 1969), pp. 26-29.

[7]For a summary of the ISI policies and incentives to foreign invest-
ments, see Baer, op. cit., ch. 4; and for an analysis of nationalist reac-
tions to foreign capital, see: Werner Baer and Mario H. Simonsen,
"American Capital and Brazilian Nationalism," reprinted in Foreign
Investment in Latin America, edited by Marvin D. Bernstein (New York:
Alfred A. Knopf, 1966), pp. 273-82.

distribution. This changed considerably in the post-World War II decades, and by 1980, investments in public utilities had practically disappeared, while manufacturing represented 68 percent of total foreign investments.

Table 2 reveals that within the manufacturing area the leading foreign investments in 1980 could be found in chemicals and pharmaceuticals, transport equipment and machinery sectors. These sectors also experienced the highest growth rates within the Brazilian economy. Substantial foreign investments could also be found in metal products and electrical machinery.

Towards the end of the second World War, the United States dominated in the origin of foreign investments, and in 1951 its proportion still amounted to almost 44 percent. As will be noted in Table 3, there has been a substantial growth in the diversification of the geographical origin of foreign capital. By 1980, the U.S. share had declined to 30 percent, while the combined share of West Germany, Japan, and Switzerland was larger than that of the U.S.

Tables 4 and 5 contain some more detailed information on the relative importance of foreign capital in a number of sectors. The former is based on the sales of the twenty largest firms in each sector. According to that survey, foreign firms are dominant in 12 sectors, including such dynamic technology industries as automobile assembly, pharmaceuticals, and electrical machinery. The remarkable fact in that survey is how dominant foreign firms are also in such more traditional sectors as textiles, food and beverages, and hygienic and cleaning goods.

Table 5 presents the results of a survey which includes almost the whole universe of firms in each sector. As is to be expected, the dominance of foreign firms is much less pronounced with this much larger coverage. In terms of sales, they exceed the 50 percent level in only seven cases; however, taking a 30 percent or higher share, one encounters 15 sectors. Foreign dominance in the universe remains in such dynamic sectors as electrical machinery, automobiles, pharmaceuticals, and construction machinery. It is considerably smaller, however, in such sectors as textiles and food products.

THE BENEFITS AND COSTS OF MULTINATIONALS: SOME GENERAL CONSIDERATIONS

Considering the current structure of foreign investments in Brazil, what are their advantages and disadvantages to the country's growth and development? I shall first summarize the arguments on both sides of the issue. This will be followed by a discussion of currently available evidence.

Benefits

The inflow of foreign capital has a positive impact on the balance of payments, especially in the early stages of the development of a new sector or when a rapid expansionary spurt occurs, as foreign firms will bring in substantial sums of foreign exchange to undertake their construction activities. This is especially the case in a country like Brazil, where the capital for long-term private borrowing is limited, where large-scale expansion of multinationals through equity offerings is also limited, and where access to long-term government credit (through the

Table 1
Sectoral Distribution of U.S. Investments in Brazil (percentages)

	1929	1940	1952		1980
Manufactures	23.7	29.2	50.6		68.0
Petroleum (distrib.)	11.9	12.9	17.1		4.7
Public Utilities (Incl. Transportation)	50.0	46.7	14.9		--
Trade	8.2	7.5	17.4		7.3
Other	6.2	3.7			
				Banking	1.7
				Finance (excl. Banking)	10.8
Total	100.0	100.0	100.0		
				Mining	1.9
				Other	5.6
				Total	100.0

Sources: Calculated from - United Nations, Foreign Capital in Latin America, New York, 1955, p. 51; Pedro S. Malan, Regis Bonelli, Marcelo de P. Abreu and Jose Eduardo de C. Pereira, Politica Economica Externa e Industrializacao no Brasil (1939/52) (Rio de Janeiro: IPEA/INPES, 1977), p. 181; U.S. Department of Commerce, Survey of Current Business, August 1981.

Table 2. Sectoral Distribution of Total Foreign Investments
And Sectoral Growth Rate

	Foreign Investments (%)		Yearly Growth Rates of Output		
	1976	1981	1967-70	1971-74	1975-80
Mining	3	3			
Manufacturing	76	73	14.2	12.0	6.9
Non-Met. Minerals	3	2	17.3	11.6	7.8
Metal Products	8	8	14.4	7.1	9.9
Machinery	8	10	22.7		7.1
Electrical Machinery	9	8	13.4	19.6	8.5
Transport Equipment	13	13	32.6	22.1	4.4
Paper and Prods.	3	2	9.1	6.7	7.7
Rubber	2	2	15.3	12.0	5.9
Chemicals & Pharm.	18	17	15.6	15.2	8.7
Textiles & Clothing	8	7	5.0	3.9	4.5
Food & Beverages	7	6	8.2	8.0	7.0
Tobacco	2	1	9.6	8.0	4.6
Public Utilities	3	-			
Services	16	20			
Other	2	4			
TOTAL	100	100			

Sources: Calculated from various issues of Conjuntura Economica, and
Boletim, Banco Central do Brasil.

Table 3. Origin of Foreign Capital in Brazil
(percentages)

	1951	1980
United States	43.9	30
Canada	30.3	4
United Kingdom	12.1	6
France	3.3	4
Uruguay	3.1	0.1
Panama	2.3	3
W. Germany		13
Switzerland		10
Sweden		2
Netherlands		2
Japan		10
Italy		3
Luxemburg		2
Other	5.0	10.9
TOTAL	100.0	100.0

Sources: Carlos Von Doellinger and Leonardo C. Cavalcanti, *Empresas Multinacionais na Industria Brasileira* (Rio de Janeiro: IPEA/INPES, 1975), p. 27; *Boletim*, Banco Central do Brasil.

Table 4.

Shares of Domestic, Foreign and State Firms in Total Sales - 1980*
(percentages)

	Domestic	Foreign	State	Total
Domestic Dominance				
Housing Construction	100.0	–	–	100.0
Sales of Motor Vehicles	100.0	–	–	100.0
Communications	98.1	–	1.9	100.0
Clothing	97.5	2.5	–	100.0
Wood & Wood Products	94.0	6.0	–	100.0
Agriculture	92.4	–	7.6	100.0
Retail Sales	92.2	7.8	–	100.0
Heavy Construction	90.1	5.5	4.4	100.0
Supermarkets	80.2	3.4	16.4	100.0
Food	73.0	27.0	–	100.0
Paper & Cellulose	70.4	26.1	3.5	100.0
Non-Metallic Minerals	64.6	35.4	–	100.0
Metal Products	60.1	39.9	–	100.0
Wholesale Commerce	45.7	42.2	12.1	100.0
Foreign Dominance				
Machinery	45.4	48.0	6.6	100.0
Electrical Machinery & Goods	44.8	55.2	–	100.0
Automotive Parts	43.5	56.5	–	100.0
Textiles	36.8	63.2	–	100.0
Transportation Products	33.2	58.4	8.4	100.0
Beverages & Tobacco	30.4	69.6	–	100.0
Hygienic & Cleaning Goods	30.0	70.0	–	100.0
Plastic & Rubber Products	27.6	69.8	2.6	100.0
Office Materials	13.6	80.0	6.4	100.0
Petroleum Distribution	10.8	59.2	30.0	100.0
Pharmaceuticals	10.0	90.0	–	100.0
Automobile Assembly	0.7	99.3	–	100.0
State Dominance				
Public Utilities	–	–	100.0	100.0
Chemicals & Petrochemicals	8.7	11.6	79.7	100.0
Mining	28.1	9.1	62.8	100.0
Steel	30.0	7.8	62.2	100.0
Transport Services	44.9	2.4	52.7	100.0

Source: "Os Melhores e Maiores," Exame, Setembro 1981.

*Each sector includes the 20 largest firms.

Table 5. Shares of Domestic, Foreign and State Firms in Assets, Sales, and Employment, 1980*

	No. of Firms	Net Assets				Sales				Employment			
		Dom.	For.	State	Total	Dom.	For.	State	Total	Dom.	For.	State	Total
Mining	48	20.9	12.7	66.4	100.0	24.9	7.4	67.7	100.0	34.5	7.1	58.4	100.0
Cement	48	80.3	19.7	–	100.0	76.5	23.5	–	100.0	83.0	17.0	–	100.0
Steel	68	33.8	3.7	62.5	100.0	35.0	7.9	57.1	100.0	41.5	10.0	48.5	100.0
Non Ferrous Metals	48	31.9	64.3	3.8	100.0	50.2	49.8	–	100.0	62.5	37.0	0.5	100.0
Misc. Metals	352	80.9	18.5	0.6	100.0	79.4	20.4	0.2	100.0	80.4	19.4	0.3	100.0
Machines, Motors, Equip.	291	64.7	33.4	1.9	100.0	58.2	38.5	3.3	100.0	61.1	37.3	1.6	100.0
Instruments, Office Equip.	28	33.8	62.7	3.5	100.0	45.1	48.8	6.1	100.0	39.4	53.8	6.8	100.0
Electrical Machines	28	32.2	67.8	–	100.0	38.9	61.1	–	100.0	42.8	57.2	–	100.0
Elect. Goods (Lamps, Utensils, etc.)	71	69.3	30.7	–	100.0	31.7	68.3	–	100.0	63.2	36.8	–	100.0
Shipbuilding	15	48.5	51.5	–	100.0	49.6	50.4	–	100.0	60.6	39.4	–	100.0
Automobiles	11	4.2	95.8	–	100.0	2.4	97.6	–	100.0	3.1	96.9	–	100.0
Tractors, Earth Moving Equip., Implements	40	49.4	50.6	–	100.0	34.2	65.8	–	100.0	53.2	46.8	–	100.0
Furniture	63	96.3	3.7	–	100.0	98.5	1.5	–	100.0	97.2	2.8	–	100.0
Wood Products	146	93.2	6.8	–	100.0	94.5	5.5	–	100.0	95.6	4.4	–	100.0
Paper and Products	138	81.8	11.2	7.0	100.0	78.5	15.4	6.1	100.0	84.0	4.0	12.0	100.0
Chemicals, Petrochem.	247	48.2	29.4	22.4	100.0	49.2	36.4	14.4	100.0	45.8	42.7	11.5	100.0
Plastics	109	81.5	18.5	–	100.0	76.7	23.3	–	100.0	84.3	15.7	–	100.0
Petroleum Ref. & Dist.	31	3.7	11.3	85.0	100.0	7.3	34.1	58.6	100.0	5.6	15.1	79.3	100.0
Pharmaceuticals	57	31.8	67.1	1.1	100.0	24.4	74.6	1.0	100.0	29.8	68.6	1.6	100.0
Perfumes, Hygienic Products	27	60.5	39.5	–	100.0	60.6	39.4	–	100.0	63.7	36.3	–	100.0
Shoes	50	98.2	1.8	–	100.0	96.8	3.2	–	100.0	94.4	5.6	–	100.0
Leather Products	54	84.3	15.7	–	100.0	72.7	27.3	–	100.0	74.8	25.2	–	100.0
Rubber Products	55	60.2	39.8	–	100.0	35.4	64.6	–	100.0	58.1	41.9	–	100.0
Textiles	328	83.7	15.7	0.6	100.0	79.0	20.3	0.7	100.0	87.3	11.4	1.3	100.0
Clothing	121	98.3	1.7	–	100.0	98.0	2.0	–	100.0	97.8	2.2	–	100.0
Milling	53	71.2	28.8	–	100.0	92.6	7.4	–	100.0	91.6	8.4	–	100.0
Meat Packing	114	93.1	5.2	1.7	100.0	91.5	7.6	0.9	100.0	91.0	6.6	2.4	100.0

Table 5 (continued)

	Number of Firms	Net Assets				Sales				Employment			
		Dom.	For.	State	Total	Dom.	For.	State	Total	Dom.	For.	State	Total
Diary Products	35	81.1	17.5	1.4	100.0	86.7	10.5	2.8	100.0	80.0	16.4	3.6	100.0
Sugar and Alchol	190	99.7	-	0.3	100.0	98.0	-	2.0	100.0	98.1	-	1.9	100.0
Vegetable Oils	66	80.3	18.8	0.9	100.0	81.4	18.5	0.1	100.0	81.3	18.5	0.2	100.0
Misc. Food Products	181	75.3	24.7	-	100.0	66.8	33.2	-	100.0	78.7	21.3	-	100.0
Beverages	100	92.4	7.5	-	100.0	84.7	15.3	-	100.0	89.9	10.1	-	100.0
Tobacco	8	4.5	95.5	-	100.0	5.7	94.3	-	100.0	12.5	87.5	-	100.0
Newspapers	17	100.0	-	-	100.0	100.0	-	-	100.0	100.0	-	-	100.0
Publishing	87	85.9	2.9	11.2	100.0	92.6	2.9	4.5	100.0	89.3	4.7	6.0	100.0
Construction	434	94.0	4.0	2.0	100.0	90.4	6.4	3.2	100.0				
Engineering Consulting	41	94.0	-	6.0	100.0	92.8	-	7.2	100.0	95.1	-	4.9	100.0
Export & Import Trade	134	69.6	19.3	11.1	100.0	68.7	16.5	14.8	100.0	65.6	27.2	7.2	100.0

Source: Compiled from information in "Quem e Quem na Economia Brasileira," Visao, 29 de Agosto, 1981.

development bank, BNDE) is not possible for foreign-controlled firms. Of course, once a foreign subsidiary is established, a substantial amount of investment financing will come from retained earnings. The latter, however, is not sufficient at times of major expansion programs.

A second benefit which foreign capital brings along is the rapid transfer of advanced technology, enabling the host country to develop new industrial sectors in a short period of time. In the case of Brazil, the rapid ISI process of the 1950's and the fast rate of industrial expansion in the late 1960's and early 1970's relied very heavily on foreign technology brought along by the subsidiaries of multinational firms. Given the limited domestic technical and financial capacity of Brazilian firms prior to the ISI process, the growth of new industrial sectors without multinationals would have required a much longer period of time than was in fact the case.

In addition to the physical know-how, multinationals also brought along new organizational or administrative technology. Complex industrial operations required a type of organization, both on the productive and bureaucratic side of a firm, which did not previously exist in the country.

Large multinational firms also influenced the technology and organization of Brazilian-owned firms. Since most relied (in some cases were made to rely through government policies) on local supplying firms for many of their inputs, they transmitted technology to those firms. In the process many Brazilian supplying firms became organizationally more efficient and improved the quality of their output as they had to adjust to the standards of their customer—the multinational firm.

The inflow of foreign capital creates employment and also upgrades the quality of the labor force as it trains both its workers and administrative staff which are drawn on the local manpower supply. It is a fact that most multinationals in Brazil are almost fully staffed by Brazilians.

Finally, the presence of a large number of multinationals in Brazil's manufacturing sector has contributed substantially to the country's program of export diversification in the late 1960's and throughout the 1970's. With an established production and marketing network throughout the world, the multinationals in Brazil were in an excellent position to facilitate the government's program to promote the export of manufactured products.[8]

Costs

Ever since Brazilian policy-makers have encouraged the influx of foreign capital to develop ISI industries, there has grown a polemical and

---

[8]There exists a substantial literature detailing some of the benefits to be gained from multinational investments. See, for instance: Joseph LaPalombara and Stephen Blank, Multinational Corporations and Developing Countries, (New York: The Conference Board, 1979), ch. 5; or Raymond Vernon, Storm over the Multinationals, (Cambridge, Mass.: Harvard University Press, 1977), ch. 7.; Carlos Von Doellinger and Leonardo C. Cavalcanti, Empresas Multinacionais na Industria Brasileira, (Rio de Janeiro: IPEA/INPES, 1975), pp. 54-78.

academic literature dealing with the problems and the negative impact of a large multinational presence in the economy's dynamic sectors.[9]

Let us briefly examine the principal negative features which have been emphasized in this literature:

Balance of Payments Impact. Since the principal motivation of multinationals in opening facilities abroad is to make a profit, sooner or later a large proportion of these profits will be repatriated to the parent firm and thus cause a drain on the foreign exchange earnings of the country.

Not only do multinationals operate abroad to make profits, but since investments in the Third World are viewed to be riskier than either at home or in other advanced industrial countries (e.g., the risk of nationalization or tight controls over operations due to a change in government, or the risk of inconvertibility of the currency due to balance of payments problems), the rate of return from such investments is expected to be higher to compensate for such risks. This attitude, which is quite understandable from the investor's point of view, will inevitably clash with the view of many groups in the host country, who will perceive the multinationals as wanting to draw a higher rate of return from a poor country than from the country of origin, where per capita income is very high.

Since most Third World countries have some type of limit on profit remittances, many multinationals are suspected of secretly transferring profits back to the parent company by engaging in transfer pricing, i.e., a situation where the parent company overcharges the subsidiary for certain imported inputs.[10] Additional motivations for the use of transfer pricing are escape from taxes and the desire to leave the impression of a lower than actual profit rate for public relations purposes. Of course, multinationals deny the practice of transfer pricing and it is generally extremely difficult, if not impossible, to produce conclusive proof of its use.

Inappropriate Technology. One set of critics fault the multinationals for not contributing to the solution of one of the major socio-economic problems of the Third World (including Brazil)--the creation of industrial employment. They import capital-intensive technology, which is not

---

[9]See, for instance: Luciano Martins, Nacao e Corporacao Multinacional (Rio de Janeiro: Editoria Paz e Terra, 1975); Alvaro Pignaton, "Capital Estrangeiro e Expansao Industrial no Brasil," Departamento de Economia, Universidade de Brasilia, Texto Para Discussao, 1973; Peter Evans, Dependent Development: The Alliance of Multinational, State and Local Capital in Brazil, (Princeton University Press, 1979); Richard S. Newfarmer and Willard F. Mueller, Multinational Corporations in Brazil and Mexico, Report to the Subcommittee on Multinational Corporations of the Committee on Foreign Relations, United States Senate (Washington, D.C.: U.S. Government Printing Office, 1975); LaPalombara and Blank, op. cit., ch. 6; Von Doellinger and Cavalcanti, op. cit., ch. IV.

[10]There exists an enormous literature on the concept of transfer pricing. See, for instance: Robert Hawkins (editor), The Economic Effects of Multinational Corporations (Greenwich, Connecticut: JAI Press, 1979), especially the articles by Thomas G. Parry and Donald R. Lessard.

adjusted for local conditions. Thus, the employment impact of multinationals has been minimal. Multinationals are not eager to spend substantial sums in trying to adapt technology to local factor availability, since that would have not much of a pay-off and one of the principal attractions of establishing subsidiaries in countries like Brazil is that this will enable them to get an extra return on research and development (R&D) expenditures which was previously undertaken for servicing the home markets.

There are other critics who are less concerned about the employment impact of multinationals and more about the unwillingness of these firms to engage in basic R&D work in the host country. Although many multinationals have laboratories of some kind as part of their operations in the host countries, these are usually part of quality control activities rather than of an effort to engage in fundamental technological research. Since technology is the most potent bargaining weapon a multinational has, it will be extremely reluctant to transfer advanced technological development capabilities to the host nation. This will be increasingly resented by the latter, as it is felt that without the involvement of citizens of the host country in R&D, there will be a permanent dependency of foreign technology and thus no chance to increase the bargaining position of the host country in negotiating for better technology transfer terms.

Finally, with R&D work concentrated in the country of the parent-company, subsidiaries are usually charged, in one form or another, for technological payments. Although this is justified on the basis that all consumers of the company's product benefit technological innovations resulting from R&D investments, and should thus contribute to reimburse the company for its expenses, one never sees a fair formula for distributing the burden of this reimbursement. In fact, some observers have claimed that technology payments from subsidiary to parent company provide opportunities for hidden remittances of profits.

Denationalization. The presence of powerful multinationals in a developing country may inhibit the development of local firms, which do not have the financial and technological means to compete. In some sectors, formerly dominant local firms may be squeezed out and/or taken over by incoming multinationals.

The denationalization issue can also be examined from a more aggregative point of view. As the most dynamic sectors of the host economy are often dominated by multinationals, there will be a trend to transfer the decision-making locus concerning levels of investment and production abroad. Multinationals are known to centralize major decisions in the parent company. The latter will develop policies with a view to optimize its world activities. The resulting decisions are not necessarily optimal from the point of view of individual host countries. This conflict of interest will be sharpened to the extent that the multinational increasingly engages in exports from the host country. For instance, though it may be optimal during a world recession for a multinational to drastically curtail its activities in the Brazilian subsidiary as compared with its home plants, few Brazilians would sympathize with such actions.

Consumption Distortions. ISI represented a move to produce domestically, goods which were formerly imported. Since the demand profile is based on the distribution of income, which was concentrated, import substitution implied the creation of a production capacity profile reflecting the existing demand profile. As multinationals were a key element in ISI, they acquired a stake in the newly established production profile and thus a vested interest in the status quo. They feared that a drastic change in the distribution of income would reduce their domestic markets. A complementary argument was that multinationals had an interest in increasing markets by influencing lower income groups to consume their products (various types of consumer durables) through advertising and credit schemes (e.g., the automobile consortia which attract consumers from lower income groups, often at the expense of more basic necessities), and thus "distorting" their consumption patterns.

Political Influence. It would be naive to assume that the presence of multinationals can be politically neutral. One does not have to go to such extreme cases as that of Chile in the 1970's, where multinationals were involved in direct political actions, or Chile and Peru in the same period, where multinationals placed direct pressures on their home governments to obtain favorable action on compensation for nationalization. In a much less dramatic way, it will be only natural for multinationals to use their political influence through their home country's diplomatic channels to influence the host country's policies-- e.g., with respect to relaxing rules on importation, price controls, labor policies, profit remittance laws, etc. Resistance to such pressures by the host government will depend on various circumstances--e.g., impending international loans or debt renegotiations, etc.

These political side-effects should be considered as one of the costs of relying on multinationals in the process of ISI and general development. If these costs are too high, due to the sensitivity of the host country's population to anything seeming to impose on the sovereignty of the country, a policy of less reliance on foreign investments would be in order, even if that would diminish the rate of growth of industrialization.

A BRIEF SURVEY OF THE EMPIRICAL EVIDENCE

Profits

It is difficult to present unambiguous information concerning the profitability of multinationals in Brazil, and also their impact on the balance of payments. The inflow of direct investments (net of reinvested earnings) has been small relative to the balance of payments needs of the country. This is born out of the fact that in 1981, direct inflow of foreign investments was less than ten percent of the foreign loans obtained by Brazil in that year. The balance of payments contributions of direct investment inflows are even smaller when one subtracts profit remittances (see Table 6). Reinvested earnings, at times represent substantially more than inflow of new funds (in 1978 the latter amounted to US $221 million, compared to US $975 for the former), while in other years the reverse is true. Table 6 also presents the profit and remittances rates based on broad balance of payments information. The former ranged from almost 16 percent in 1971 to 5.5 percent in 1980, while in the same period, profit rates in the U.S. averaged about 14.2 percent.[11] The data in Table 7, taken from the balance sheets of the 50 largest firms in each ownership category, reveals even higher profits rates (though domestic firms' rates are higher than those of multinationals).

Returning to Table 6, it will be noted that the rate of profit remittance, as a percentage of capital stock, was fairly stable, averaging about 4.2 percent. It would thus seem that multinationals are well within the limits placed on such remittances by the Brazilian government. The law makes any remittance about 12 percent per year over registered original investment plus reinvestments subject to severe taxation.[12]

On the face of it, multinationals in Brazil do not seem to be making excessive profits, whether when compared to local enterprises or to firms in the countries of origin, and are rather moderate in repatriating profits. The major question which arises is about the use of hidden ways to transfer profits. Little evidence exists to date about the usage of transfer pricing. The opportunities for its usage exist since much of the foreign trade of multinationals takes place within the firm. In the early 1970's, over 70 percent of multinational sales took place within the parent system.[13] Also, a survey of multinational firms, in the 1975-77 period, shows that in most sectors multinationals run negative trade balances, which provided (or reflect) the opportunity to engage in some type of transfer price activities (see Table 8).

It is difficult to obtain specific information about technology payments, which might be a way to circumvent restrictions on profit remittances. Since the 1960's, legislation to control technology payments has been ample. The payment of royalties is only allowed when a foreign company has less than 50 percent control of a firm in Brazil. Technology and licensing agreements are also subject to a considerable amount of restrictions and scrutiny. When royalties or technical

---

[11]For the U.S. this is the profit after income taxes as a percent of stockholders' equity, yearly average for 1973-80, in Economic Report of the President, February 1982 (Washington, D.C.: U.S. Government Printing Office, 1982).

[12]Mario Henrique Simonsen, "O Brasil e as Multinacionais," in Multinacionais: Os Limites da Soberania, edited by Getulio Carvalho, (Rio de Janeiro: Editora da Fundacao Getulio Vargas, 1977), p. 63.

[13]Richard S. Newfarmer and Willard F. Mueller, Multinational Corporations in Brazil and Mexico, Report to the Subcommittee of Multinational Corporations of the Committee on Foreign Relations, United States Senate (Washington, D.C.: U.S. Government Printing Office, 1975) p. 128.

Table 6
Stock, Flows, and Earnings of Foreign Capital in Brazil

	Total Direct Investments (US$ Millions)	Direct Investments in Industry (US$ Millions)
1967	3,728	–
1969	–	1,420
1973	4,579	3,603
1976	9,005	6,886
1978	13,740	10,593
1980	17,480	13,005
1981 (June)	17,495	–

		(US$ Millions)		
	Inflow of Direct Foreign Investments	Re-Investment of Earnings	Profit Remittance	Foreign Loans
1977	–	–	458	–
1978	221	975	564	13,811
1979	964	721	740	11,228
1980	1,101	411	544	12,300
1981	1,500	–	–	16,700

	Rate of Profit (Reinvested earnings + Remitted Profits as % of capital stock)	Rate of Remittance (Remitted Profits as % of capital stock)
1971	15.8%	4.1%
1972	11.6%	4.7%
1973	12.2%	4.5%
1974	11.1%	4.4%
1978	11.2%	4.1%
1979	9.1%	4.6%
1980	5.5%	3.1%

Source: Von Doellinger and Cavalcanti, op. cit., pp. 89-90; Banco Central do Brasil, Boletim, various issues.

Table 7
Comparative Performance of Domestic Private, Multinational and
State Firms in Brazil - Profits as a Percent of New Assets

	Domestic Private	Multinationals	State Firms
1977	25.2	23.4	7.8
1978	13.7	13.5	4.8
1979	11.8	17.7	3.1
1980	19.1	15.6	2.3

Source: "Melhores e Maiores," Edicao Especial, Exame, Setembro 1981, pp. 122-23. Based on 50 largest firms in each category.

Table 8. Brazil: Foreign Trade Balance of Firms by Ownership Category
(US$ Millions)

	State Enterprises			Private Domestic			Multinationals		
	1975	1976	1977	1975	1976	1977	1975	1976	1977
Automobile Producers	-	-	-	-	-	-	69.0	-8.2	235.4
Auto Parts	-	-	-	-25.8	-8.7	10.2	-86.0	-55.4	-22.2
Tractors	-	-	-	-7.7	-6.6	0.3	-124.5	-148.0	-54.2
Machinery	-1.7	-15.9	-9.9	-51.7	-52.4	-49.4	-152.2	-90.3	-82.2
Food, Tobacco, Beverages	-2.1	-5.1	-	-7.1	12.4	5.5	332.5	289.2	557.2
Chemicals, Pharmaceut., Hygienic articles	-4,458.1	-175.7	-103.8	-122.8	-162.6	-183.6	-767.2	-968.4	-763.2
Textiles, Clothing, Shoes	-	-	-	-34.1	-24.2	-19.5	2.8	-12.9	32.8
Fertilizers	-10.5	-14.0	-5.6	-137.8	-103.7	-136.2	-78.7	-67.4	-100.9
Non Metallic Minerals	-2.1	-0.6	-0.9	-3.6	-2.4	-2.2	-47.5	-83.8	-37.5
Tires	-	-	-	-1.7	-3.6	-0.4	-98.4	-139.7	-99.7
Office Equipment	-	-	-	1.4	-	-	-146.0	-90.1	-17.2
Electrical Equipment	-0.9	170.1	162.3	-13.0	-62.9	-80.1	-444.1	-270.3	-154.6
Steel & Metal Products	-	-	-	156.8	115.7	124.8	-78.0	-102.5	-86.4
Shipbuilding	-	-	-	-150.7	-58.6	-95.6	-59.5	-57.8	-89.8
Construction	-	-	-	-29.4	-42.2	-26.1	-1.2	-4.7	-0.9
Paper & Cellulose	-	-	-	17.9	17.4	-2.4	-80.4	-67.2	-22.5
Public Utilities	-614.7	-481.1	-571.1	-137.8	-25.9	-34.0	-37.5	-43.7	-25.1
Miscellaneous	156.8	18.6	204.1	-57.6	-67.2	-42.3	-99.6	-120.2	-124.9

Source: SEPLAN, unpublished sources.

Table 9. Indebtedness of Domestic, Multinational
and State Enterprises
(50 largest in each category)

	1977	1978	1979	1980
General Indebtedness (% of net assets)				
Domestic Firms	57.0	56.0	56.8	57.0
Multinationals	60.0	57.8	63.7	62.4
State Enterprises	47.7	51.9	58.4	59.9

Source: Same as Table 7.

assistance payments are allowed, they cannot exceed five percent of gross sales[14] It has been estimated that in 1973 and 1974, technical assistance payments amounted to only US $136 million and US $176 million respectively. These are small numbers considering that they also include domestic firms.[15]

Another way of getting around profit remittance restrictions is through increased foreign borrowing for expansion purposes, as there are no restrictions on the payments of interest on foreign loans. Although it is well known that a large part of the growth of Brazil's foreign debt in the 1970's was due to the borrowing of state enterprises, a substantial amount was also done by multinationals. As the latter have no access to official long-term credit (from the BNDE system), they have a good justification for borrowing abroad. Unfortunately, published Central Bank data do not provide a breakdown of borrowers by ownership type. The only indirect evidence available is from a survey of the 50 largest firms in each ownership category, shown in Table 9. It will be noted that multinationals are more in debt than either domestic Brazilian or state firms.

Technology
Relatively little systematic work has been done to date on the technological behavior of multinationals in Brazil. The best work to date

---

[14]Mario Henrique Simonsen, "O Brasil e as Multinacionais," in Multinacionais: Os Limites de Soberania, edited by Getulio Carvalho, (Rio de Janeiro: Fundacao Getulio Vargas, 1979), p. 65; Carlos Von Doellinger and Leonardo C. Cavalcanti, Empresas Multinacionais na Industria Brazileira.

[15]Von Doellinger and Cavalcanti, op. cit., p. 95.

is that of Morley and Smith on the metal working industries.[16] Comparing the operations of U.S. multinationals in their U.S. and Brazilian plants, they found that the former "...use far more automatics and special purpose machines..."[17] However, they also found that "...At U.S. output levels, all the capital goods producers that we visited in Brazil indicated that they would use about the same degree of automation as their U.S. parent, and we doubt that they would change this decision even if labor costs were substantially lower."[18] They noted that in metal stamping there was much less automation in loading and unloading devices. And they conclude that "...all the evidence we have reported... points to a substantial modification of production processes by multinationals in Brazil ...They also tend to substitute labor for capital in...the materials handling or support services of the production process..."[19] The basic cause for differences between production techniques of multinationals in their parent vs. their Brazilian plants was found to "...stem from scale differentials, not cheap labor. At home country output levels most firms said that they would use home country production techniques in Brazil despite the fact that the cost of labor is only one-fifth of what it is in the United States."[20]

In a study of Brazil's electrical industry, Newfarmer and Marsh compared multinational and domestic firms. They found that the latter employ more labor per unit of capital than the former.[21]

However, even if adjustments of technology are made by some multinationals, it is doubtful that this will have much of an impact on the general employment picture, since most of multinational investments are in sectors which are inherently capital intensive. It should be noted that in the import substitution era of the 1950's, many multinationals established themselves in Brazil by importing second-hand equipment. This could be interpreted as a deliberate choice at the time in favor of more labor intensive techniques. With the emphasis on export diversification since the second half of the 1960's, both multinational and domestic firms have based their expansion on new equipment, using the latest technology.

---

[16]Samuel A. Morley and Gordon W. Smith, "The Choice of Technology: Multinational Firms in Brazil," Economic Development and Cultural Change, January 1977.

[17]Ibid., p. 254.

[18]Ibid., p. 255.

[19]Ibid., p. 257.

[20]Ibid., p. 261.

[21]Richard S. Newfarmer and Lawrence C. Marsh, "Foreign Ownership, Market Structure and Industrial Performance: Brazil's Electrical Industry," mimeographed, Department of Economics, University of Notre Dame, November 1979, p. 17.

144

Firms perceived this as necessary in order to effectively compete in the international market.[22]

As far as the development of new technology thorugh research and development in Brazil is concerned, the efforts of multinationals are relatively
small. Evans found that in Brazil "...affiliates allocate about one-fifth
the expenditures to R&D that their parents do...If multinationals
allocated to R&D in Brazil the same proportion of local sales as they do
in the United States, Brazilian expenditures would have been almost $150
million in 1972 instead of under $30 million."[23] One might add that even
the little that was spent on R&D in Brazil was not necessarily pure
research expenditures, as it is difficult to separate quality control work
in laboratories from genuine frontier research.

Equity Considerations
To the extent that income distribution is related to the technological
characteristics of industries, multinationals can be viewed as having
contributed towards the increased concentration of income in Brazil, i.e.,
their high capital/labor ratios helps to explain the observed income
distribution trends. This has occurred in spite of the better remunera-
tion of employees in multinational as compared to domestic private
firms. In 1972, for instance, average salaries paid by multinationals in
the manufacturing sector were 30 percent higher than domestic firms. This
has to be counter-balanced by the fact that productivity in the former was
over 50 percent higher than in the latter.[24]

Multinationals do have an interest in promoting the sales of the products
they produce in Brazil, and to the extent that their production profile
reflects the demand profile, which, in turn, is based on a concentrated
distribution of income, they will either support policies which do not
disturb the status quo and/or they will influence consumers through
advertising and/or credit schemes (like the car consortia). Whether this
will "distort" the consumption structure of the lower income classes is a
matter of substantial ideological controversy.

Denationalization
Various trends can be observed when the Brazilian economy is examined over
the past 40 years. In the public utilities and mining sectors, there has
been a strong nationalization trend. In fact, in the former sector, the
multinational presence has disappeared. To the extent that multinationals
had a dominant position in rapidly growing new sectors (like the
automobile, electrical machinery and other industries), whose weight in
the economy was growing, the relative power of multinationals were
certainly expanding. Finally, in some sectors denationalization occurred
through direct takeovers of domestic firms.

---

[22]Werner Baer, "Technology, Employment and Development: Empirical
Findings," World Development, Vol. 4, No. 2, 1976, p. 129. For the
arguments concerning the ineffectiveness of more labor intensive
techniques on general employment creation, see: Werner Baer and Larry
Samuelson, "Toward a Service-Oriented Growth Strategy," World
Delvelopment, Vol. 9, No. 6, 1981.

[23]Evans, op. cit., pp. 177-78.

[24]Von Doellinger and Cavalcanti, op. cit., pp. 67-68.

Evans documented the denationalization process in the Brazilian pharmaceutical industry, which was once dominated by local firms, but which, after World War II gradually experienced a denationalization process, so that by the mid-1970's foreign firms controlled over 85 percent of the market. Evans identifies the importance of new products resulting from R&D, which became increasingly central to profits, as one of the main causes for the decline of local firms. The denationalization process occurred mainly by the acquisition by multinationals of local firms.[25] Newfarmer's study of the Brazilian electrical industry traces a continued trend of denationalization throughout the 1960's and 1970's, so that by the mid-1970's almost 80 percent of the industry was in the hands of multinationals. Much of the growth of the latter was due to acquisitions.[26]

GOVERNMENT POLICIES AND THE BEHAVIOR OF THE MULTINATIONALS IN BRAZIL

Although the import-substitution process has implied a reliance on multinationals in many sectors and their strengthening through various incentive programs, and although similar favors were granted to them during the period of export promotions, the Brazilian government has taken many actions to control their behavior and influence. Let us briefly list some of the government measures which acted as a countervailing force:

Control of Remittances
In its control of profit remittances and payments for technology the Central Bank and other government agencies have become increasingly sophisticated in monitoring payments. Of course, this does not mean that transfer pricing practices are totally under control.

The BNDE System
The complex credit system of the government was designed to strengthen the domestic private sector and state enterprises. By excluding foreign firms from this system, some degree of balance was restored in the "tripe," that is, the ownership structure in the Brazilian economy between domestic private, multinational and state firms. This, for instance, made it possible for the domestic private sector to expand considerably in the capital goods sector in the 1970's.[27] Also, by requiring firms to be over 50 percent owned by domestic capital to have access to government credit, local firms acquired an important bargaining tool in setting up joint ventures with multinationals.

State Enterprises
The rapid growth of state enterprises in such key sectors as steel, mining, petrochemicals, and others, has also acted as a countervailing

---

[25]Evans, op. cit., pp. 121-131.

[26]Richard S. Newfarmer, "TNC Takeovers in Brazil: The Uneven Distribution of Benefits in the Market for Firms," World Development, Vol. 7, Number 1, January 1979, pp. 25-43.

[27]This is discussed in detail in: Annibal V. Villela and Werner Baer, O Setor Privado Nacional: Problemas e Politicas Para Seu Fortalecimento, (Rio de Janeiro: IPEA/INPES, 1980), ch. III.

measure. This is becoming increasingly evident since the mid-1970's as Brazil has been developing a strategy to develop its raw material resources and related industries. The development of the bauxite mining and aluminum industry, of the Carajas resources, of some new petrochemical and steel complexes, are based on joint ventures between state enterprises and multinationals, with the former holding the dominant shares of the ventures. Brazil's state enterprises are large, technologically sophisticated, and financially backed by the government, and are thus in a good position to face multinationals on a fairly even level in bargaining about technology, profit sharing, etc.[28]

Market Controls.
The Brazilian government's occasional use of a policy called "reserva de mercado" also represents an attempt to check on relative growth of multinationals and to give an incentive to local firms to enter new technologically advanced fields. One of the best examples was the attempt to restrict the market for minicomputers to a reduced number of firms which would be predominantly domestic in character, i.e., more than 50 percent controlled by local firms.

MULTINATIONAL BEHAVIOR IN THE 1980'S

Although many key sectors of Brazil's industry are dominated by multinationals and decisions are thus made abroad, it is not clear to date whether, on balance, decisions have been favorable to multinational world strategy but harmful to the interests of Brazil. Multinationals have collaborated with the government's policies of export diversification, as a growing percentage of their output is being exported. Of course, this was not only done to acquire good-will, as multinationals were amply rewarded for this collaboration through the export-incentive program. It is also noteworthy that with the 1981-82 Brazilian recession, many multinationals have substantially increased their exports to compensate for local market declines. The huge growth of automobile exports is a case in point, as over US $2 billion were exported in 1981. Also, to date, the recession in industrialized countries has not led multinationals to decrease their Brazilian operations. On the other hand, multinationals continue to shy away from basic R&D in Brazil.

It should be clear from this short review that the presence of multinationals has brought benefits and costs to Brazil. It is, of course, a very subjective matter to attempt to manufacture numbers and weights to measure where the country comes out on a net basis. There is some evidence that Brazil's authorities have learned how to police multinationals more effectively than in the past without scaring them away, and thus to increase the net benefits which can be drawn from them. The increased sophistication of Brazilian officials in dealing more effectively with multinationals is also helped by the fact that there is a greater geographical diversification in their origin, which adds some leverage to their bargaining position.

---

[28]For greater details, see: Villela and Baer, op. cit., ch. I; also Baer, The Brazilian Economy..., op. cit., ch. 7, "Brazil's Extended Public Sector."

Comments by Tulio Duran on Werner Baer's
"Foreign Investment in Brazil: Their Benefits and Costs"

Professor Baer's paper is divided into three main parts. They are an historical perspective of foreign investment in Brazil, a cost benefit approach to the role of Multinational Corporations (MNC's) in the Brazilian economy and some empirical evidence on MNC performance in Brazil. I will concentrate my comments on the cost benefit approach.

Professor Baer pointed out four main benefits for Brazil due to the presence of the MNC in the Brazilian economic environment. These are:

a) Capital inflow for direct investment in construction activities;

b) Technology transfer in new sectors accelerating the import substitution process;

c) Creation of new jobs using Brazilian manpower, and;

d) Export diversification and geographical expansion using MNC distribution channels.

Five major sources of cost to the Brazilian economy were cited:

a) Negative impact on the balance of payments due to the capital outflow of profits;

b) Inappropriate technology. The extensive use of capital intensive technology in trying to avoid labor costs due to regulations;

c) Denationalization. Policy decision-making for dynamic sectors done abroad;

d) Distortion in consumption patterns. Marketing and credit policies employed to attract low income individuals toward the consumption of durable goods, thereby distorting consumption patterns;

e) Political influence. As the MNC's political influence is not neutral, it could influence the overall political economy strategy and the design of regulations to the benefit of MNC's.

The main problems in dealing with the presence of MNC's in a distorted economy like Brazil's is to correct the regulations that are distorting the economic environment. For example:

1. In terms of the direct investment versus foreign loans, the legislation on direct investments at the margin is more severe than that on the loan procedure. So, a MNC would prefer to make a loan abroad rather than to undertake direct investment. So, part of MNC direct investment is concealed in the foreign debt.

2. The limitation of profit and royalty remittances due to regulation, provides incentive for subsidiaries of MNC's in Brazil to overprice inputs imported from the home country in order to conceal the remittance of profits.[1]

3. The control of MNC operations in Brazil is very weak, though it is really is a worldwide problem, appropriately treated at the level of a world body, like the United Nations. The response to MNC's rapid growth in the share of total Brazilian economic activity has been the increased participation of state owned enterprises with a shrinking share for private Brazilian capital participation in the economy.

---

[1] As an example, see the case study for the pharmecuetical industry dor by J. Frenkel, _Finep Staff Papers_.

INFLATION AND RECESSION FATE OR POLITICAL CHOICE IN BRAZIL TODAY?

Claudio R. Contador

INTRODUCTION

One of the striking features of the Brazilian economy is the stubbornness of the recent inflationary process, even under a severe stabilization program since 1981. As a result most people, including influential economists in the government, are prone to support a change in the economic strategy.

A second feature is the belief that the economic policy has been following a cyclical path of mistakes and successes. As displayed in Tables 1 and 2, the average growth of the Gross Domestic Product (GDP) reached 3.1 percent with inflation over 56 percent in the period 1962-67. Both mean rates were far from the historical perspective: the inflation higher than any other previous period, and the real growth lower than the historical 7.2 percent rate. In the following six years there was a large improvement: in 1968-73 the growth of real product reached 11.5 percent, inflation declined from 25 percent to nearly 11 percent, and the exports rocketed from less than US$ 2 billion to US$ 6.2 billion. Thereafter, from 1974 to 1979, the real growth rate declined once again while inflation soared to 40 percent.

In 1980 a new strategy was implemented to speed real growth and, at the same time, decrease inflation and adjust the balance of payments, in an attempt to repeat the performance of 1968-72. However, the efforts were unsuccessful in almost every aspect. In fact the real GDP grew 8 percent, but the cost was too high in terms of inflation (110 percent) and of foreign trade deficit (US$ 2.8 billion). The economic conditions of 1981 showed a huge change. For the first time in four decades the GDP dropped 3.5 percent and industrial output decreased 8.4 percent. Although agriculture's performance was excellent and services growth positive, the net overall result was negative. On the other hand, the trade balance turned from a US$ 2.8 billion deficit in 1980 to a US$ 1.2 billion surplus in 1981. The other benefit of the 1981 recession was the decline of the domestic inflation rate from 110 percent in December 1980, to 95 percent at the end of 1981. At a first glance, the comparison between end-to-endfigures is not impressive, but the fall was really significant, con-

TABLE 1: GROWTH OF REAL PRODUCT IN BRAZIL

(Average Annual Rates)

PERIOD	GROSS DOMESTIC PRODUCTS	AGRICULTURE	INDUSTRY
1947–1955	6.8	4.8	9.0
1956–1961	7.3	5.2	10.4
1962–1967	3.5	4.1	3.5
1968–1974	10.0	3.7	12.2
1975–1981	5.2	5.0	5.1
1977	5.4	11.8	3.9
1978	4.8	-2.6	7.4
1979	6.7	5.0	6.6
1980	7.9	6.3	7.9
1981	-3.5	6.8	-8.4

SOURCE: Getulio Vargas Foundation

FIGURE 1

REAL GROWTH AND IDLE CAPACITY
IN BRAZIL

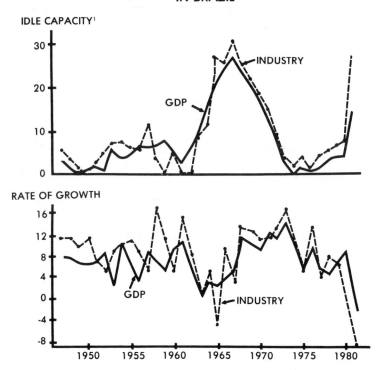

Measured by difference between potential and actual product.

TABLE 2: INFLATION IN BRAZIL
(December to December rates)

PERIOD	GENERAL PRICES	WHOLESALE PRICES	COST OF LIVING INDEX
1947–1958	15.6	16.2	15.1
1959–1964	57.0	56.1	56.9
1965–1973	23.7	23.3	25.1
1974–1978	37.9	37.6	38.2
1979–1981	94.2	98.5	85.9
1977	38.8	35.5	43.1
1978	40.8	42.9	38.1
1979	77.2	80.1	76.0
1980	110.2	121.3	86.3
1981	95.2	94.3	95.3

SOURCE: Getulio Vargas Foundation

FIGURE 2
RATE OF INFLATION IN BRAZIL
GENERAL PRICE INDEX

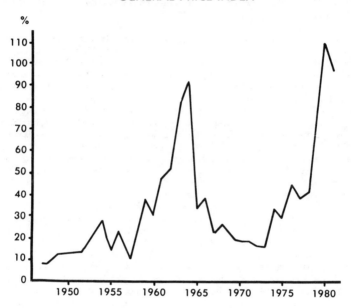

sidering that the public's expectations at the beginning of 1981 was around 150 percent. Most of the fall in inflation was due to agricultural prices whose rate of inflation decreased from 130 percent to 85 percent in 1981. The rate of inflation of wholesale industrial prices fell only from 110 percent in December 1980 to 100 percent in 1981.

Until recently, a prospect of low or negative growth of real GDP was implausible in the minds of politicians, businessmen, and public at large. After all, we thought that the dynamics of the Brazilian economy were different from most industrialized countries. Although the orthodox view of the Phillips curve kept telling us that a trade-off exists between inflation and real growth in the short run, we were prepared to accept that the aim of reducing inflation would be accomplished through a temporary fall in GDP growth and a higher unemployment, but we believed economic growth would still be positive.

Even under the most severe stabilization policy in the late 1964-66 there was no decline in the level of real GDP. The fall of sixty points of inflation (from 90 percent to 30 percent) cost only four points off the historical rate of the real GDP growth. If past experience has any value to predict the future, as economists believe, one should expect that the 1981 recession was accompanied by a large fall in inflation.

The official argument for the economic failure in 1980, 1981 and even the inflationary pressures of the late 70s, was to transfer the blame to the real shocks that the Brazilian economy has been subjected to, in particular the oil crisis of 1973 and 1979, the international interest rates turmoil in 1980 and 1981, and the domestic wage policy since 1980. However, up to now we can only guess the actual impact of these factors, as no strong empirical evidence has been presented. Moreover, how do we distinguish between the effects of political errors and those of external disturbances? Has the control of aggregate demand became a useless tool as proposed by the supply side economics, or is it simply inappropriate under the current circumstances?

This paper deals with two issues, both related to inflation. First, it presents a sketchy discussion of the theoretical points of view, and second, it tries to predict the overall movements of inflation and future growth.

THE ORTHODOX VIEW OF THE TRADE-OFF BETWEEN INFLATION AND GROWTH

Since the path-breaking paper of Phillips[1] in 1958, the main concern of macro-economic policy has been how to reconcile measures of fighting inflation with the social needs of decreasing, or at least not augmenting, unemployment in the short run. Truly speaking, other economists had looked into the relationship between unemployment and inflation well

---

[1]A.W. Phillips, "The Relation Between Unemployment and the Rate of Change of Money Wage Rates in the United Kingdom, 1861-1957" *Economica*, vol. 25, November 1958, pp. 283-99.

before 1958,[2] or at the same time,[3] but the relationship that would reinviogorate modern macroeconomic policy bears Phillips' name.

Phillips applied the conventional economic postulates to the labor market in the United Kingdom. As one would expect, when there is excess demand for commodities, prices are predicted to rise and the derived demand for labor should be affected in the same way. The now-famous graph of empirical evidence showed a negative nonlinear relation between wage inflation and unemployment.

The importance of Phillips' findings caught the politicians' interest. The policy implications were the most important; if there is a stable trade-off between inflation and unemployment, then it would be possible to choose and attain a specific point on the Phillips curve representing the optimal combinations elected by the public and the policy makers.

It also meant that unemployment could be reduced permanently if society accepted a higher rate of inflation. Or on the contrary, if people want a zero rate of inflation, they would have to accept a higher rate of unemployment. In Phillips' mind, we could buy either employment forever at the price of a given rate of inflation, or a lower or zero inflation rate, accepting higher unemployment.

Since then, a large number of economists have done much additional research, both theoretical and empirical. Most of them have confirmed the core of Phillips' message that there exists a negative relation, but rejected other aspects of this naive model. One of the main theoretical revisions was that the trade-off exists only or mostly in the short run; but that in the long run there would be no trade-off.[4] Because of market frictions, unemployment would exist even when there is no excess demand in each market and the economy at general equilibrium. In this approach, the equilibrium rate of unemployment is called the "natural rate", a real phenomenon determined only by other real variables.

Now the trade-off between inflation and unemployment has become temporary. There is no way of "buying" employment anymore; we can only "borrow" it now at the cost of accelerating prices in the future. Along a static Phillips curve, an upward shift in the aggregate demand decreases unemployment and raises inflation. However, as soon as people readjust their expectations of inflation, the Phillips curve shifts upwards until actual inflation and expectations become equal. When this occurs, unemployment returns to its "natural rate". Any further attempt to

---

[2]Irving Fisher, "A Statistical Relation Between Unemployment and Price Changes" International Labour Review, Vol. 13, June 1926, pp. 185-92, reprinted in Journal of Political Economy, Vol. 81, March/April 1973, pp. 496-502.

[3]Lawrence R. Klein and Robert J. Ball, "Some Econometrics of the Determination of Absolute Prices and Wages", Economic Journal, Vol. 69, September 1959, pp. 465-82.

[4]Milton Friedman, "The Role of Monetary Policy", American Economic Review, Vol. 58, March 1968, pp. 1-17.

decrease unemployment ultimately spurs the rate of inflation, revising the expectations of inflation and pulling the unemployment rate back to its original position. Therefore the long run Phillips curve is vertical, and the accelerationist hypothesis states that the only way of keeping the unemployment rate permanently below the economy's natural rate is continuously fooling people by raising the rate of inflation to non-expected levels.

The Phillips curve has originated several theoretical and empirical versions. There exist numerous papers on the issue in Brazil, and all of them confirm the accelerationist hypothesis.[5] However the absence of unemployment figures imposes a statistical problem for research in Brazil, and the GDP gap--the relative difference between actual and potential levels--has been used to represent idle capacity and labor unemployment.

According to some empirical studies,[6] there exists a stable short-run trade-off between inflation and GDP gap: each point percentage of decline in inflation is related to a one percentage point increase in idle capacity. In the long run, the impact of inflation expectations compensates for the shift in aggregate demand and the Phillips curve becomes vertical.

The political question of this conclusion is disturbing; if GDP growth cannot be raised permanently, away from its historical path, what role remains for demand policies? Some economists argue that if there is a positive rate of time discount, it may be a good political project to speed real growth now and reap its benefits in the short run, even at the cost of a higher rate of inflation later on.

It is interesting to note that the Brazilian government seems to be well aware of the benefits and costs of stabilization programs, even though conflicting measures seem to be adopted. The experiences of 1980 and 1981 provide good examples of this issue.

THE SECOND VIEW OF THE TRADE-OFF

The conventional view of the Phillips curve assumes that all pressures come from the demand side and then the aggregate supply curve shows a stable behaviour with no shifts over the time. This hypothesis presumes no supply shocks, except those shifts due to the inflation expectations. Since all disturbances derive from the aggregate demand, inflation can be

---

[5]Edmund S. Phelps, "Phillips curves, Expectations of Inflation, an Optimal Unemployment Over Time", Economica, Vol. 34, August 1967, pp. 254-81.

[6]Unfortunately most of them are published only in Portuguese: Claudio R. Contador, "Crescimento Economico e o Combate a Inflacao", Revista Brasileira de Economica, January 1977, and "Recessao ou Inflacao? As Faces do Debate", Conjuntura Economica, August 1980; A.C. Lemgruber, "A Inflacao Brasileira e a Controversia sobre a Aceleracao Inflacionaria", Revisita Brasileira de Economia, July 1974.

reduced only by controlling aggregate demand, which imposes a short-run increase in unemployment.

Nevertheless, this approach cannot explain some actual movements, unless it resorts heavily to changes in inflation expectations. For instance, the conventional view leaves no room to explain declining inflation together with lowering unemployment and high rates of real growth, as they occurred in Brazil during the period, between 1968 and 1973--the so-called "economic miracle." Neither provides a good explanation for the period 1974-1979. In both periods changes in inflation expectations played an important but not exclusive role.

For understanding the cycles of inflation and growth we have to resort to an eclectic reasoning. We have to accept that relative prices change during the growth of general prices, and that relative price movements entail allocative adjustments.

In this view, shifts in the aggregate demand comprise only a part of the process. The rise in the prices of final goods and services is transmitted to the prices of factors, and the aggregate supply also shifts upwards. For didactic puposes, let us divide the dynamic movements of inflation and unemployment into four phases, as shown in Figure 3. Pressures in aggregate demand diminish unemployment, speed the real growth above the historical rate, and raise inflation--phase I--until expectations and cost adjustments are revised upwards and unemployment raises together with inflation--phase II. The public's worries and the political crises due to accelerating prices cause government to adopt a stabilization program. In the short run, it means forcing people to revise downwards their inflation expectations and/or to impose changes in their standard of living and to accept costly adjustments.

This is accomplished with an increase in unemployment and fall in the actual rate of real growth below its natural path in phase III. The lagged effects allow the subsequent phase IV to be characterized by both declining inflation and unemployment, until the idle capacity pushes inflation upwards, and the whole process starts all over again. Therefore we should expect that the dynamics of inflation and unemployment (or GDP gap or other related measures) would follow a theoretical clockwise movement as shown in Figure 3.

Of course, one may not agree with the reasoning, but one is forced to accept the empirical experience. Figure 4 presents the Brazilian experience since 1963, and Figures 5 and 6 show the same phenomena for eight industrialized economies. All cases display the same pattern of clockwise movements. The conventional view of the trade-off states that inflation can be decreased by controlling aggregate demand only in phase III. If we accept the past evidence, as displayed in Figures 4, 5, and 6, we then have reason to suspect that the political attempt in 1979-80 to revive "growth-with-decreasing-inflation" was untimely. That strategy would be efficient only at the end of phase III or at the beginning of phase IV, but never in phase II. Neither the idle capacity was sufficient to sustain a large shift in demand without accelerating prices, nor were inflation expectations declining. Therefore, as several economists predicted, the eight percent growth in GDP could only be attained at the cost of higher inflation.

FIGURE 3

THE THEORETICAL MOVEMENTS OF
INFLATION AND UNEMPLOYMENT

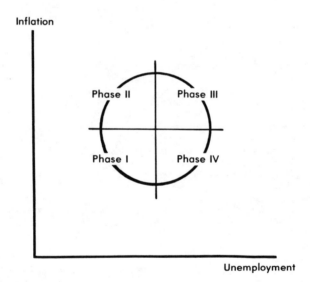

FIGURE 4

THE MOVEMENTS OF INFLATION[1] AND UNEMPLOYMENT[2] IN BRAZIL

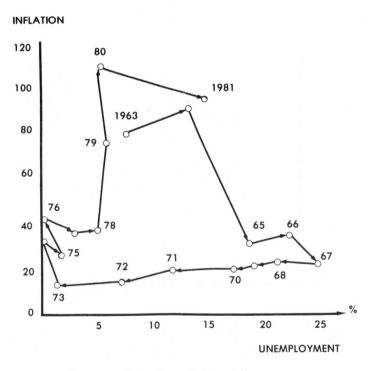

1. Measured by General Price Index
2. Measured by GDP gap

FIGURE 5

THE MOVEMENTS OF INFLATION AND

UNEMPLOYMENT : THE INTERNATIONAL EVIDENCE

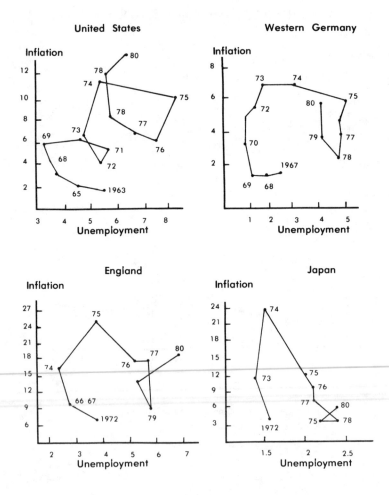

FIGURE 6

THE MOVEMENTS OF INFLATION AND UNEMPLOYMENT:
THE INTERNATIONAL EVIDENCE

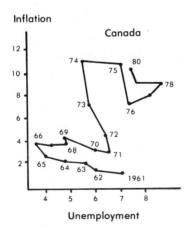

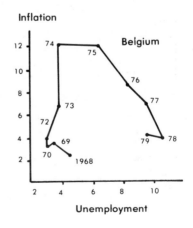

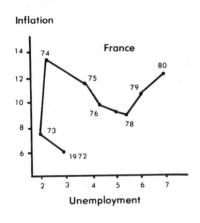

However, those opposing this argument could question why the same reasoning fails to explain the 1981-82 recession. After all, the idle capacity at mid-1981 was almost the same as that of 1967, and it was expected that inflation would slow down very rapidly at the end of 1981 and the beginning of 1982.

Before proceeding, we should recall that this model can describe the cyclical movements of inflation and real growth only when the disturbance stems from the demand side. When the disturbances come from the supply side, that is, when supply shocks occur, this approach fails to explain and predict the overall trends of inflation and growth. For dealing with these cases we need another model.

GROWTH AND INFLATION UNDER SUPPLY SHOCKS

After 1973, the oil shocks forced us to revise our understanding of the conventional trade-off. It is interesting to note that even before 1973, institutional arrangements, particularly index-linking, introduced distortions and "autonomous" effects on costs of production, but they remained mostly ignored. More recently, in 1979, a change in the wage policy imposed new pressures on aggregate supply. Due to these facts, the short-run aggregate supply is no longer stable. Its upward shift starts an inflationary process that differs from that entailed by demand-pull shifts.

Figure 7 displays the changes in prices and real income when supply shocks occur.[7] The picture should be read as in dynamic growth; changes in price level mean changes above the previous rate, and the same is valid for real income. The initial aggregate supply is indicated by SS; the aggregate demand by DD; y^e is the full employment (or potential) real GDP; and P, the general price level. At period t_0, the economy faces an idle capacity equal to the difference between potential and actual GDP (= y^e - y_0) and general price level P_0. Be definition, aggregate supply becomes more and more inelastic as the economy approaches full-employment. When the GDP gap is large aggregate supply is relatively elastic. At full employment (y^e), it becomes vertical.

First, let us assume a shift in aggregate demand. The orthodox view tells us that if income rises from y_0 to y_1, then prices increase from P_0 to P_1. If the economy were previously at the "natural rate of unemployment", the increase in real growth will be temporary, for factor costs will end up rising. The supply shifts to S'S, and the former idle capacity is restored. Note that in terms of GDP gap and inflation, the movement from point A to B coincides with phase I and from point B to C, with phase II in Figure 3. When inflation becomes unbearable, a severe stabilization policy is implemented, aggregate demand shifts downward from D'D' to DD and inflation declines only at the cost of higher unemployment. The movement CE corresponds to phase III in Figure 3. During the next period, the smaller change in prices of goods and services is transferred to

---

[7]A more detailed exposition can be found in A.C. Harberger "Uma Visao Moderna do Fenomeno da Inflacao", Revista Brasileira de Economia, Vol. 32, January/March 1978, pp. 69-91.

FIGURE 7
CHANGES IN PRICES
AND OUTPUT

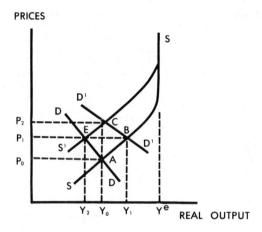

factor prices and the economy ends up at the initial position A.   The movement EA is the same as that displayed by Phase IV in Figure 3.

However, when the economy faces supply shocks as those entailed by the oil crisis, the new wage policy, and so on, the inflationary process stems from shifts in aggregate supply.   The same Figure 7 deals with this case.   Now the increase in factor prices induces a shift in aggregate supply from SS to S'S, prices rise to P_1 and real income falls from y_0 to y_2.   The new equilibrium is at point E, where unemployment is higher than before.   An expansionary demand policy is called on to restore the previously lower level of unemployment: the aggregate demand shifts upward from DD to D'D' and the new equilibrium is at C.

While demand inflation can be reduced by a temporary increase in unemployment and a lower rate of real growth, supply shocks raise two difficulties.   First, it is more painful to fight inflation through demand policies because the impact on unemployment is enormous.   Second, in general it is not easy to discern real from monetary disturbances and there is always a chance of adopting the wrong remedy.   For both reasons, most countries are more prone to inflation nowadays, than in the period prior to 1973.   It also means that we should expect dynamic movements of inflation and unemployment moving northeast.   The evidence for the United States, Western Germany, and England, in Figure 5, and France and Canada in Figure 6 will probably become the basis of a standard pattern for other economies, including Brazil.

If so, we should expect that under these circumstances demand policies will become tools less efficient than in the past.

MEASURING SUPPLY SHOCKS

By definition, an economic shock is any non-expected disturbance, or in a less restrictive sense, any change beyond that necessary to permit the real growth of the economy.   Thus, nominal or monetary shocks can be measured by the excess change in the nominal stock of money, when we take into account the effect of real income growth, the changes in expectations of inflation and in interest rates as well as in other variables related to the demand for money.   A recent study[8] dealt with this question and provides estimates of the most important shocks affecting the Brazilian economy.

The most pervasive real shocks come from the oil crises, the wage policy, and the exchange policy.   The first disturbance may be represented by the increase of the price of oil denominated in dollars.   The wage policy shock is more difficult to deal with, but a simple way of expressing it could be by the difference between the nominal change in wages and the expected rate of change in cost of living index.   Finally, the exchange rate disturbance is measured by the difference between the nominal change

---

[8]Claudio R. Contador, "Monetary Correction in Brazil: Myth and Reality" paper presented at the Second International Conference on the Financial Development of Latin America and the Caribbean, Caracas, Venezuela, April, 1981.

in cruzeiros and the change in the ratio of domestic and foreign relative price indices.

Table 3 summarizes the statistical data needed to identify the magnitude of each shock over time. Until 1972, monetary shocks were more important than real shocks. Note also that the wage and exchange rate policies favored the decline in inflation since the changes were mostly negative. Therefore the orthodox view of fighting inflation through demand policies was efficient under these conditions. In 1973 and 1974, the world oil prices rose 140 percent comprising one of the most severe real shocks faced by the Brazilian economy to date. Thereafter, and in particular in 1980, additional shocks sprang from oil prices, wage adjustments and exchange rate policy. Thus we should accept the proposition that the demand policies would be less efficient in controlling inflation and more pervasive in terms of raising unemployemnt.

If so, what can be said about growth and inflation in the years ahead? Certainly, if we want to diminish the rate of inflation to something around 20-30 percent, we will have to face growth rates lower than the historical rate of seven percent. It means that the combination of inflation and GDP gap must move downward and to the right in Figure 4. As long as capital formation is sustained, the growth slowdown is temporary, while the adjustments in the balance of payments are not completed. Later on, let us say after 1985, a new revival (and unfortunately also temporary), with rates higher than seven percent, will be possible by exhausting the idle capacity in industry. Until then we must be patient.

CONCLUSION

This paper has discussed some issues related to the recent conditions of inflation and growth in Brazil. We have shown that the naive view of a negative relationship between inflation and unemployment or GDP gap in the short run does not deal with supply shocks. Therefore the strategy recommended by the demand policies fails to decrease inflation and at the same time imposes higher unemployment.

The 1980 inflationary eruption, followed by the 1981 recession with only a slight decrease in inflation, has been attributed to wrong economic policies. In fact, when focusing only on these two variables, one is easily distracted away from the different nature of the source of inflation.

Today the supply shocks entail the most pervasive effects on the stabilization policy dilemma. Therefore the performance of macro-economic policies cannot be evaluated by just comparing the results with those of the past. Honestly, we still need better ways of appraising economic strategies under real shocks.

TABLE 3. NOMINAL AND REAL "SHOCKS" IN THE BRAZILIAN ECONOMY MEASURED BY ANNUAL GROWTH RATES AT YEAR-END (percentage)

Year	Inflation	GNP Gap	Nominal Monetary Shocks	Supply Shocks		
				Wages	Oil	Exchange Rate
1965	56.8	19.9	77.1	-15.3	-1.6	-14.1
1966	38.0	23.9	-19.8	-18.5	0.6	-8.0
1967	28.3	26.7	49.6	-10.2	9.4	-6.0
1968	24.2	22.2	12.5	-5.2	-8.6	3.3
1969	20.8	19.2	25.5	-5.1	1.5	1.6
1970	19.9	17.5	13.3	-2.6	20.9	6.6
1971	20.3	12.5	19.4	-2.6	4.0	-0.9
1972	17.3	8.5	28.8	-1.8	-7.1	-7.1
1973	14.9	2.1	28.0	-1.5	27.3	-15.4
1974	28.7	.0	23.5	3.4	88.6	-8.2
1975	27.9	1.5	54.0	5.7	23.7	-9.3
1976	41.2	.0	23.3	9.9	-8.0	-0.3
1977	42.6	1.0	45.6	3.9	1.9	-7.3
1978	38.7	3.3	28.2	0.1	1.1	-10.6
1979	53.9	3.9	72.8	10.7	33.4	6.6
1980	100.2	3.2	99.9	28.8	67.5	30.1
1981	109.9	14.7	82.1	13.4	19.4	-9.8

SOURCE: See text.

Comments by Samuel A. Morley on Claudio Contador's, "Inflation and
Recession: Fate or Political Choice in Brazil Today"

Contador's paper makes a convincing case that the recent upsurge of
inflation in Brazil is the result of a series of supply shocks, not the
lagged effects of excess demand.   The evidence for a supply shock is
persuasive.   During the last several years, Brazil has suffered through
the doubling of oil prices, a bad harvest, a maxi-devaluation and a change
in the wage indexing system.   Each of these shifts the supply curve
upwards which tends to raise prices and reduce output both at the same
time.

In this comment, I would like to extend Contador's analysis by focusing on
the policy responses and possible cures for a supply shock inflation.
Basically, in response to a supply side bottleneck, a society must either
accept a rise in the relative price of the scarce good (in this case,
foreign exchange), or face a reduction in the overall level of income.
Either remedy reduces the demand for foreign exchange and enables society
to live with the lower level of supply that is available.   However, the
cost of the recession remedy exceeds by far the cost of changing relative
prices, since it implies large amounts of output foregone and
unemployment.   Yet societies often seem more willing to have recessions in
response to supply shocks than to change relative prices.   In some cases,
the recessions are the mechanism by which relative prices are forced to
change, and in other cases, they are simply a temporary "quantity
adjustment" to the bottleneck.

In response to a supply shock a government can confine itself to the
traditional tools of demand management, or it can intervene into the wage
price system to change relative prices directly.   The latter is generally
hazardous politically.   Suppose, therefore, that a government decides to
use the traditional instruments of demand management only.   There are
three possible responses: neutral, contractionary and accommodating.   In
the first case, aggregate demand is maintained at the pre-supply-shock
level.   There will be a rise in inflation accompanied by a recession as
the supply curve shifts left up the stationary demand curve.   Second, the
government can try to offset the inflation by a very contractionary policy
which reduces demand enough to keep inflation rates down, in spite of the
supply shock.   Finally, one can accommodate the supply shock by expanding

the money supply sufficiently to avoid the supply-side recession. This is what Brazil did in 1970-80. Unfortunately, this is very likely to convert a one-time supply shock into a permanently higher inflation. In the Brazilian case, with its wage-indexing system, the effect of the higher inflation was to lower the average ex-post real wage and, presumably, also the relative cost of home goods. Because the indexing scheme is not instananeous, inflation has a negative effect on the real wage. Thus, in the accommodative policy, the economy lives with the bottleneck by allowing a higher inflation rate to change relative prices by means of a higher inflation rate. The country avoids the supply shock or bottleneck recession at the cost of a permanently higher inflation rate. This was the Brazilian solution in 1979-80. The country "borrowed" prosperity from the future and grew faster than it should have. Now Brazil is faced with the other side of that coin--either higher inflation or recession or perhaps both.

I would now like to think a bit about the economic effects of recession, as opposed to inflation, as a way of a living within a bottleneck. As I have said, a bottleneck requires a change in relative prices, and the question therefore is whether recession is a good way to bring about such a change. I would argue that it is not. It is always difficult to change relative prices in a market economy, particularly when there is indexing. In general, with indexing and markup pricing the relative price structure remains the same. Devaluations tend to be immediately translated into higher wages and home goods prices. In that case, recessions tend to have little effect on relative prices; they do little to cure a bottleneck. Rather recessions allow the country to live within the bottleneck, temporarily, by having a lower income level. But that lasts only as long as the country stays in the recession, and is, therefore, a terribly costly sort of remedy.

Eventually, it is likely that contractionary demand management can work. If one maintains the recession long enough, the price of home goods and wages should go down relative to the prices of traded goods. But I think that an extended recession is a very inefficient way to bring this change in relative prices about. The reason is that prices are insensitive to the level of demand and therefore recession has little effect on the inflation rate. Slack does not significantly change relative price or the real wage, with the result that most of the adjustment falls on quantities, rather than prices. Therefore, it is likely to take prolonged recession to produce even a small movement in relative prices.

People should look back at the relatively successful stabilization of 1964-66 in Brazil for lessons for the present. In that period, an incomes policy was imposed under which wages and prices were forced down by an effective system of wage and price controls, at the same time that demand was being contracted. There was a change in relative prices, but very little recession compared to what Brazil is going through now. The point is, that contractionary monetary policy was complemented by policies which acted directly on prices and wages. Acting just on the demand side, leaving the market (or unemployment) to bring the reduction in wages and home goods prices, is likely to be both long and costly. The recession may appear to cure the balance of payments deficit, but the cure will not outlast the recession unless the recession also forces a change in relative prices.

Two additional points have been widely discussed at this conference. First, does the new system of indexing make it harder to control inflation? In my opinion, it does not. The culprit is the flat supply curve or the insensitivity of prices to the level of demand. If the supply curve were upward sloped, a reduction in demand would reduce inflation and the effect would be magnified under the new system. One could get a lower inflation rate by driving down the profit rate or the real wage through either price or wage controls. But indexing per se is not the problem, the problem is a set of income demands which imply a large balance of payments deficit at full employment.

One final point with regard to indexing and productivity. If one has an indexing system which includes a productivity adjustment, that produc- tivity must be adjusted in some manner for supply shocks. Events such as a rise in the price of oil or a bad harvest are like a tax on GNP. Someone must pay that tax. If everyone is allowed to have the increase in productivity in their particular industry, then someone must have some massive declines in real income. If not, the price system will impose the tax on an unprotected group through general inflation. Therefore, if there are to be productivity adjustments in the general wage indexing system, there must be an agreement that the sum total of all the particular adjustments add up to no more than the real rate of growth of productivity. It cannot be more, otherwise the system will generate bursts of inflation or recession whenever there is a supply shock.

REMARKS ON BRAZILIAN INFLATION AND WAGE POLICY

Roberto Macedo

This paper deals with wage indexation and inflation in Brazil. Contrary to most subjects that have dealt with in this volume so far, it emphasizes internal problems. I think that in Brazil there is now a tendency to over-emphasize external problems and not to realize that we have major domestic ones. I have been saying this especially since the governmental authorities have been trying to either import scapegoats or export problems, blaming everything on external causes instead of acknowledging that a large part of the problems we face in terms of inflation are due to our own mistakes.

At the outset it should be made clear that we do not have full indexation of wages in Brazil. We have the so-called staggered wage indexation, staggered in the sense that indexation occurs from period to period. Until November 1979, this staggered indexation was on an annual basis, so you had a collective readjustment according to the wage policy laws once every year. In November 1979, the wage policy was revised, in the sense that the government adopted semi-annual wage indexation, together with other changes in the wage policy. These changes caused much discussion in Brazil regarding economic effects.

I was away from Brazil during 1980, and when I arrived back in 1981 I was asked to give my opinion of the relation between wage policy and inflation.

After studying the subject I decided to write a paper.[1] I found the available discussion unclear. In particular, I realized that some of the pariticipants did not know all the details of the new wage policy, nor was the definition of the so-called inflationary impact clear as it could mean several things which I will point out later. So, in discussing this

---

[1]Later published as "Wage Indexation and Inflation: The Recent Brazilian Experience," in Rudiger Dornbusch and Mario H. Simonsen, eds., Inflation Debt and Indexation. Cambridge: MIT Press, 1983.

question of the effect of the wage policy on inflation, I shall separate three points.

The first is an attempt to make clearer what we mean by an inflationary impact. The second, and I think maybe the most important contribution of my paper, is to emphasize the effect which occurred during the transition from one policy to another. Most of the discussion that had been going on in Brazil about the effects of wage policy, simply ignored what happened during the transition from the former to the new policy. And the third, is an attempt, very crude I would say, to show that the impact of the wage policy occurs not only in terms of cost, but in terms of aggregate demand as well.

I shall have to touch on some descriptive material because to analyze the impact of wage policy, it is very important to make its meaning clear, as well as the nature of the changes introduced by the government in November 1979. The following is an illustrative example of the mechanisms by which this wage policy operates. If you are, say, a bank clerk in Brazil, you are entitled to a collective wage re-adjustment. Before 1979 every year, and after that every six months. You are represented as an industry group by a union, which by the time of year the previous contract ends (we call this a basis date) gets into negotiations with the representatives of the firms. Since, in general, they do not reach an agreement, because the workers ask for more and the firms offer less, the case goes to court, in which the judge handles the dispute following the rulings of the law. These rulings mean that you are entitled to a collective wage rate readjustment. This is a minimum rate to which all permanent workers are entitled. It does not mean that everyone in the economy is going to receive this rate that the government authorized. Firms may give less if market conditions are such that they can make a turnover of the labor force, and then hire people according to the market rates. The government has no direct influence on the absolute level of wages, it just gives wage readjustments. So, if you are on a job, in which you are entitled to a wage readjustment and you are fired, then you are going to negotiate a new wage level in your next employment. The level of this new wage has nothing to do, at least on a direct basis, with the wage policy established by the government.

On the other hand, firms can give more if they find it convenient to do so. There is nothing that forbids this. Let us say that if the government gives 40 percent, they could give 45-46 percent. So, it depends very much on market conditions and on the wage policy followed by the employers themselves. At least in the short run, since firms cannot promote a complete turnover of the labor force, the rates established by the government establishes a minimum level of readjustment for the so-called formal sector of the economy. Public workers, are not affected by these rates. They have adjustments more or less every year and did not receive the semi-annual readjustment after the new wage policy was introduced. This readjustment for public workers is given on ad hoc basis, and it more or less follows the rate of inflation, but proportionately below it.

In 1979, the government changed the law giving annual readjustments and it introduced six major changes. The first one, which is considered most important, is the above mentioned adoption of semi-annual collective readjustments, instead of the annual readjustments of the previous policy. The second is the introduction of a national consumer price index to serve as a basis for the new wage policy. Previously we had a wage readjustment formula having among its components the rate of inflation in the previous year. But, this formula was abandoned in favor of a single number given by the rate of change of the national consumer price index, which I call the INPC. The third one was the establishment of rates of adjustment differentiated by wage level. In the past, the policy was to give a flat rate for all workers. Since 1979, it has been mandatory to give, let us say, variable rates of readjustment that are lower for higher wages. The fourth measure is the introduction of a "spread" over the nominal rate of readjustment, based on the increase of productivity for each industry group. So on your basis date, for instance, if your industry group is bank clerks, you get an annual readjustment in September and then the semi-annual one six months later. But only in September, do you get an additional increase in accordance with the rate of growth of productivity in each industry group. The fifth measure, which has not been realized to some extent, is that the government has started to announce, at least one month before the base date, the readjustment to which you are entitled. For instance, bank clerks having their basis date in September, in the past would know the rate of readjustment to which they were entitled by around the middle of September. This system changed, so that by early August they know the rate of adjustment that they will receive in September. This is important, in terms of expectations of wages in the future, especially in the transition period, which I am going to deal with later. The sixth change is also very important, particularly in this transition context. In order to move from the old policy to the new one, the government had to compensate those industry groups which had already passed more than six months from their pevious readjustment. This had an important inflationary effect because the immediate impact of wage policy was broader, in the sense that the rate published by the government then covered a much larger group of workers.

Why was the wage policy introduced? It was introduced due to pressures by the workers which emerged, not necessarily in 1979, but that can be identified as early as in 1974. At the outset of the first oil crisis, rates of inflation doubled in Brazil. So the logic behind the wage policy was linked to the doubling inflation rate. It is intuitive to see that, if you double the inflation rate and you reduce the period between readjustmnts to half, then yu maintain your average real wage over a period of, say, one year. But it is important to emphasize that this scheme will work only if inflation does not change again. And this is crucial to an understanding of what happened after the wage policy was introduced.

I now turn to the impact on inflation, given this descriptive material on the wage policy. I decided to address myself to three points in terms of trying to clarify what is meant by inflationary impact of new wage policy. First, was the new wage policy a major factor behind the inflationary outburst which became evident in 1979? Second, did the new wage policy further accelerate this outburst of inflation? And finally, as it added additional fuel to inflation, was it explosive, in the sense of resulting in higher and higher rates of inflation?

To deal with the first question, I assembled a set of price indexes on the Brazilian economy. Annual rates of change on a quarterly basis from 1977-1979 are calculated for a general price index, bank credit to the private sector, the price of gasoline, and the wholesale prices for agricultural products. It is clear from these figures that inflation accelerated in the third quarter of 1979. So my conclusion, based upon examining these figures, is that you cannot blame the wage policy, which was introduced late in the fourth quarter, for this initial outburst in the rate of inflation. Although it would be possible to conceive of some effect of the wage policy on expectations, because the law went earlier to Congress, this would be very hard to prove.

The second question concerning the inflationary character of the wage policy, in terms of adding to the inflationary process, required devising a particular methodology to analyze it. So, at this point, the question is did the new wage policy contribute to a further increase in the rate of inflation? I have an affirmative answer to it, upon which I shall elaborate. On the basis of my beliefs and experience in Brazil, I opted for a non-orthodox manner of dealing with inflationary problems, in which you have some external or supply shocks (external not in the limited sense of coming from abroad, although clearly they can come from abroad as in the case of the oil shock) some of them arising from internal causes. The poor agricultural crops in 1978 and 1979 which led to an autonomous increase in the prices of agricultural products, in particular food, exemplifies the latter.

In my non-strict view of external shocks, you can have this type of outburst beginning with a particular cause, however it then becomes necessary to place attention not on the initial cause itself, but rather on the process by which these shocks are transferred from one group to society to another. I think I can summarize this approach by taking the increase in oil prices in the middle of 1979 and trying to analyze how the economy responded to it. I see the new indexation mechanism as an attempt to prevent workers from having a loss in real wages. But it failed because the government was not able to prevent firms from responding to this attempt by increasing prices. Rather, it allowed it explicitly, as it authorized the transfer of the costs of the wage policy to prices. So in the end, in my view, the workers did not gain from this change in the wage policy, in terms of real wages.

To check the effect of the wage policy, I looked first at the cost pressures that emerged from it, and then I made an attempt to show that it also had an important effect on aggregate demand. But in dealing with those cost pressures, I had a problem due to an institutional change which I insist was very important. When the government adopted the new wage policy, it had to compensate those industry groups which had their readjustments more than six months before the new wage policy went into effect. So let us compare what happened in terms of cost pressure, before that new wage policy went into effect, after it went into effect, and also during the transition period.

For instance, around mid-1979, the government would publish every month a rate of readjustment. But this would affect only the industry groups having their basis date in that particular month. When the government turned to the new policy and published a given rate of readjustment, then it started to affect not only the industry groups that had their basis date in that month, but also those who also had their basis date six months before. So the new wage policy started to increase the coverage of the rates that were established as guidelines for the nation. Therefore, I have a problem of how to translate the different coverages of the guidelines as a measure of the cost caused pressures imposed by the wage policy. In a particular case, month of November 1979, I have to measure the effect of the transition mechanism that the government established. In my estimation, the effect of the transition measures adopted by the government was such that in November 1979, the rate established by the government had a coverage four times greater than in the previous month. In order to measure these changes, I decided to resort to a new index. In Brazil it is a national sport to build new price indices, so I decided to build my own, which I call the index of coverage of readjustments of the wage policy.

What I did was to simulate a big wage bill for the whole economy, assuming that at the beginning of the period one twelfth of it was readjusted every month, and so I applied the rate published by the government in this fashion. In addition I took into consideration that in the transition from one policy to another, it was necessary to increase the coverage of readjustment by giving it to all industry groups which had been entitled to their first semi-annual readjustment in that particular month. The results are very important ones, particularly for the transition period. In November 1979, the annual rate of adjustment implicit in the rates established by the government moved to 54.5 percent from 50.0 in October, but if we look at this new index, we can see that the difference between the two months is significantly larger.

The important point to emphasize here is that when I measure the effect of the rates, in terms of the coverage, you see a different picture by using my index. It shows a larger difference between the previous wage policy and the new wage policy. In particular, from October to November, my index grew sharply, by 15 percent. If you compare this to the change in the price index in that particular month, which was around five percent, you can see that there was a real atempt to either recover or increase real wages, given the effect of the wage policy in terms of cost.

Given this change in the guidelines imposed by the government, you have not only a cost pressure, but a demand effect as well. Let us first address the question of the cost pressure. I assume that firms will try to respond to this attempt to protect workers from inflation by transferring these costs over to prices. The question is, did the government do anything to prevent this? Did they enact any kind of price controls? Did they adopt any mechanism that would prevent this transferring of increasing wage cost to prices? The answer is no, and not merely no, but quite to the contrary. By the time that the wage guidelines went into effect, the government had a "so called" price control committee, which was supposed to try and control prices, especially for industrial goods. But, it was to my surprise that I found only fourteen days after the wage policy went into effect, the government had already established the rules for the transferring of the additional costs of the wage policy to prices.

So the government gave to the workers with one hand and took it away with the other, by practically accepting as unavoidable the transferring of these additional costs to price. It should be clear that my point of view is that it would be foolhardy to say that you cannot transfer any of the cost increases to price. In any case, the government did not prevent, and, in fact, did facilitate the transfer of these additional costs to price.

Now let us turn to the demand effect. This demand effect is very important given some institutional aspects of the Brazilian economy. The wage policy was established in November, so it immediately affected the so-called 13th wage which is paid in December, at least a part of it. Recall that one of the features of the policy was that the government anticipated by more than one month the date by which workers would know the rate of the adjustment to which they were entitled. So one could imagine the situation of workers around November. They knew that they were going to have semi-annual readjustments, also that their thirteenth wage would be higher, and that inflation was growing, but they did not know by how. So, in my opinion, they had at least the expectation that their real wage would be higher in the future, because while although they did not know which rate of inflation would prevail they were, in general, optimistic that it was not going to increase substantially. Then they proceeded to spend and this was compounded because this is the period in which you have Christmas shopping.

According to a retailer from Sao Paulo, December 1979 reminded him of the years of the "Miracle Period" because "we sold everything we had due to the very high demand for our products." So I think there was an important effect from the point of view of demand. To substantiate this effect, I looked at some figures of sales of consumer goods. In regard to the sales of durable goods at the wholesale level in the period 1979-1981, 1979 was taken as the base because it shows the usual pattern of seasonal variation of these sales in the Brazilian economy. In general, they tend to fall in the first semester of the year and they perk up in the second semester. So they reach their highest level in the second semester of the year. In this regard, 1979 was a typical year, but if you look at 1980, the pattern of seasonal change observed is different now. You have higher sales in the first semester, and lower sales in the second semester. In my view, this is a result of the attempt by firms to replenish their stocks which had dwindled due to higher sales in December and also to the fact that the effect of wage policy on demand continued over the first semester of the year. After that, the inflation rates started to increase very rapidly. So by the second semester, this effect is exhausted because workers by then knew that prices had increased and their real wages had fallen once again.

The third point that my paper addressed was, as I said before, the hypothesis of an explosive impact on inflation. I found that this is not the case because given the Brazilian wage structure and the differentiated rates of readjustment given by the policy, there is evidence showing that the elasticity of the wage bill with respect to the rates established after the introduction of the new wage policy is slightly less than one. In other words, the new wage policy brought inflation one step higher, but after that its effect can be considered deflationary, although at a very slow rate. I took this point from the existing literature, but in retrospect I am not quite confident about it. It certainly deserves further investigation.

This completes my analysis of the wage policy, not only on the side of cost, but on the side of demand. As it can be seen, it is very difficult to isolate the effects because in 1980 the government established a ceiling on interest rates and on the indexation that applies to savings accounts, all this boosting consumption expenditure and the aggregate demand. There was also a devaluation in December 1979, over the crawling peg mechanism applied by the government and adding new fuel to inflation.

As a final comment, I would like to add that in Brazil, there are those who concluded with me that the wage policy led to higher rates of inflation, but they also conclude that for this reason it should be abolished. There is no conclusion of this type found in my paper. In my view this is a political issue, even if you can prove that the wage policy was inflationary, although this is not a point that is held on the basis of public opinion in Brazil. The workers still believe that it was very favorable and that you have to stick to this wage policy. Even though, if you look at the inflation rate now, what would be needed to maintain real wages would be an indexation every two or three months. So real wages are clearly not being maintained. I think the way out of this impasse would be a kind of political compromise in which the workers would accept wage restraint in exchange for political participation, particularly in the area of wage and price controls or guidelines. More to the point, what I have in mind is an incomes policy package, ruled by a tripartite committee of workers, businessmen and government officials, which would try to stop or at least to reduce substantially the dog-chasing-tail inflation cum indexation that we have. But, this is nothing but a dream, given the political and institutional barriers that this idea faces in Brazil.

Comments by Fred Levy on Roberto Macedo's, "Remarks on
Brazilian Inflation and Wage Policy"

Brazil's current wage policy was introduced during a period of
accelerating inflation and in the wake of strikes celebrating the
progressive political opening. By providing automatic wage adjustment for
increases in the cost of living, the wage policy was intended, in part, to
reduce the range of conflict in wage bargaining and thus reduce strike
activity. A number of Government officials now believe, however, that the
wage policy itself is an important element in perpetuating, if not
accelerating, the inflation.

In analyzing this relationship, three groups of questions must be
answered:

1. Has the policy been effective--i.e., have nominal wages been
    increased in accordance with the wage formula, or is evasion common?

2. If effective, how have wage increases compared with growth in labor
    productivity, and how have the resultant changes in unit labor costs,
    if any, impacted profits, employment, output, and the inter-industry
    pattern of supply and demand?

3. Is the policy sustainable beyond the short run?

Macedo answers the first question essentially in the affirmative.
Although hard data is scarce, Macedo points to the costliness to employers
of high rates of labor turnover and the ease of passing cost increases on
through higher prices to show that employers have had little incentive to
evade the legal adjustments. Moreover, in view of productivity growth and
the lag between price increases and wage adjustment, average real wages
have risen little, with the exception of the initial one-time impact of
the shift to a semi-annual, as opposed to annual, adjustment. Not
explored is the apparent compression of wage differentials implied, if
employers are adhering to the tapered adjustment formula; further
reference is made to this below. Finally, however, Macedo does note that
the tapered adjustment formula tends to create greater wage pressures in
firms which use low-skilled labor intensely, as compared to high-skill
intensity operations.

Although the policy is being widely adhered to, Macedo finds that it is not playing a major role in the present inflation. The introduction of semi-annual adjustment probably served to propel inflation to a new and higher plateau, but the adjustment lag and modest real average wage increase generated by the formula prevent its inflationary charge from becoming explosive. In passing, the paper suggests that the wage adjustment policy may contribute to unemployment, but this point is not pursued.

Further empirical analysis would be needed to support the above conclusions, but Macedo's logic, as far as it goes, is persuasive. Crucially absent, however, is a forward look at question 3. Is the present wage policy sustainable and consistent with the Government's medium-term objectives of reducing inflation, improving Brazil's external accounts, and resuming economic growth? To what extent is the benignity of the wage policy dependent on the combined acceleration of inflation and recession which the Brazilian economy has been experiencing?

With inflation accelerating, the lagged adjustment formula prevents real wages from rising. By the same token, however, the formula would cause real wages to rise during periods of decelerating inflation itself and could become an obstacle to deceleration. At a constant rate of inflation, the formula mandates a ten percent per annum real wage increase for the large number of workers in the lowest pay categories. Quite apart from its impact on aggregate demand, such a rate of pay increase, far in excess of likely productivity gains, could only be non-inflationary if offset by a compression of the wage structure, falling profit rates, and/or the substantial disemployment of low-wage labor. All three appear to have occurred to some degree during the 1981 recession. But, as the economy recovers, and the labor market tightens, the old wage structure could well reassert itself with all pay rates rising at least as rapidly as the lowest wage rates--i.e., at ten percent above the inflation rate if the present formula prevailed. Therefore, although the wage policy may not have been a significant factor in the inflation of the past year, it does appear to greatly complicate the future trade-off between growth, employment, balance-of-payments improvement, and price stabilization.

BRAZIL'S FOREIGN INDEBTEDNESS--DETERMINANTS AND LIMITS

Antonio Carlos Lembruger

During the time period corresponding to the two oil shocks, i.e., between 1973 and 1981, Brazil's foreign debt grew at a yearly rate of 22 percent, going up from US$ 12.6 billion to US$ 61.4 billion. It is undoubtedly quite a substantial growth rate, which immediately raises two questions: (a) what are the factors responsible for this growth rate? (b) what were the international financial market conditions to favor the availability of funds to finance this increase of indebtedness and, at the same time, to roll over the debt at every instance? These are fundamental questions, if we are to analyze future trends either with respect to Brazil's demand for funds or to the international credit supply.

Although this is not the proper place for a formal demonstration, it is easy to notice that the foreign debt growth rate relies basically on five determinants: (i) the (positive or negative) growth of international reserves; (ii) the magnitude of the trade deficit (or surplus) (iii) the magnitude of the services deficit (or surplus) excluding interest and dividend payments; (iv) the cost of borrowing foreign funds or, more simply, the international interest rate; and (v) the volume of foreign investments discounting remittance of dividends. Furthermore, the annual amount of amortizations added to those five determinants if one intends to look at the gross amount of loan resources required by a country each year.

In the Brazilian case, if it were at all possible to establish a simplified ranking by importance, we could say that between 1974 and 1976, and again in 1979 and 1980, the main factor was undoubtedly the trade balance deficit. Within this context, the shocks were actually the chief element to explain the process of indebtedness during those years. We should also remember that, except for 1974, the non-oil trade balance always showed a surplus. However, in 1977/78 and again in 1981, in spite of the good results shown by the trade balance--even including oil--the debt kept climbing and that is obviously explained by the feedback influence of the international interest rate on the existing debt.

Indeed, the fast growth of the foreign debt between 1973 and 1977 (26 percent a year as an average) transferred to the following years a process of accelerating interest payments, which would acquire even further relative significance as of 1979/80 with the boom of international interest rates, both in nominal and real terms. Therefore, in recent years--and certainly in 1982--the major element in Brazil's foreign indebtedness became the international interest rate.

In fact, it can be proved that--assuming constant international reserves, foreign investments equal to remitted dividends and a trade surplus basically similar to the services deficit (excluding interests payments and dividends)--the growth rate of the net foreign debt tends to be exactly the same as the cost of foreign borrowing or the international interest rate. More generally, based on the present Brazilian situation, this means that the foreign debt growth is equal to the international interest plus something if the trade balance and other services do badly, or minus something if the trade balance and other services do well.

Still another element should be added, which bears an influence on the Brazilian annual gross demand for funds--the amount of amortizations. Like interest payments, the yearly amortizations of the debt in the last few years reflected the faster growth of the debt during the first oil shock, as well as an overlapping of maturities brought about by a shortening of minimum loan maturities during that time period (1974 to 1978). To put it plainly, it could be said that Brazil's present gross borrowing need is basically the amount required to pay back both interest and amortizations, i.e., to service the debt.

Just as a quantitative illustration of some of the points made in the present analysis, Brazil had, in 1981: a gross debt of US$ 61.4 billion, US$ 7.5 in reserves, US$ 9.2 billion in net interest payments and US$ 7.7 billion in amortizations. The latter two amounts accounted for 20 percent of the 1980 net debt (gross debt less reserves) and 14 percent of the 1980 gross debt, respectively. The 1981 current account deficit was US$ 11.7 billion, of which US$ 1.2 billion corresponded to the trade surplus, US$ 2.6 billion to the deficit in other services, and US$ 1.1 billion to dividend payments, while foreign investments added up to US$ 2.3 billion.

It seems likely that, in 1982, we shall reach the hypothetical situation illustrated before: a net borrowing requirement designed to cover the interest payments of the existing debt (estimated at US$ 9.5 billion), in addition to anticipated amortizations of US$ 9 billion which will have to be rolled over. This adds up to a gross borrowing requirement of US$ 18.5 billion. The trade surplus and the investment inflow will be sufficient only to cover the deficit from other services and the remittance of dividends, and we can predict almost constant reserves.

It is important to point out that, from the required US$ 18.5 billion in loans, a substantial share (about 15 percent) is usually raised from non-banking or non-commercial sources.

Despite the high growth rates as far as indebtedness is concerned, Brazil has not found many difficulties in raising the necessary funds in the international market. There were, of course, sizeable reserve losses in 1974-75 and again in 1979-80, besides sharp increases in the country's average spreads in 1975-77 and again in 1980-81. But, as a whole, Brazil was able to finance most of its foreign resource requirements throughout the years since 1974, with funds from the Euromarket.

International market conditions undeniably favored the recycling of funds to countries like Brazil. Between 1973 and 1981, international banking assets grew at an average rate of 24 percent to 25 percent a year, increasing six times, from US$ 300 billion in 1973 to US$ 1.8 trillion in 1981. This was made possible by an ample international dollar supply and by the increase of OPEC surpluses. Petrodollar recycling was brilliantly undertaken by the international financial market, and deficit-prone countries like Brazil, insofar as they were willing to accept the rules of the game, were able to obtain the funds needed. The Euromarket was able to adjust entirely to the new situation that arose since 1973 with strong balance of payments imbalances and extreme volatility as to exchange and interest rates.

After having considered the fast growth of Brazilian debt—and of international credit as well—between 1973 and 1981, it is reasonable to question future trends.

It is hardly likely that the international credit supply will continue to rise at the same fast pace. The larger banks no longer want to let their international assets grow more than their capital. Balance of payments imbalances should be smaller, with the eventual disappearance of the OPEC surplus. In the US, prospects are of a very sharp drop of inflation and monetary expansion. Therefore, it is unthinkable that yearly growth rates of 24 to 25 percent in international credit will be maintained. But neither can we choose the other extreme of conceiving that the process of international financial expansion is about to end. On the contrary: there is still room for growth as regards the banks' international operations which, after all, respond to market incentives—in their particular case, to spreads.

In simpler terms, we could say that, as of 1982, a limit was set on the potential growth of the Brazilian foreign debt as a result of the likely growth of international credit in the next few years—which can be optimistically estimated at 15 percent a year.

Therefore, and bearing in mind the previously mentioned relationships, the strategy of Brazilian economy's foreign sector will have to take this basic limit into account. On the one hand, in order not to rely on the probability of favorable moves of international interest rates, the external debt will be required to grow less than the international interest rate. On the other hand, exports will have to grow more that the international interest rate. To accomplish this, increasing trade surpluses will be vital not only to cover the services deficit, but to start generating extra surpluses to finance the interest account as well. It is important that those surpluses are obtained together with a fast export growth. It is not the same to achieve a US$ 2 billion surplus and US$ 28 billion in exports than to have the same surplus compared to US$ 26 billion in exports: the implications in both instances are entirely different for those who analyze foreign indebtedness as related to exports.

As we have stated, at medium term, the debt tends to grow at the same rate as the international interest rate minus something if both the trade and services balance turn out well. Thus, it is necessary that this subtractive factor increases gradually throughout the years, until it reaches a certain point in time—possibly within the next ten years—when the debt growth rate will be zero. Until then, Brazil's foreign debt will keep increasing. But the growth in the next few years will have to be much lower than the 22 percent in 1973-1981. And more important still: there is every indication that this growth rate will tend to decline, going down from 15 percent or 16 percent in 1982.

It is very important that the country manages to keep its exports growing in the future at satisfactory rates, above the debt growth rate and above the international interest rate. In this respect, 1982 prospects are unfavorable, since exports should grow well below 15 percent. Brazil's trade surplus in 1982 should be significant--probably US$ 2 billion--but in the long run it is necessary that surpluses are kept parallel to a fast export increase. Experts in international trade know that controls on imports end up by penalizing exports and, similarly, the fostering of exports turn out by encouraging imports--it is the old story of the two-way avenue. The opening in Brazil's foreign trade is a necessity--and any excessive control on imports will ultimately affect the very process of the country's economic opening in financial terms, which has become an arithmetical need due to the magnitude of our current account deficits.

The 1982 current account deficit should add up to US$ 12 billion (US$ 9.5 billion in interest, US$ 1.3 billion in dividends, US$ 3.2 billion in services less a US$ 2 billion trade balance). A first impression might be that, in spite of all efforts, the country does not seem to be making any headway towards adjusting its foreign sector, since the deficit is expected to be the same as in 1981. But, dynamically, the foreign situation is clearly better--and this is translated into a declining trend of the foreign debt growth rate. Even if the annual amounts to be raised remain high in absolute terms (grossly US$ 15.5 billion will be necessary from banking sources in 1982), the fact is that, in relative terms, those amounts are much lower than the ones borrowed by Brazil between 1974 and 1981. Even if the current account deficit and the gross borrowing remain constant in the next 2 or 3 years, the foreign debt growth rate should decrease. But, undoubtedly, increasing trade surpluses will be required to make these figures really consistent with real facts.

SHORT-RUN ECONOMIC POLICY IN BRAZIL

John Williamson

The subject of this paper is short run macroeconomic policy: specifically, where I think short run macroeconomic policy should lead Brazil, given that one starts from a position of severe stagflation. This is, of course, not a specifically Brazilian phenomenon, but one that has recently characterized the world as a whole--although inflation has now dropped off quite dramatically in a number of the leading countries. I will comeback to the explanation for that, and the sustainability of that decline, in due course.

I suggest that an important professional function of economists is to introduce a longer time scale into the economic policy process, and to attempt to restrain the sort of short-run idiocies which were seen in Brazil in 1979-80. And not only in Brazil does this happen: you can name just about any change of government in Britain in the last couple of decades and identify similar instances. (The unique feature of Margaret Thatcher is that she did not do a U-turn when she discovered that the policies initially adopted were not very good ones.)

One needs, therefore, to frame short run policy in terms of a coherent long run framework. The great failure of Keynesian demand management policy as it was practiced is the 1950s and 1960s was the lack of such a framework. Maybe it is not possible to fine tune, but one can clearly do some tuning: one does not have to have recessions as big as the current one. The problem with activist demand management as it was practiced in the past was not inability to hit targets, but rather the lack of attention to ensuring the long run consistency of the targets that were being pursued. There are two major long-run constraints, and it is about those, and the extent to which they constrain Brazilian policy at the present time, that I speak.

The first constraint is of course inflation. Figure 1 shows unemployment against inflation. The interaction between the Phillips's model of the inflationary process and political pressures, which react myopically first to over-high inflation and then to excessive unemployment, generate the sort of cyclical process illustrated by the loop. What we would like to

184

do, presumably, is to identify what is the natural rate of unemployment (U_n)--the long run sustainable rate of unemployment--and zero in toward a point like A. If we start from a

Figure 1

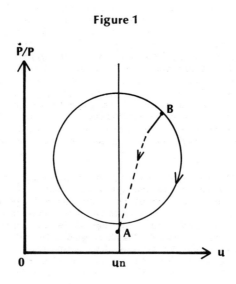

position of stagflation like B, then the optimal strategy would be something like the dotted line. One would want to go immediately rather close to the long run sustainable level of unemployment, because the costs of excess capacity are very great. Creating more excess capacity is a very inefficient way of decelerating the rate of inflation. But one would have to keep some margin of slack to keep some pressure to decelerate inflation over time. The great trick about anti-inflationary policy in my view is to identify circumstances in which it is possible to get a rapid deceleration of inflation for relatively little cost. It is also possible to envisage positive supply shocks, and, indeed, the reason for the comparative success of Brazilian stabilization policy in 1965 was precisely, a positive supply shock, in the form of a bumper harvest that year. So then, the strategy would be to attempt to maintain demand at some sort of appropriate level, avoiding pressures to accelerate inflation but maybe not aiming for particularly rapid reduction, until one of these nice shocks (like a reduction in the price of petroleum) comes along.

I do not think that I would want to rely purely on a Phillips curve type of model to explain inflation in Brazil. Essentially the model I think in terms of, is one that seems to be in the back of the minds of many Brazilian economists. Indeed, I formalized it, to the extent I have formalized it, during my period in Brazil. I found a hint of it in Roberto Macedo's paper. It is essentially a two sector model, in which one has a fixprice sector where the participants are in a position to enforce given real income claims, interacting with a flexprice sector, which in the Brazilian case is clearly the agricultural sector. This is a very illuminating model with which to analyze a number of questions. You can get a Phillips curve type of relationship out of the whole model even if there is an absolutely horizontal supply curve in the fixprice sector, even if there is no Phillips curve relationship in its traditional form there. The way this arises is that monetary restriction leads to a fall in output in the fixprice sector and a fall of prices in the flexprice sector, so real income is squeezed in the flexprice sector, and that enables people in the fixprice sector to satisfy their real income demands. Having cut back demand to the necessary level, one can then go about decelerating inflation, and one can question whether indexation helps that process along or not. One quickly comes to the conclusion that indexation may be helpful if the alternative is a situation in which the real income claims would be built in _ex ante_ on the basis of inflation expectations that were unduly pessimistic. On the other hand, indexation can speed up the process of inflationary acceleration which results from any incompatibility between the level of real income claims in the fixprice sector.

One can also build in supply shocks, which raise the price of agricultural products and so increase the incompatibility of real income claims in the fixprice sector, and hence accelerate the whole inflationary process. If there is a passive monetary policy which is aiming for a particular level of demand, and then that level of demand becomes incompatible with the avoidance of accelerating inflation, something has to give. If a restrictive monetary policy is adopted, then it operates by cutting back demand which affects the real income of the flexprice sector and the real output of the fixprice sector. This is a useful model not only to understand what's happening in Brazil, but also to understand what's happening in the world right now. The reason that inflation has declined dramatically, in the past three months, appears to be that monetary restriction has indeed been pushed to the point where real incomes in the flexprice sector have been cut back. That is manifest in the disastrous balance of payments prospects facing the whole of the Third World, including, on this occasion, OPEC, certainly including Latin America, and including Africa (where there are terms of trade deteriorations of 20-30-40 percent), as the most disastrous. It includes also, incidentally, the farm sector here in the United States, where projected real farm income for this year is the lowest since the Great Depression. Yes, monetary restriction is breaking the inflationary process, but it is doing so by creating a very considerable depression. As and when output recovers from that depression, the inflationary process is going to start again. If you believe this, as opposed to it all being explained by inflationary expectations, then simply reducing inflation to zero for a few months, even for a year or two, isn't going to get inflation out of the system. What is necessary, however, to eliminate inflation is to cut back real income claims in the fixprice sector to levels that are consistent with a satisfactory level of demand in the world as a whole. And that adjustment, we simply don't see any sign as of yet on the world level. This means that the second constraint on Brazilian demand management policy, which is the external constraint, is more problematic than it otherwise would be.

At the external level there are really two types of constraints operating: there's a short run reserve constraint, and a long run indebtedness constraint. There seems to be a question as to whether the reserve constraint is binding in Brazil at the moment. At a conference on

IMF conditionality, Edmar Bacha presented a paper about why Brazil hasn't been to the fund in the last couple of years. Bacha said that Brazil had done the things that were necessary to go to the Fund, but that it didn't want to go. However, as soon as the bankers thought it was a desirable country to lend to again, Delfim could get the economy moving by a more expansionary policy, while the Fund would have stopped that. His thesis was that in the short run, Brazil is very much constrained by the level of reserves, and that it is just not possible to accept a higher level of income because of that. We had a very different story from a conference participant, who told us that in fact bankers were dying to lend to Brazil given current margins, and wondered why Brazil didn't cut the margins. Or, what Brazil would presumably prefer to do is expand income and borrow some more if things were really as easy as he says. So that's one type of constraint. It's a short run reserve constraint. Does it exist? I don't know; we have conflicting stories on that. The long run external constraint comes from the level of indebtedness; one doesn't want to get ever deeper into debt in relationship to other relevant magnitudes. In particular, one doesn't want debt to expand without limit relative to income. That's a problem which I don't think Brazil is facing. After making the adjustment that one should, when doing inflation accounting on the balance of payments deficit, the current account deficit was something like $7 billion last year, which is perhaps 3 percent of Brazilian GNP. That is a good but below the trend rate of growth, so I don't see anything alarming. On those grounds I would argue that Brazil could in fact afford a bigger current account deficit. So it seems to me that it's the reserve constraint that is the key one. To the extent that, the constraint is not binding, then I would argue that appropriate Brazilian policy at this time is to relax, but not overrelax. Policy has to remain cautious, for the world as a whole is in a recession and that means that the balance of payments gives a smaller margin to play with. Furthermore, inflation is not something that should be forgotten, it should be kept on a downward trend. Hence realization should, in my view, be fairly cautious.

Let me just make one final point about monetary policy, because I feel strongly that Brazilian monetary policy is not as bad as sometimes suggested. I don't think that Brazil could have an independent monetary policy, because exchange rate policy is geared to the maintenance of competitiveness in international trade and interest rate policy is geared to maintaining a capital inflow, and that the two together essentially determine monetary policy. But that seems to me a perfectly sensible way to use monetary policy--much more sensible than what is happening in the U.S. and the U.K., where people are busy pursuing fluctuations in real exchange rates which are far more damaging than any ill-consequences that I can think of from the lack of an independent monetary policy.

LONG RUN PERSPECTIVES

Stan Czamanski

While this conference is concerned mainly with short-run developments, I would like to formulate a few comments dealing with the broader background issues of long-run problems and discernible trends.

Brazil is the most recent among the countries which have been reclassified by the World Bank from underdeveloped to developed status. Its progress has not only been an outstanding success, but it also has several features of great general interest. It is a well-known, albeit somewhat surprising fact that a significant proportion of the newly developed countries and the most rapidly growing countries in transition are lacking natural resources or conditions for successful agriculture, while many of the poor and stagnant countries are well endowed by nature. Of the several possible explanations for this phenomenon, one that has attracted considerable attention may perhaps be called "the staple mentality," or "staple trap"; terms following the staple theory of economic growth advanced by economic historians.

According to a modern version of this theory, a country possessing a natural resource such as good conditions for producing an agricultural staple will maximize its per capita returns by employing its factors of production in agricultural activities. Assuming the existence of an abundant supply of land and of labor, and a relative scarcity of capital, returns to capital will be higher in activities with high land/capital and labor/capital ratios than in those with high labor/capital ratios, but using negligible quantities of the third factor—land. Under those circumstances, there are not incentives for investing in manufacturing, which by its very nature is usually more capital intensive and does not utilize directly, unprocessed natural resources. There is here some divergence between individual and social goals, for in the long run industrialization is the core of development. Extensive agriculture or mineral extraction not only puts the country at the mercy of fluctuations in world demand for the staple, but further does not require the acquisition of substantial technical and organizational skills, and hence does not lead to the formation of a trained, diversified labor force or to the emergence of Schumpeterian entrepreneurs. In short, plantation type agriculture not only results in an unbalanced income distribution and socio-political tensions, but in the long run fails to promote the growth of human capital, without which the attainment of developed status is impossible.

Among the large countries, richly endowed by nature, Brazil is almost unique in its determined policies aimed at industrialization which came to be known as the "Brazilian model." For such policies invariably involve a lowering of the present standards of living for the sake of benefits likely to accrue beyond the time horizon of political decision makers.

Since market forces would not induce private capital investments in manufacturing, government policies led to the emergence of partial state capitalism, with huge government owned enterprises run by salaried technocrats who became a new managerial class. Simultaneously, multinational corporations were encouraged to invest in key industries, sometimes in partnerships with the government. Forced savings accumulated through regressive, largely indirect taxation, provided the necessary funds for direct industrial investments and for such indispensable elements of the infrastructure as roads or power plants. The industrial growth of Brazil and its impressive human capital are witnesses to the success of this policy.

The process of rapid industrialization and the policies which brought it about raised, however, several problems, some of which emerged as difficult to resolve dilemmas. Industrialization brought about massive shifts of population, since by its very nature industrial organization cannot be forced into a spatial settlement pattern which evolved over a long period of time for the needs of a largely agricultural society. The emerging, often exaggerated, hopes of finding employment in the rapidly growing cities led to massive rural to urban migration. The numbers of these newcomers exceeded the expanding job opportunities, leaving in most Brazilian cities vast pools of destitute mostly illiterate unemployed.

This serious and apparently growing problem raised some questions about a possible divergence between the factor proportions typical of the new industries and local factor availabilities. Several unrelated studies have shown that capital intensities in local plants of multinational corporations and in government-owned enterprises were only about one third of those typical of corresponding plants in the United States, but this hardly answers the question of proper mix of newly established industries. The real choice, largely dependent upon Government policies, is between, on the one hand, modern, capital-intensive industries generating important internal and external economies of scale and leading to the emergence of a new class of managers, engineers, and technicians and on the other hand traditional sectors like garments, textiles, or leather with low capital-labor ratios, creating employment opportunities but with limited prospects for the future.

Two other problems are related to the spatial dimensions of Brazilian economic development. In recent decades most Brazilian cities were mushrooming, but these developments were overshadowed by the explosive growth of Sao Paulo, and to a lesser extent of Rio de Janeiro. For a while, Sao Paulo was the fastest growing city in the world. This vast agglomeration of population and of industrial plants is, however, inadequately endowed with basic urban services and suffers from excessive densities. Both are the result of the systematic diversion of government funds to the building up of industrial infrastructure and of direct productive investments at the expense of housing and of urban facilities. The massive inflow of rural migrants, who could not be accommodated in the existing housing stock, by new construction, led to the phenomenon of favelas or vast squatter settlements, typical of many Latin American cities. In Sao Paulo, with its larger and more vigorous urban economy, they seem to comprise some 300,000 inhabitants, but in Rio de Janeiro they may well constitute one third of the urban population.

The perceived dangers of overurbanization led the Brazilian Government to adopt a policy of fostering the development of middle sized cities. The financial resources which have been put into these programs have been so far quite inadequate to cope with the problem, but more importantly, it is doubtful whether a dispersion of urban population would result in more convenient living conditions. Smaller cities may be cheaper to invest and to run in per capita terms, but this is largely due to the fact that their inhabitants enjoy a much lower level of amenities. Some services such as theaters, universities, or specialized hospitals can obviously not be made available to inhabitants of smaller cities although their lack is next to impossible to quantify. Moreover, some studies initiated by me at the University of Sao Paulo seem to indicate, that for many services the per capita costs are inversely proportional to the density of population and thus indirectly also to the size of the urban agglomeration. On purely economic grounds, it appears that large urban agglomerations are cheaper to service than smaller towns. Moreover, some studies seem to suggest that the huge Brazilian metropolitan areas may not have yet attained their maximum sustainable size.

Finally, the rapid industrialization conflicts to some extent with the Brazilian policy of frontier development--of pushing the frontier of the settled area in a north-western direction. This policy has been followed for many decades, and in fact, precedes, the massive industrialization drive of the last twenty years. The idea of opening up the hinterland has important social, psychological, and political dimensions, but one of its objectives is to exploit the over-abundant, natural resources of Brazil. The most recent developments in the Carajas region are as much an attempt at extending the frontier as of taking advantage of the high marginal productivities of capital connected with investments in sub-soil resources.

SUMMING UP

Roberto Fendt

Some of the results of the workshop were much more optimistic than
expected. In particular, only John Williamson mentioned the long-term
debt problem. It was not a dominant theme throughout the conference. I
will take for granted that probably most people agree with his comments on
the fact that the long term debt is not that much of a problem, at least
in the way some people used to think. On the short run reserve
constraint, I would be a little more cautious on the current Brazilian
position.

In several instances in the past, we went through highly explicit
stabilization programs, and were forced to adjust to events brought on by
balance of payments disequilibria. We came out of the events of the
Depression without scars, in part due to positive supply shocks. The
existence of idle capacity, the fact that we were able to go through a new
round of import substitution, is the experience of Brazil that Albert
Fishlow probably had in mind when he spoke of pursuing import substition
as an option for current times. At the same time, we should not forget
the fact that at that time price and wage flexibility were the order of
the day, and that helped to make adjustment easier.

During the 1964-67 stabilization period, there were again positive supply
shocks. The recovery of the public debt was possible due to a consistent
plan which involved not only taxes, but the recovery of the internal debt
in Brazil as well. At the same time, savings were also recovered by the
introduction of the monetary correction. Concurrently, wage policy played
a role which is completely different from the role described in Macedo's
exposition. Of course, the existence of a very peculiar phase in the
business cycle on a world wide scale, had major impact. It was possible
for Brazil to integrate, at that moment in time, and pursue simultaneously
both import substitution and export promotion. No doubt, this was also
due to the fact that we had considerable idle capacity in the period
because of the recession. It became quite clear to me that not only does
this group believe that the margin for maneuvering is quite small these
days, but also that the definition of policy is blurred. We believe that
certainly the main instruments of ecomomic policy are not being utilized
in the direction that would produce the best results. And, in some

instances, as in the case of commercial policy, quite probably the policy is producing nothing but numerous counterproductive measures, both on the attempt to provide protection and at the same time the attempt to circumvent it.

I understand that monetary policy today is in such a situation that it would be very difficult to go through any adjustment period, whatever change is suggested. Larry Sjastaad suggested that one of the main explanations for the very high real rates of interests in Brazil is the ceiling on expansion based on domestic liabilities. The way monetary policy is organized in the country is such that to get rid of those ceilings on the expansion of credit based on domestic liabilities, will necessarily require a very long time period for this elimination to be carried out. Otherwise, the market for public securities, the financing of the government debt and the very existence of the financial markets will be severely affected.

There can be very few doubts that the public sector deficit is the main factor in this story. However, we did not discuss in detail, what to do for the future. There is in the minds of policy makers the idea that we will finish all the investment programs which are underway, but after that, we will stop and see what happens. This kind of attitude has been clearly manifest over the last several months. Regarding major projects in the public sector, it has been unambiguously signaled to the domestic capital goods industry that no new projects will be forthcoming. The idea that the public sector deficit, including the state enterprises, might start to come into control from 1983 on, is very appealing, but at the same time, the major question mark remains what to do with the incredibly large domestic capital goods industry.

Everyone discussed the issue of real interest rates in Brazil, and no doubt very few of us disagree that if international rates remain where they are, and as Brazil devalues at the rate of domestic inflation, we'll be paying very high nominal international interest rates plus all the fees involved.

The gentleman who suggested that the spread is too high, I guess had in mind that Brazil pays 2 1/4 percent. The spread in reality is probably closer to 4-5 percent, if you include the very fact that banks deduct interest payments here, use their income tax payments in Brazil against their tax liabilities in the U.S., and the front end fees themselves. I think that whatever happens to the conduct of monetary policy, real interest rates will continue to be very high. I can't imagine how a major recovery producing results could develop with real rates of interest so high.

I was not convinced through our discussions that the opening of the political process will necessarily lead to a resurgence of populism in Brazil, in such a way as to create a new dilemma for the conduct of economic policy. As I understand the nature of political process in Brazil, at the present time everybody is concerned with the institutionalization of the process. I'm not saying that in the future some populist pressures might not appear, but I don't see them as a major short-term problem. Therefore, it is my feeling that the political opportunity, at this point in time, is a major constructive force for the conduct of an economic program, which if consistent, can lead to results over the short term.